Spatial Regression Models for the Social Sciences

Advanced Quantitative Techniques in the Social Sciences

Series Editor: Shenyang Guo, *Washington University in St. Louis*

VOLUMES IN THE SERIES

1. HIERARCHICAL LINEAR MODELS: Applications and Data Analysis Methods, 2nd Edition
   Stephen W. Raudenbush and Antony S. Bryk

2. MULTIVARIATE ANALYSIS OF CATEGORICAL DATA: Theory
   John P. van de Geer

3. MULTIVARIATE ANALYSIS OF CATEGORICAL DATA: Applications
   John P. van de Geer

4. STATISTICAL MODELS FOR ORDINAL VARIABLES
   Clifford C. Clogg and Edward S. Shihadeh

5. FACET THEORY: Form and Content
   Ingwer Borg and Samuel Shye

6. LATENT CLASS AND DISCRETE LATENT TRAIT MODELS: Similarities and Differences
   Ton Heinen

7. REGRESSION MODELS FOR CATEGORICAL AND LIMITED DEPENDENT VARIABLES
   J. Scott Long

8. LOG-LINEAR MODELS FOR EVENT HISTORIES
   Jeroen K. Vermunt

9. MULTIVARIATE TAXOMETRIC PROCEDURES: Distinguishing Types From Continua
   Niels G. Waller and Paul E. Meehl

10. STRUCTURAL EQUATION MODELING: Foundations and Extensions, 2nd Edition
    David Kaplan

11. REGRESSION ANALYSIS: A Constructive Critique
    Richard A. Berk

11. PROPENSITY SCORE ANALYSIS: Statistical Methods and Applications, 2nd Edition
    Shenyang Guo and Mark W. Fraser

12. INTERACTION EFFECTS IN LINEAR AND GENERALIZED LINEAR MODELS: Examples and Applications Using Stata®
    Robert L. Kaufman

13. MODELS FOR SOCIAL NETWORKS WITH STATISTICAL APPLICATIONS
    Suraj Bandyopadhyay, A.R. Rao, and Bikas K. Sinha

14. SPATIAL REGRESSION MODELS FOR THE SOCIAL SCIENCES
    Guangqing Chi and Jun Zhu

Spatial Regression Models for the Social Sciences

Guangqing Chi
The Pennsylvania State University, USA

Jun Zhu
University of Wisconsin—Madison, USA

$SAGE

Los Angeles | London | New Delhi
Singapore | Washington DC | Melbourne

SAGE

FOR INFORMATION:

SAGE Publications, Inc.
2455 Teller Road
Thousand Oaks, California 91320
E-mail: order@sagepub.com

SAGE Publications Ltd.
1 Oliver's Yard
55 City Road
London EC1Y 1SP
United Kingdom

SAGE Publications India Pvt. Ltd.
B 1/I 1 Mohan Cooperative Industrial Area
Mathura Road, New Delhi 110 044
India

SAGE Publications Asia-Pacific Pte. Ltd.
18 Cross Street #10-10/11/12
China Square Central
Singapore 048423

Acquisitions Editor: Helen Salmon
Editorial Assistant: Megan O'Hefferman
Content Development Editor: Chelsea Neve
Production Editor: Tori Mirsadjadi
Copy Editor: Gillian Dickens
Typesetter: C&M Digitals (P) Ltd.
Proofreader: Liann Lech
Indexer: Michael Ferreira
Cover Designer: Candice Harman
Marketing Manager: Susannah Goldes

Copyright © 2020 by SAGE Publications, Inc.

All rights reserved. Except as permitted by U.S. copyright law, no part of this work may be reproduced or distributed in any form or by any means, or stored in a database or retrieval system, without permission in writing from the publisher.

All third party trademarks referenced or depicted herein are included solely for the purpose of illustration and are the property of their respective owners. Reference to these trademarks in no way indicates any relationship with, or endorsement by, the trademark owner.

The R Foundation owns the copyright to R software and licenses it under the GNU General Public License 2.0, Https://www.r-project.org/COPYING. The R content depicted in this book is included solely for purposes of illustration and is owned by The R Foundation and in no way indicates any relationship with, or endorsement by The R Foundation. The R software logo as it appears in this book is available at https://www.r-project.org/logo/ and is copyright protected by The R Foundation and licensed under Creative Commons Attribution-ShareAlike 4.0 International license (CC-BY-SA 4.0) https://creativecommons.org/licenses/by-sa/4.0/.

Printed in the United States of America

Library of Congress Cataloging-in-Publication Data

Names: Chi, Guangqing, author. | Zhu, Jun (Professor of statistics), author.

Title: Spatial regression models for the social sciences / Guangqing Chi, The Pennsylvania State University, USA, Jun Zhu, University of Wisconsin–Madison, USA.

Description: Los Angeles : SAGE, [2020] | Includes bibliographical references and index.

Identifiers: LCCN 2018050719 | ISBN 9781544302072 (hardcover : alk. paper)

Subjects: LCSH: Spatial analysis (Statistics) | Social sciences—Statistical methods.

Classification: LCC HA30.6 .C45 2020 | DDC 519.5/3—dc23 LC record available at https://lccn.loc.gov/2018050719

This book is printed on acid-free paper.

19 20 21 22 23 10 9 8 7 6 5 4 3 2 1

BRIEF CONTENTS

Series Editor's Introduction	xv
Preface	xvii
Acknowledgments	xix
About the Authors	xxi

Chapter 1	•	Introduction	1
Chapter 2	•	Exploratory Spatial Data Analysis	21
Chapter 3	•	Models Dealing With Spatial Dependence	55
Chapter 4	•	Advanced Models Dealing With Spatial Dependence	85
Chapter 5	•	Models Dealing With Spatial Heterogeneity	113
Chapter 6	•	Models Dealing With Both Spatial Dependence and Spatial Heterogeneity	139
Chapter 7	•	Advanced Spatial Regression Models	155
Chapter 8	•	Practical Considerations for Spatial Data Analysis	183

Appendix A: Spatial Data Sources	217
Appendix B: Results Using Forty Spatial Weight Matrices available on the website at study.sagepub.com/researchmethods/ quantitative-statistical-research/chi	
Glossary	221
References	223
Index	235

DETAILED CONTENTS

Series Editor's Introduction   xv
Preface   xvii
Acknowledgments   xix
About the Authors   xxi

Chapter 1 • Introduction   1

Learning Objectives   1
    1.1 Spatial Thinking in the Social Sciences   3
    1.2 Introduction to Spatial Effects   4
       1.2.1 Spatial Analysis, Spatial Data Analysis, and Geographic Analysis   5
       1.2.2 Four Types of Spatial Data Analysis   6
    1.3 Introduction to the Data Example   7
       1.3.1 Population Change as a Spatial Process   8
       1.3.2 The State of Wisconsin in the United States: The Study Area   11
       1.3.3 Minor Civil Division (MCD): The Spatial Unit of Analysis   13
       1.3.4 Population Change in Wisconsin   16
    1.4 Structure of the Book   18
    Study Questions   19

Chapter 2 • Exploratory Spatial Data Analysis   21

Learning Objectives   21
    2.1 Exploratory Data Analysis   22
       2.1.1 The Methods   22
       2.1.2 Data Example   23
    2.2 Neighborhood Structure and Spatial Weight Matrix   33
       2.2.1 What Is a Neighborhood Structure?   33
       2.2.2 What Is a Spatial Weight Matrix?   35
       2.2.3 Why Should We Use a Spatial Weight Matrix?   39
       2.2.4 Which Spatial Weight Matrix Should We Use?   39
       2.2.5 Issues With Spatial Weight Matrices and Solutions   40
       2.2.6 Data Example   41
    2.3 Spatial Autocorrelation, Dependence, and Heterogeneity   41
    2.4 Exploratory Spatial Data Analysis   43
       2.4.1 Visualizing Spatial Data   43
       2.4.2 Moran's I Statistic   44
       2.4.3 Geary's c Statistic   46
       2.4.4 Local Indicator of Spatial Association (LISA)   47
       2.4.5 Data Example   49
    Study Questions   53

Chapter 3 • Models Dealing With Spatial Dependence — 55

Learning Objectives — 55

3.1 Standard Linear Regression and Diagnostics for Spatial Dependence — 56
- **3.1.1 Standard Linear Regression** — 56
- **3.1.2 Diagnostics for Spatial Dependence** — 58
- **3.1.3 Model Evaluation** — 59
- **3.1.4 When Do We Need to Account for Spatial Dependence?** — 59
- **3.1.5 Data Example** — 60

3.2 Spatial Lag Models — 65
- **3.2.1 What Is a Spatial Lag Model?** — 65
- **3.2.2 Model Fitting via Maximum Likelihood** — 66
- **3.2.3 Model Diagnostics** — 67
- **3.2.4 When Is a Spatial Lag Model Needed?** — 67
- **3.2.5 Which Spatial Weight Matrix to Use in a Spatial Lag Model?** — 68
- **3.2.6 Cautions About Spatial Lag Models** — 68
- **3.2.7 Data Example** — 69

3.3 Spatial Error Models — 74
- **3.3.1 What Is a Spatial Error Model?** — 74
- **3.3.2 Model Fitting via Maximum Likelihood** — 76
- **3.3.3 Model Diagnostics** — 77
- **3.3.4 When Is a Spatial Error Model Needed?** — 77
- **3.3.5 Which Spatial Weight Matrix to Use in a Spatial Error Model?** — 78
- **3.3.6 Spatial Lag Models or Spatial Error Models?** — 78
- **3.3.7 Spatial Models: SAR, CAR, and SMA** — 79
- **3.3.8 Data Example** — 80

Study Questions — 83

Chapter 4 • Advanced Models Dealing With Spatial Dependence — 85

Learning Objectives — 85

4.1 Spatial Error Models With Spatially Lagged Responses — 86
- **4.1.1 What Is a Spatial Error Model With Spatially Lagged Responses?** — 86
- **4.1.2 Why and When Is an SEMSLR Needed?** — 87
- **4.1.3 Model Fitting** — 87
- **4.1.4 Which Spatial Weight Matrices Should Be Used in an SEMSLR?** — 88
- **4.1.5 Data Example** — 89

4.2 Spatial Cross-Regressive Models — 93
- **4.2.1 What Is a Spatial Cross-Regressive Model?** — 93
- **4.2.2 Model Fitting** — 93
- **4.2.3 When Is a Spatial Cross-Regressive Model Needed?** — 94
- **4.2.4 Which Spatial Weight Matrices Should Be Used in a Spatial Cross-Regressive Model?** — 95
- **4.2.5 Data Example** — 95

4.3 Multilevel Linear Regression — 98
- **4.3.1 What Is an MLR Model?** — 100
- **4.3.2 MLR Model Diagnostics** — 103

4.3.3 Cautions About MLR Models	104
4.3.4 Data Example	104
Study Questions	110

Chapter 5 • Models Dealing With Spatial Heterogeneity — 113

Learning Objectives — 113

5.1 Aspatial Regression Methods	115
5.1.1 The Methods	115
5.1.2 Data Example	116
5.2 Spatial Regime Models	122
5.2.1 The Methods	122
5.2.2 Model Fitting	125
5.2.3 Data Example	126
5.3 Geographically Weighted Regression	127
5.3.1 The Limitations of Spatial Regime Models	127
5.3.2 Model Specifications of GWR	129
5.3.3 Spatial Weight Matrices for GWR Models	130
5.3.4 Model Fitting	131
5.3.5 Model Diagnostics	131
5.3.6 Strength and Limitation of GWR	132
5.3.7 Data Example	133
Study Questions	138

Chapter 6 • Models Dealing With Both Spatial Dependence and Spatial Heterogeneity — 139

Learning Objectives — 139

6.1 Spatial Regime Lag Models	140
6.2 Spatial Regime Error Models	141
6.3 Spatial Regime Error and Lag Models	142
6.4 Model Fitting	144
6.5 Data Example	144
Study Questions	153

Chapter 7 • Advanced Spatial Regression Models — 155

Learning Objectives — 155

7.1 Spatio-temporal Regression Models	156
7.1.1 Why Use Spatio-temporal Regression Models?	156
7.1.2 Two General Approaches for Spatio-temporal Regression Modeling	157
7.1.3 From Standard Linear Regression to Spatio-temporal Regression	157
7.1.4 How to Fit the Spatio-temporal Regression Model	161
7.1.5 Data Example	163
7.2 Spatial Regression Forecasting Models	167
7.2.1 What Is a Standard Regression Forecasting Model?	168
7.2.2 What Is a Spatial Regression Forecasting Model?	169
7.2.3 What Spatial Weight Matrices Should We Use in a Spatial Regression Forecasting Model?	171

7.2.4 Practical Considerations in Forecasting	171
7.2.5 Data Example	171
7.3 Geographically Weighted Regression for Forecasting	176
7.3.1 The Methods	176
7.3.2 Data Example	177
Study Questions	182

Chapter 8 • Practical Considerations for Spatial Data Analysis — 183

Learning Objectives — 183

8.1 Data Example of U.S. Poverty in R	184
8.1.1 Standard Exploratory Data Analysis	185
8.1.2 Standard Linear Regression	188
8.1.3 Neighborhood Structure and Spatial Weight Matrix	195
8.1.4 Exploratory Spatial Data Analysis	197
8.1.5 Spatial Linear Regression	201
8.2 General Procedure for Spatial Social Data Analysis	210
8.2.1 Reducing Data Dimensions	211
8.2.2 Selecting an Appropriate Spatial Weight Matrix	212
8.2.3 Spatial Regression Modeling With Spatial Dependence and Spatial Heterogeneity	213
8.2.4 Multitemporal Comparison of Variable Presence and Coefficient Influence	215
Study Questions	215

Appendix A: Spatial Data Sources	**217**

Appendix B: Results Using Forty Spatial Weight Matrices
available on the website at study.sagepub.com/researchmethods/
quantitative-statistical-research/chi

Glossary	**221**
References	**223**
Index	**235**

LIST OF FIGURES

Figure 1.1	The geography of Wisconsin, United States Source: Chi and Marcouiller (2011). Note: The urbanized areas are based on the 2000 Census Urban Areas.	12
Figure 1.2	Wisconsin population growth since 1840 Source: Decennial censuses, U.S. Census Bureau.	13
Figure 1.3	The classification of rural, suburban, and urban minor civil divisions (MCDs) in Wisconsin Source: Chi (2012).	15
Figure 1.4	Population change at the minor civil division (MCD) level in 1970–1980, 1980–1990, 1990–2000, and 2000–2010 in Wisconsin	17
Figure 2.1	Independent variables Source: Chi (2010b). Note: (a) The proportion of old population (sixty-five years and older) at the minor civil division (MCD) level in 2000 in Wisconsin, (b) the unemployment rate at the MCD level in 2000 in Wisconsin, (c) locations of major commercial airports in Wisconsin and neighboring states, (d) proximity to major commercial airports at the MCD level in Wisconsin and neighboring states, (e) forest coverage in Wisconsin, (f) the proportion of forest coverage in Wisconsin, (g) undevelopable land as of 2001 in Wisconsin, and (h) the proportion of land available for development at the MCD level as of 2001 in Wisconsin.	28
Figure 2.2	Contiguity neighborhood structure: (a) rook's case and (b) queen's case	34
Figure 2.3	A 4 × 4 lattice	36
Figure 2.4	A 16 × 16 spatial weight matrix without row standardization	37
Figure 2.5	A 16 × 16 spatial weight matrix with row standardization	37
Figure 2.6	Moran scatterplot of population change at the minor civil division (MCD) level from 2000 to 2010 in Wisconsin	51
Figure 2.7	LISA of population change at the minor civil division (MCD) level from 2000 to 2010 in Wisconsin	52
Figure 3.1	Residuals of the standard linear regression	64
Figure 3.2	Residuals of the spatial lag model based on the 4-nearest neighbor weight matrix	71
Figure 3.3	Residuals of the spatial lag model based on the 20-mile general distance weight matrix	74

Figure 3.4	Coefficient estimates of land developability in spatial lag models	75
Figure 3.5	Residuals of the spatial error model based on the 4-nearest neighbor weight matrix	82
Figure 4.1	Residuals of the spatial error model with spatially lagged responses (SEMSLR) Note: The 4-nearest neighbor weight matrix is used for calculating the spatially lagged responses; the 20-mile general distance weight matrix is used for controlling for the spatial error dependence.	92
Figure 4.2	Residuals of the spatial cross-regressive model	98
Figure 4.3	Moran's *I* statistics of the spatial cross-regressive model residuals	99
Figure 4.4	The Public Use Microdata Areas (PUMAs) in Wisconsin, 2000	105
Figure 5.1	Residuals of the standard linear regression model with urban-rural classifications	118
Figure 5.2	Residuals of the standard linear regression model with urban-rural classifications and interaction variables	120
Figure 5.3	Residuals of the standard linear regression models across the urban-rural continuum	121
Figure 5.4	Moran's *I* statistics of the spatial regime model residuals	128
Figure 5.5	Local coefficient estimates of initial geographically weighted regression (GWR)	135
Figure 5.6	The *t*-values of initial geographically weighted regression (GWR) coefficients	136
Figure 5.7	Local coefficients and *t*-values of final geographically weighted regression (GWR)	137
Figure 6.1	Coefficient estimates of the spatial regime lag model (SRLM)	146
Figure 6.2	Residuals of the spatial regime lag model (SRLM)	147
Figure 6.3	Coefficient estimates of the spatial regime error model (SREM)	148
Figure 6.4	Residuals of the spatial regime error model (SREM)	149
Figure 6.5	Moran's *I* statistics of the spatial regime lag model (SRLM) residuals	150
Figure 6.6	Coefficient estimates of the spatial regime error and lag model (SRELM) Note: The 4-nearest neighbor weight matrix is used for calculating the spatially lagged responses; the 30-mile general distance weight matrix is used for controlling for the spatial error dependence.	152
Figure 6.7	Residuals of the spatial regime error and lag model (SRELM)	152
Figure 7.1	Moran's *I* statistics for residuals of a standard linear regression model	165
Figure 7.2	Residuals of the spatio-temporal regression model based on the 4-nearest neighbor weight matrix	166

Figure 7.3	Moran's *I* statistics for the previous growth variable	172
Figure 7.4	Residuals of the initial spatial regression model	174
Figure 7.5	Residuals of the final spatial regression model	175
Figure 7.6	Local coefficients of the final geographically weighted regression (GWR) model	180
Figure 7.7	The *t*-values of the final geographically weighted regression (GWR) coefficients	181
Figure 7.8	Local R^2 of the geographically weighted regression (GWR) model	182
Figure 8.1	Histogram of poverty (a) and scatterplot between the poverty rate and the female employment rate (b)	188
Figure 8.2	Quantile-quantile (Q-Q) plot of the standard linear regression model residuals	194
Figure 8.3	Quantile-quantile (Q-Q) plot of the standard linear regression model residuals with the response variable transformed	194
Figure 8.4	Neighborhood structure for the counties in the contiguous United States	197
Figure 8.5	Poverty rate (a) and female employment rate (b) in 2000 Data source: The U.S. Census Bureau's Decennial Census in 2000.	198
Figure 8.6	Residuals versus fitted values of the spatial lag model	205

SERIES EDITOR'S INTRODUCTION

I am very pleased to introduce Guangqing Chi and Jun Zhu's volume *Spatial Regression Models for the Social Sciences*. Over the past few decades there has been a rapid increase in the use of spatial data to discern spatial effects in social science research due to the upsurge in the availability of geographically referenced data and the availability of user-friendly spatial data analysis software packages. However, many of the empirical studies remain at a stage that is descriptive and exploratory in nature, because many studies are geo-mapping or spatial overlay using geocoding technology. Regression-typed analyses exploring causal or correlational spatial effects are relatively sparse. Some studies employed multilevel regression models with random effects but failed to address the departure from the independent errors assumption at high levels. For contiguous geographic units, spatial lag models, spatial error models, spatial regime models, geographically weighted regression, spatio-temporal regression models, and geographically weighted regression for forecasting are more salient than the multilevel regression model. In essence, these models address the spatial dependence and heterogeneity issues more sophisticatedly by fully exploring the neighborhood structure embedded in an appropriately developed spatial weight matrix.

This volume describes all these latest advances in spatial regression models in a relatively accessible fashion for a broad range of readers conducting social scientific research. It describes the statistical principles, main features, strengths and limitations, and illustrating examples in a clear, succinct, and comprehensive fashion. The book is well organized to discuss lattice (or areal) data analysis using spatial regression methods.

This volume aims to help social scientists learn practical and useful statistical methods for spatial regression with relative ease. The authors have made efforts to limit the use of mathematic notations, derivations, and proofs but present the core materials in a comprehensive and easy-to-follow manner. Each chapter begins with learning objectives and ends with study questions to help readers get focused. For most methods discussed in the volume the authors focus on one case study with one data set for addressing specific research questions rather than different studies with different data sets, variables, and/or research questions. This pedagogical approach makes the learning of spatial regression models relatively easy. In summary, this very much needed book fills a gap in statistical analysis of geo-referenced spatial lattice data for social sciences.

Shenyang Guo
Series Editor

PREFACE

The past few decades have seen rapid development in spatial regression methods, which have been introduced in a large number of books and journal articles. However, when teaching spatial regression models and methods to social scientists, the authors had difficulty recommending a suitable textbook for students in the social sciences to read. Many of the existing textbooks are either too technical for social scientists or are limited in scope, partly due to the rapid development in the methods. A textbook that provides relatively comprehensive coverage of spatial regression methods for social scientists and introduces the methods in an easy-to-follow approach is much needed.

Therefore, we have attempted to write this as a primer type of textbook for social scientists who would like a quick start to learning spatial regression methods. While the methods are many and counting, we have decided to focus on the methods that are commonly used by social scientists and tend to be useful to them. These methods include exploratory spatial data analysis, methods dealing with spatial dependence and/or spatial heterogeneity, and more advanced spatial regression models.

WHY THIS BOOK?

There are a number of existing books on spatial regression methods in the field of spatial statistics. They provide comprehensive coverage of some, if not all, of the three main components of spatial statistics: spatial point pattern analysis, lattice (or areal) data analysis (i.e., spatial regression models and methods), and/or geostatistics; a few books also address spatial interactive data analysis. However, these textbooks tend to be written for natural scientists or regional scientists and require that readers have a good understanding of mathematical statistics. In addition, they are not necessarily tailored to areal (or lattice) data analysis in social science research, which is the most useful component, at least presently. This is not a criticism of these books; rather, we simply see a lack of a spatial regression textbook for social scientists interested in learning the models and methods in a comprehensive and easy-to-follow manner and with limited training in mathematical statistics. This is where our book comes in: like these other books, it discusses spatial regression models and methods, and unlike the other books, it is written specifically for social scientists.

The distinguishing features of this book include the following:

1. It is geared toward social scientists who are familiar with standard regression methods and would like to learn spatial regression models and methods.

2. It provides relatively comprehensive coverage of spatial regression models and methods for social scientists.

3. The spatial regression models that it covers are commonly used by social scientists and are of interest to them.

4. It introduces the spatial regression models and methods in a generally easy-to-follow manner.

5. All figures and illustrations have color versions available at **study.sagepub.com/researchmethods/quantitative-statistical-research/chi**

WHO IS THIS BOOK FOR?

This book could be particularly useful for social scientists who are familiar with standard regression methods and desire to learn spatial regression models and methods. It can be used as an introductory book to get to know spatial regression methods and apply them readily. It can also be used for a one-semester quantitative social science course at both undergraduate and graduate levels.

In addition, this book could be useful for social scientists who are interested in using spatial regression methods in their research. This includes instructors, researchers, and students in a wide range of social science disciplines such as sociology, demography, criminology, anthropology, human geography, economics, education, communication, history, law, political science, psychology, urban studies and planning, and others. The book may serve these social scientists as both a textbook and a reference book.

Although it is chiefly intended to be a core textbook for social science courses that focus on areal (or lattice) data analysis using spatial regression models and methods, it could serve as a supplemental textbook for social science courses that provide a more general coverage of regression methods.

A website for the book at **study.sagepub.com/researchmethods/quantitative-statistical-research/chi** contains color versions of the figures from the book, together with the tables that form Appendix B: Results Using Forty Spatial Weight Matrices.

ACKNOWLEDGMENTS

In 2008, we published an article titled "Spatial Regression Models for Demographic Analysis" in the journal *Population Research and Policy Review* to introduce spatial regression models for demographic research. It was well received, largely because spatial regression models were still new to social scientists at that time. Around 2010, we started to write a book of spatial regression models and methods *for* social scientists. Between now and then, we have presented the book idea and many rounds of revision in a variety of venues, and the feedback has been positive and enthusiastic: There does appear to be a need for such a spatial regression method book for social scientists.

This book is not a work that is solely ours; rather, it is a work collectively accomplished by us with tremendous support from our mentors, colleagues, students, editors, friends, and families. First, we would like to thank our students, Donghui Wang, Maria Kamenetsky, Supriya Joshi, and Taylor Hackemack, for having provided assistance with figures, tables, and data analysis.

We received valuable advice and suggestions from mentors and colleagues. Paul Voss was instrumental in teaching Guangqing Chi spatial regression methods. Stephanie Bohon, David Levinson, Stephen Matthews, David Plane, Stuart Sweeney, Tse-Chuan Yang, and Stephen Ventura provided advice and suggestions for our book.

We would also like to thank the institutions where we work(ed) during the development of the book: The Pennsylvania State University, University of Wisconsin–Madison, Mississippi State University, and South Dakota State University. This book is supported in part by the National Science Foundation (Awards CMMI-1541136, OPP-1745369, DGE-1806874, and SES-1823633), the National Aeronautics and Space Administration (Award NNX15AP81G), the U.S. Department of Transportation (Award DTRT12GUTC14), and the National Institutes of Health (Awards P2C HD041025 and U24 AA027684).

This book would not be possible without the tremendous support from the SAGE team. Helen Salmon, our Acquisitions Editor, was essential in guiding us to revise the book to be high quality and to tailor it better for our readers. Professor Shenyang

Guo, the Editor of the Advanced Quantitative Techniques in the Social Sciences Series, has provided insightful comments for our book. Megan O'Heffernan has been very helpful in assisting us during the final touches of the book. Also, reviewers provided many constructive comments and suggestions, which have helped us revise this book from a reference book into a textbook that is more pedagogical. They are J. S. Onesimo Sandoval, Saint Louis University; Daoqin Tong, Arizona State University; Peter Rogerson, University of Buffalo; Wenwu Tang, University of North Carolina at Charlotte; Changjoo Kim, University of Cincinnati; and Karen Kemp, University of Southern California.

We are grateful to Cindy Sheffield Michaels, now Editor of Special Publications for ASHRAE, for having worked with us from the very beginning. She not only edited the content and format but also provided constructive suggestions to make the book readable from the reader's perspective. What's more important, she encouraged us to move this book project forward when we ran out of steam, several times.

Guangqing's eldest daughter, Claire, has asked multiple times when the book will be published, because Guangqing promised her at the very early stages of this project that he would acknowledge his family so that Claire's name will show up in a book. So, Guangqing's last but not the least acknowledgment goes to his family—Yunjuan Jiang, Claire Chi, Gloria Chi, and Lydia Chi—for their patience and support. As for Jun, she would like to take this opportunity to express her deep gratitude toward all those who have mentored her with kindness and compassion, especially her parents, academic advisers, and colleague mentors.

Guangqing Chi and Jun Zhu
October 2018

ABOUT THE AUTHORS

Guangqing Chi is Associate Professor of Rural Sociology and Demography in the Department of Agricultural Economics, Sociology, and Education with courtesy appointments in the Department of Sociology and Criminology and Department of Public Health Sciences at The Pennsylvania State University. He also serves as Director of the Computational and Spatial Analysis Core of the Social Science Research Institute and Population Research Institute. Dr. Chi is an environmental demographer. His research examines the interactions between population change and the built and natural environments. He pursues his research program within interwoven research projects on climate change, land use, and community resilience, with an emphasis on environmental migration and critical infrastructure/transportation and population change within the smart cities framework. Most recently, Dr. Chi has applied his expertise in big data to study issues of generalizability and reproducibility of Twitter data for population and social science research. He also studies environmental migration, including projects on coupled migrant-pasture systems in Central Asia, permafrost erosion and coastal communities in the Arctic, and ecological migration in China. Dr. Chi's research has been supported through grants from national and state agencies, including the National Science Foundation, National Institutes of Health, National Aeronautics and Space Administration, and U.S. Department of Transportation. He has published more than 50 articles in peer-reviewed journals. His research on gasoline prices and traffic safety has been highlighted more than 2,000 times by various news media outlets, such as National Public Radio and *Huffington Post*.

Jun Zhu is Professor of Statistics at the University of Wisconsin–Madison. She is a faculty member in the Department of Statistics and the Department of Entomology, as well as a faculty affiliate with the Center for Demography and Ecology and the Department of Biostatistics and Medical Informatics. The main components of her research activities are statistical methodological research and scientific collaborative research. Her statistical methodological research concerns developing statistical methodology for analyzing spatially referenced data (spatial statistics) and spatial data repeatedly sampled over time (spatio-temporal statistics) that arise often in the biological, physical, and social sciences. Her collaborative research concerns applying modern statistical methods, especially spatial and spatio-temporal statistics, to studies of agricultural, biological, ecological, environmental, and social systems conducted by research scientists. Dr. Zhu's methodological and collaborative research projects have been supported by the Environmental Protection Agency, National Institutes of Health, National Science Foundation, U.S. Department of Agriculture, U.S. Department of Defense, and U.S. Geographical Society. She is a Fellow of the American Statistical Association and a recipient of the Distinguished Achievement Medal in its Section of Statistics and the Environment.

Sara Miller McCune founded SAGE Publishing in 1965 to support the dissemination of usable knowledge and educate a global community. SAGE publishes more than 1000 journals and over 800 new books each year, spanning a wide range of subject areas. Our growing selection of library products includes archives, data, case studies and video. SAGE remains majority owned by our founder and after her lifetime will become owned by a charitable trust that secures the company's continued independence.

Los Angeles | London | New Delhi | Singapore | Washington DC | Melbourne

1

INTRODUCTION

> **LEARNING OBJECTIVES**
>
> - Understand the current status of spatial social science research.
> - Understand basic concepts and terminologies related to spatial effects.
> - Familiarize yourself with the primary data example of population change that is used throughout this book.

This is a book for social scientists who want to learn spatial regression models with relative ease. But first of all, why should social scientists care about studying spatial regression models? Many statistical methods could be useful to social science research; learning any of them could take one considerable effort and also sometimes involve a steep learning curve.

We believe that quantitative social scientists, especially those who deal with aggregated quantitative data, can benefit from learning and using spatial regression models from at least three perspectives—theoretical, methodological, and practical. First, *theoretically,* many phenomena of the social sciences exhibit spatial effects. This has been explained both explicitly and implicitly by many theories and examined in many empirical studies. Second, *methodologically,* the standard linear regression analysis may not be reliable when the independence assumption of the model is not adequately met; if spatial effects are not properly accounted for, estimation and statistical inference may be unreliable (e.g., the effects of explanatory variables may be overstated or understated). Third, *practically,* the past twenty years have experienced a rapid increase in the use of spatial regression models for social science research—first human geography and regional science and then other social science disciplines, including anthropology, criminology, demography, economics, political science, urban studies and urban planning, and sociology. The bar for quantitative social science research has been raised, and conducting spatial regression analysis can be methodologically more rigorous in many research areas.

Why has there been a rapid increase in the use of spatial regression models for social science research? Because in addition to the recognition of their usefulness in social science research, spatial regression models have also become more accessible for social scientists to explore (Chi & Zhu, 2008). Multiple factors are associated with this increased accessibility, such as the following:

- the upsurge in the availability of geographically referenced data,
- the development of user-friendly spatial data analysis software packages, and
- increased computing power combined with affordable computers.

Geographically referenced data from geographic information system (GIS) sources and remote sensing images are often useful for social scientists and can be easily added to geo-referenced social science databases. Three resources are especially useful for researchers conducting spatial demographic analysis: the topologically integrated geographic encoding and reference (TIGER) system products; census summary files of 1980, 1990, 2000, and 2010, as well as the American Community Survey data; and sociological and demographic survey databases companioned with the geocoding technique. Moreover, development of spatial statistical software packages has been rapid in the past two decades, via products such as ArcGIS, GeoDa, GWR, MATLAB, Python, SAS, SpaceStat, S-plus, SPSS, Stata, and WinBugs. Improved computing power together with inexpensive personal computers has made conducting spatial regression analysis more affordable for social scientists. Furthermore, greater opportunities for studying spatial regression have arisen due to the larger number of textbooks, journal articles, and conference presentations advancing or using spatial data analytical tools (Entwisle, 2007; Florax & Van der Vlist, 2003; Logan, 2012). And this number is only growing.

Considering the opportunities for and development in spatial regression methods, we assert that it is an opportune time for social scientists to make better use of spatial regression methods and apply them to social science research. We believe that spatial regression models and methods can be learned with relative ease, and this book is intended to help readers do just that.

1.1 SPATIAL THINKING IN THE SOCIAL SCIENCES

Many phenomena of the social sciences exhibit spatial effects; this has been addressed both explicitly and implicitly in many theories and empirical studies. It would be useful to review the spatial thinking and theories as well as the empirical studies in the social sciences to build a foundation and make a case for spatial regression models in social science research. However, doing so is challenging considering that there is a large amount of spatial theories and empirical studies in the social sciences, and certain theories and studies are limited to specific social science disciplines. With both the benefit and the challenge in mind, and considering that this book is about spatial regression models rather than spatial theories, in this section, we provide a brief overview of the current status of spatial theories and empirical studies across social science disciplines.

Most social science disciplines and their subdisciplines have addressed the spatial dimension of their phenomena of study, although the extent to which they have done so varies greatly (Goodchild & Janelle, 2004). The Center for Spatially Integrated Social Science (CSISS) Classics provides a list of classic readings that contribute to spatial thinking in the social sciences.[1] Overall, spatial thinking in social science disciplines and subdisciplines can be addressed from multiple perspectives.

First, spatial thinking and theories have originated largely from human geography and regional science. Space and place are in the "blood" of human geographers and regional scientists, who almost always consider space and/or place in their research. They provide the core spatial theories and use them to investigate and explain a wide range of social phenomena. Some spatial thinking and theories have been developed in other social science disciplines but not as extensively as in human geography and regional science. Most existing empirical studies of spatial social sciences, although conducted in a variety of social science disciplines, cite the work of human geography and regional science.

Second, spatial methodologies have been developed by human and physical geographers, regional scientists, economists, statisticians, and others. These methodologies, which are discussed in Section 1.2, include spatial analysis techniques such as GIS and remote sensing image processes as well as statistical methods for spatial data analysis such as spatial point pattern analysis, lattice (or areal) data analysis (where the spatial regression models and methods described in this book fall), geostatistics, and spatial interactive data analysis. The development of

---

[1]www.csiss.org/classics

spatial methodologies enables and facilitates spatial thinking and theories to be applied to empirical studies of social science research.

Third, the application of spatial thinking and methodologies has experienced a rapid increase in the past two decades in many social science disciplines and subdisciplines (other than geography and regional science), including anthropology; criminology; demography; economics; political science (international studies, political economy, public administration); urban studies and urban planning; sociology; and interdisciplinary areas (such as area studies, development studies, environmental studies, and public health). Their data, when geographically referenced, can be analyzed using spatial methods. The rise in the application of spatial thinking and methodologies in these disciplines is largely due to the increased availability of geographically referenced data (i.e., spatial data), more user-friendly software packages for analyzing spatial data, and the rapid advances in robust and affordable computing power, as previously discussed.

Finally, spatial thinking and methodologies are seen as potentially beneficial to the humanities and social sciences such as communication, education, history, law, linguistics, and psychology from at least two perspectives. One, at the individual level, the socioeconomic and physical environments where the individual is located have effects on the individual; these environments can be seen as the "spatial" elements. Two, if individuals or observations are geocoded, which becomes increasingly easy to do with the development of geocoding techniques, the spatial dimension could be incorporated into empirical analysis using spatial methodologies. As a matter of fact, spatial thinking has already been developed in or for the disciplines of communication, history, and linguistics. Refer to the CSISS Classics for the relevant work.

It should be noted that the discussion here on spatial social science research is far from complete; rather, it is limited to our incomplete understanding of fields outside our own areas of expertise. Many books, journal issues, book chapters, journal articles, and websites provide overviews of spatial social science research. We suggest that readers look into these resources as well as spatial social science research in their own disciplines, if available, for more comprehensive understanding of spatial thinking and theories, methodologies, and applications.

1.2 INTRODUCTION TO SPATIAL EFFECTS

What are spatial effects, spatial analysis, spatial data analysis, spatial statistics, spatial autocorrelation, spatial dependence, and spatial heterogeneity? A newcomer to spatial regression models could easily be confused by the numerous concepts and terminologies associated with the models. This section introduces concepts related to spatial effects and the relevant terminologies used in the existing literature. We organize these concepts and terminologies into two categories:

- Spatial analysis versus spatial data analysis versus geographic analysis
- Four types of spatial data analyses

1.2.1 Spatial Analysis, Spatial Data Analysis, and Geographic Analysis

Spatial data refer to data that are geographically referenced and represent phenomena that are located in space. More specifically, spatial data refer to data that not only have the values or attributes related to the phenomena of interest but also the geographical or locational information of the observations. While aspatial data analysis uses only the former, spatial data analysis uses both. In a broad sense, spatial data analysis is the quantitative study of spatial data (Bailey & Gatrell, 1995). *Spatial analysis* is sometimes used interchangeably with *spatial data analysis, geographic analysis, spatial information analysis,* and *geographic information analysis* in the existing literature. While these terms refer to different things and have different foci, the boundary among them is somehow not clear and not completely agreed upon among researchers from different disciplines. For the purposes of this book, we understand spatial analysis as being composed of spatial data analysis and geographic analysis. The spatial regression models and methods are a specific set of tools for spatial data analysis.

Spatial data refer to data that are referenced geographically and represent phenomena located in space.

Spatial data analysis describes, models, and explains spatial data, from which we can make inferences about the phenomena under study and make predictions for areas where observations have not been sampled (Bailey & Gatrell, 1995). A spatial data analysis is conducted instead of aspatial data analysis if the data have spatial information and the spatial arrangements in the data or in the interpretation of the results are given explicit consideration. In particular, spatial data analysis is about using statistical methods to analyze spatial data; in the existing literature, this is often referred to as *spatial statistics.*

Spatial data analysis describes, models, and explains spatial data and enables us to make inferences and predictions.

Geographic analysis (or geographic information analysis or spatial information analysis) examines spatial data locations, attributes, and feature relations using geographic analysis techniques, and it also extracts or creates new information from spatial data (O'Sullivan & Unwin, 2010). Examples of geographic analysis are spatial overlay, spatial interpolation, network analysis, three-dimensional analysis,

Geographic analysis extracts or creates new information from spatial data and examines spatial data locations, attributes, and feature relations.

geocoding, terrain analysis, and others by using GIS software (e.g., ESRI) that uses GIS and remote sensing images. Geographic analysis methods and tools have been developed mostly by geographers, geologists, and environmental scientists and have been used by researchers from a wide range of fields.

1.2.2 Four Types of Spatial Data Analysis

There are four types of spatial data analysis as categorized in existing spatial statistics and spatial econometrics literature (see, e.g., Bailey & Gatrell, 1995; Cressie, 1993; Schabenberger & Gotway, 2005; Waller & Gotway, 2004):

- spatial point pattern analysis,
- areal data analysis,
- geostatistics, and
- spatial interactive data analysis.

Each of these types of analysis has its own set of objectives and approaches.

Spatial point patterns consist of event locations in a spatial domain of interest.

Spatial point patterns (or spatial point processes) consist of the locations of events occurring in a spatial domain of interest (see, e.g., Baddeley, Rubak, & Turner, 2015; Cressie, 1993; Møller & Waagepetersen, 2003). A goal of spatial point pattern analysis often is to determine or quantify spatial patterns in the form of regularity or clustering (as deviation from randomness) or in relation to covariates. For example, disease mapping, for which the data often consist of locations of disease occurrences and are spatially referenced, is focused on the description and analysis of geographic variations in a disease (such as randomness, regularity, and clustering) and seeks explanations from demographic, environmental, behavioral, socioeconomic, genetic, and infectious risk factors (Elliott & Wartenberg, 2004; Waller & Gotway, 2004).

Areal data are spatial data observed over regular grid cells or aggregated to irregular areal regions.

Areal data refer to spatial data observed over regular grid cells (or pixels) as seen in remotely sensed data or spatial data aggregated to irregular areal regions such as counties and census tracts; such data are often referred to as lattice data and are sometimes referred to as regional data (see, e.g., Schabenberger & Gotway, 2005; Waller & Gotway, 2004). Areal data analysis aims to quantify the spatial pattern of an attribute on a spatial lattice or region (regular or irregular) through a specific neighborhood structure and examines the relations between the attribute and the potential explanatory variables while accounting for spatial effects. Spatial regression modeling is a common approach used in areal data analysis. For the purposes of this book, the term *areal data analysis* is used.

Geostatistical data refer to spatial data sampled at point locations that are continuous in space. The objectives of geostatistics are similar to those of areal data analysis, but geostatistics aims to also predict attribute values at locations that are not sampled (see, e.g., Cressie, 1993; Goodchild, 1992; Stein, 1999). Geostatistics is common in geology, soil science, and forest resource management research. For example, petroleum geologists estimate hydrocarbon fuel distribution based on a small number of hydrocarbon samples from known locations using geostatistical methods. Two key differences distinguish geostatistics from areal data analysis:

- geostatistical data are geographically referenced to specific point locations while areal data are geographically referenced to areal regions, and
- geostatistics generally measures spatial dependence by distance-based functions while areal data analysis often uses neighborhood structures.

> **Geostatistical data** are spatial data from point locations continuous in space.

Spatial interaction data refer to the "flows" between origins and destinations (see, e.g., Bailey & Gatrell, 1995). Spatial interaction data analysis attempts to quantify the arrangement of flows and build models for origin and destination interactions in terms of the geographical accessibility of destinations versus origins as well as the "push factors" of origins and "pull factors" of destinations. Spatial interaction data analysis is often used in transportation planning, migration studies, and other research that has flow information.

> **Spatial interaction data** are the "flows" between origins and destinations.

In this book, we restrict our attention to **areal data analysis,** as it is currently the spatial data analysis approach most used in the social sciences. The other methods discussed (point data analysis, geostatistics, and spatial interaction data analysis) are useful for social science studies as well, however. For example, geographers conduct demographic studies using geostatistics (e.g., Cowen & Jensen, 1998; Jensen et al., 1994; Langford, Maguire, & Unwin, 1991; Langford & Unwin, 1994; Mennis, 2003), and epidemiological and social network researchers use point data analysis and spatial interaction data analysis, respectively.

> **Areal data analysis** is the focus of this book because it is the spatial approach currently most used in the social sciences.

1.3 INTRODUCTION TO THE DATA EXAMPLE

As we addressed in the Preface, the goal of this book is to help social scientists learn practical and useful statistical methods for spatial regression with relative ease. Our approach is to use concrete social data examples and in-depth analyses to illustrate the statistical concepts, models, and methods while keeping the use of statistical formulas and proofs at a minimum. No background of mathematical statistics is assumed of readers.

For ease of presentation, for most methods discussed in this book, we focus on one case study with one primary data example for addressing specific research questions rather than different studies with different data sets, variables, and/or research questions. Readers are encouraged to think about how their own data could be analyzed to address their research questions while reading our data analyses.

> The data example used throughout this book is a possible template for readers to consider how their own data can be analyzed to address their research questions.

In the primary data example for this book, the state of Wisconsin in the United States is the study area of interest. We illustrate the use of spatial regression models and methods by studying *population change* as the response variable in relation to a variety of factors spatially and temporally at the minor civil division (MCD) level. In this book, population change is specifically referred to as a change in population size; that is, the outcome could be either population growth or population decline. Population change is a familiar subject to most social scientists and has been considered an essential component in many social science disciplines, making this data example quite accessible to many social scientists.

In the following subsections, we first review why and how population change is seen as a spatial phenomenon in several social science disciplines. There are two purposes for doing this. One, population change is the primary data example used throughout this book for demonstrating the use of spatial regression models, and thus it deserves a thorough understanding on its spatial dimension to build the theoretical foundation for spatially analyzing population change. Two, many social science phenomena are studied in multiple social science disciplines with different approaches; researchers often review and adopt approaches from other disciplines. Our review of population change as a spatial phenomenon (or spatial process) can serve as a template for studying the spatial effects of other social phenomena. We then briefly introduce the state of Wisconsin to readers who are not familiar with it and follow with a description of the MCD, which is the spatial unit of analysis. Finally, we present descriptive statistics of population change in Wisconsin.

1.3.1 Population Change as a Spatial Process

Population change is considered spatially both explicitly and implicitly in existing social science literature. Population change is theorized and modeled spatially and explicitly in human geography (including population geography, geographic information sciences, transportation geography, and health geography); regional science; and environmental planning. These fields have well-established theories and methodologies for spatial data analysis of population change.

Researchers in population geography are interested in the spatial variation of population distribution, growth, composition, and migration; they seek to explain the population patterns that can be attributed to spatial regularities and processes (Bailey, 2005; Trewartha, 1953). Tobler's (1970) first law of geography states that everything is related to everything else, but nearer things more so. Population geography's spatial diffusion theory argues that population growth forces spread (spillover) into surrounding areas (Hudson, 1972), which implies that population growth is spatially dependent.

Researchers in regional economics explain and model changes in land use patterns, which are nearly always associated with population change (Boarnet, 1998; Cervero, 2003). For example, the growth pole theory explains, through the concepts of spread and backwash, the mutual geographic dependence of economic growth and development, which in turn leads to population change (Perroux, 1955). The central place theory puts population in a hierarchy of urban places, where the movement of populations, firms, and goods is determined by the associated costs and city sizes (Christaller, 1966). In the "new" economic geography theory, Krugman (1991) adds space to the endogenous growth and studies the process of city network formation over time.

In environmental planning, researchers study how land use changes are encouraged or discouraged by the physical environment and the socioeconomic conditions and how this, in turn, leads to population change. The approach is generally empirical, usually using GIS overlay methods to answer what-if questions. There is also similar work on developable lands (Cowen & Jensen, 1998), qualitative (Lewis, 1996) and quantitative (Cardille, Ventura, & Turner, 2001) environmental corridors, growth management factors (Land Information and Computer Graphics Facility, 2000, 2002), and a land developability index (Chi, 2010b).

Population change as a spatial process is also implicitly suggested and considered in theories of sociology (especially urban sociology, rural sociology, and sociological human ecology) and demography (especially spatial demography, rural demography, and applied demography). The spatial process of population change has already been formally incorporated into demographic models and empirical studies (Entwisle, 2007). In addition, researchers often use maps to illustrate spatial patterns and population change with multiple time frames. For a review of the large body of literature on this research, see Entwisle (2007), Fossett (2005), Logan (2012), Reibel (2007), Voss (2007), and the position paper collection *Future Directions in Spatial Demography* released jointly by University of California, Santa Barbara; Pennsylvania State University; and the National Institutes of Health Advanced Spatial Analysis Training Program.[2]

Rural demographers study population's spatial dimension, conducting research on population distribution and migration. They argue that migrants prefer somewhat rural or truly "sub"-urban locations within commutable distances of large cities (Brown, Fuguitt, Heaton, & Waseem, 1997; Fuguitt & Zuiches, 1975). Applied demographers often use the idea of neighbors for small-area population estimation and forecasting. For instance, they may adjust populations projected at the municipal level so that they agree with their parent county's projections; this neighborhood context, however, is different from the spatial effects that we address in this book. Recent population forecasting research has used a modified spatio-temporal regression approach (e.g., Chi & Voss, 2011) and a geographically weighted regression approach (e.g., Chi & Wang, 2017) to formally incorporate spatial effects into the modeling.

Sociological human ecology, or the study of how human beings are affected by the environment in space and time (McKenzie, 1924), also informs sociologists of the spatial distribution of population (Berry & Kasarda, 1977; Frisbie & Kasarda, 1988). Hawley (1950) considers one of human ecology's main topics to be spatial differentiation within urban systems, whereas Robinson (1950) views human ecology studies as using spatial information rather than individual units. And Logan and Molotch (1987) espouse that the analytical basis for urban systems in human ecology is spatial relations.

Segregation studies, one of the largest bodies of urban sociological research, likewise suggest population distribution has spatial effects (Charles, 2003; Fossett, 2005). There are several theoretical approaches explaining segregation: the spatial assimilation approach claims differences in socioeconomic statuses and associated lifestyles cause it (Galster, 1988), the place stratification approach states discrimination causes it (Alba & Logan, 1993; Massey & Denton, 1993), and the suburbanization explanation argues the suburbanization process leads to segregation (Chi & Parisi, 2011).

The spatial dimension of population dynamics is also studied by neo-Marxists, who mainly focus on population redistribution. They explain that capitalism's pursuit

---

[2] www.ncgia.ucsb.edu/projects/spatial-demography/docs/All-position-papers.pdf

of profit leads to how cities are structured, how land is used, and how population changes (Hall, 1988; Jaret, 1983). They also argue that the basis of urban development in the United States is capital accumulation (Gordon, 1978; Hill, 1977; Mollenkopf, 1975, 1981). As Hill (1977) explains, because capital accumulation occurs in an environment that is spatially structured, the geographical form and spatial patterning that it takes is (at least provisionally) urbanism.

Although there is a large body of literature on spatial demography, demography has not yet fully integrated spatial statistics and analysis methods (Hugo, Champion, & Lattes, 2003). Sociologists and demographers can benefit from the advances in spatial techniques and the availability of spatial data as these tools become more accessible and well known to develop new theories and ask new demographic and sociological questions (Chi & Zhu, 2008). Sociological and demographic perspectives of population change can be strengthened further as more researchers incorporate the spatial effects of proximity, continuity, and contagion from geography and regional science's spatially explicit theories into new theories. For a summary of the literature, see Entwisle (2007), Fossett (2005), Reibel (2007), and Voss (2007).

It should be noted that this list of the explicit and implicit spatial theories of population change is far from complete. The implicit spatial theories come mostly from sociological and demographic perspectives, which the authors are familiar with; theories from other social science disciplines regarding population change as a spatial process are not discussed here.

1.3.2 The State of Wisconsin in the United States: The Study Area

Our case study focuses on population changes during the period of 1970 to 2010 at the MCD level in the state of Wisconsin in relation to the spatial and temporal variations of a multitude of explanatory variables. Wisconsin, located in the upper Midwest of the United States, borders Minnesota, Iowa, Illinois, and Michigan, as well as the Mississippi River, Lake Michigan, and Lake Superior (Figure 1.1). Wisconsin contains 34.8 million acres (excluding the Mississippi River and Great Lakes areas in the state), and inland lakes constitute 3 percent of the state's total surface area (Wisconsin Legislative Reference Bureau, 2005).

Although Wisconsin became the thirtieth state in 1848, the written history of the state dates to more than 300 years ago, when around 20,000 Native Americans and French explorers were first arriving (Wisconsin Legislative Reference Bureau,

FIGURE 1.1 ◆ The geography of Wisconsin, United States

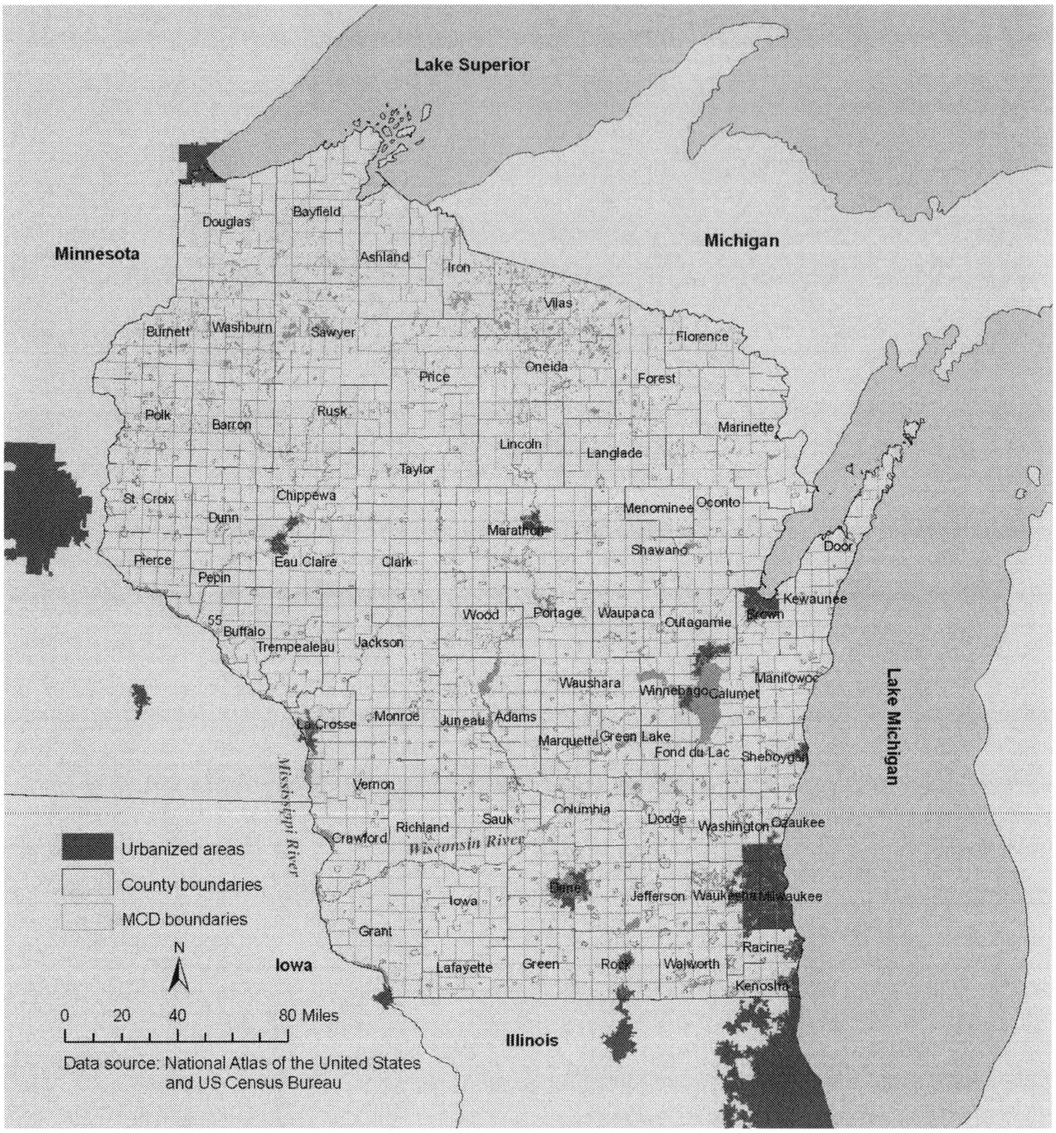

Source: Chi and Marcouiller (2011).

Note: The urbanized areas are based on the 2000 Census Urban Areas.

2005). The years between 1824 and 1861 saw the first wave of immigration to Wisconsin, due to lead mining in the southwestern corner of the state (Figure 1.2). As the years passed, immigration continued, and in the early years of its statehood, Wisconsin became a major area for wheat farming. As the wheat industry moved to the northern and western parts of the state after the Civil War, the lumber industry became important for the northern half of the state (1870s to 1890s), as did the dairy industry for the state as a whole (1880s and 1890s). The heavy machinery and

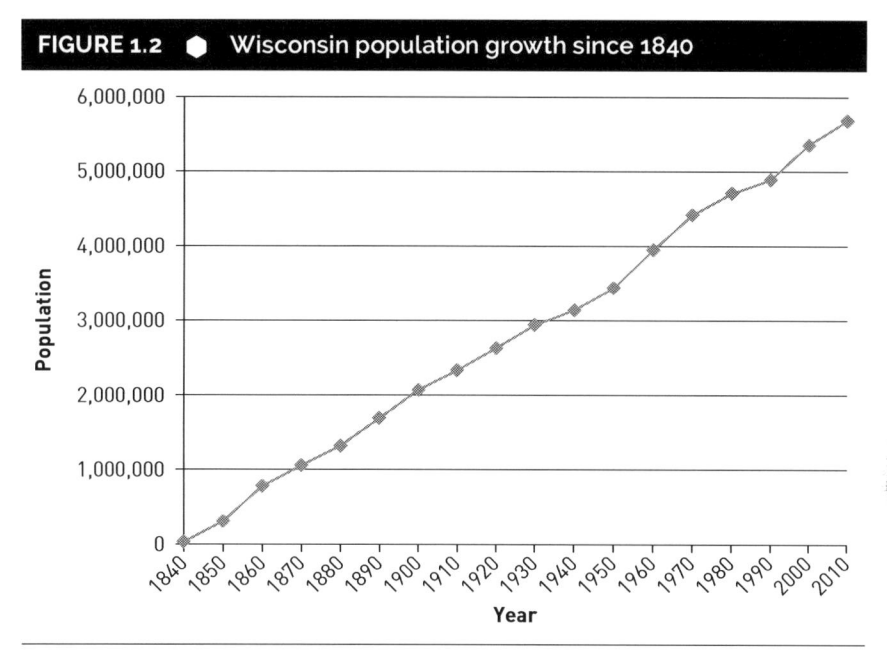

FIGURE 1.2 ● Wisconsin population growth since 1840

Source: Decennial censuses, U.S. Census Bureau.

brewing industries grew and developed dramatically in Wisconsin until the end of the nineteenth century. By the middle of the twentieth century, the large-scale European immigration had ended. During this time, the lumber industry faded and the brewing industry disappeared temporarily, while the heavy machinery manufacturing, paper, and dairy industries thrived. Tourism has since emerged as a major industry for the entire state, and other industries have been concentrated in its eastern and southeastern areas. In the 1980s, the state grew less than 4 percent (the smallest increase in the state's history); the 1990s saw 9.6 percent population growth and the 2000s saw 6.0 percent growth.

1.3.3 Minor Civil Division (MCD): The Spatial Unit of Analysis

MCDs are designated on the basis of legal entities rather than on population sizes and are recognized in twenty-eight U.S. states. Each MCD (a city, a village, or a town) is a functioning governmental unit with elected officials who provide services and raise revenues. The particular data set to be analyzed in our case study consists of 1,837 adjusted MCDs in Wisconsin. Wisconsin has seventy-two counties, and the MCDs are county subdivisions. They are exhaustive political territories that are mutually exclusive and nonnested. Wisconsin is composed of some large cities and surrounding neighboring suburbs; multiple small villages, towns, and cities; and low-density rural areas. It is therefore a typical MCD state.

In Wisconsin from 1970 to 2010, the MCD boundaries were unstable—over time, boundaries of existing MCDs shift, new MCDs are created, former MCDs disappear, the names of MCDs change, and the jurisdictional statuses of the MCDs change (e.g., towns become villages and villages become cities). Changes such as these required that we adjust the data to establish a data set that is spatially consistent over time. We applied three rules: new MCDs are merged into the original MCDs from which they emerged; disappearing MCD problems are solved by dissolving the original MCDs into their current "home" MCDs; and occasionally, several distinct MCDs are dissolved into one super-MCD. The adjustments resulted in a data set of 1,837 MCDs. Among these, the sizes of the MCDs range from 0.1 to 368 square miles, with an average size of 29.6 square miles. In 2010, the populations of MCDs ranged from 40 to 594,833 persons, with an average population of 3,097 persons.

For the purpose of illustrating spatial regression models dealing with spatial heterogeneity, in Sections 5.1 and 5.2, we further classify the MCDs into rural, suburban, and urban areas. Many classifications of rural, suburban, and urban areas have been used in existing research, and a single, standard classification does not exist (Chi, 2012). Our classification in this book is based on the 2000 Census Urban Areas and 2000 Metropolitan and Micropolitan Statistical Areas (MMSAs) defined by the U.S. Office of Management and Budget. Our classification system consists of the following: MCDs that fall into the Census Urban Areas we call urban areas, MCDs that fall into the MMSAs but not into the Census Urban Areas we call suburban areas, and MCDs that fall out of both the MMSAs and the Census Urban Areas we call rural areas (Figure 1.3). This categorization may be useful for evaluation purposes but does not necessarily accurately reflect the actual conditions in Wisconsin.

Studying population change at the MCD level has two advantages. The first one is the relevance of MCDs to planning and public policy making. In most parts of Wisconsin, census tracts have average sizes similar to MCDs and may serve as an alternative spatial unit of analysis. However, census tracts are geographic units delineated by the U.S. Census Bureau and do not have specific political or social meanings. MCDs, on the other hand, are functioning governmental units. The second advantage is that studying population change at subcounty levels, such as the MCD level, can provide insights into possible local dynamics that may not be captured by analysis at the county level or higher. For example, changes in transportation accessibility may not have major impacts on population change at county levels or higher, but they may have great impacts at subcounty levels. The changes

FIGURE 1.3 ● The classification of rural, suburban, and urban MCDs in Wisconsin

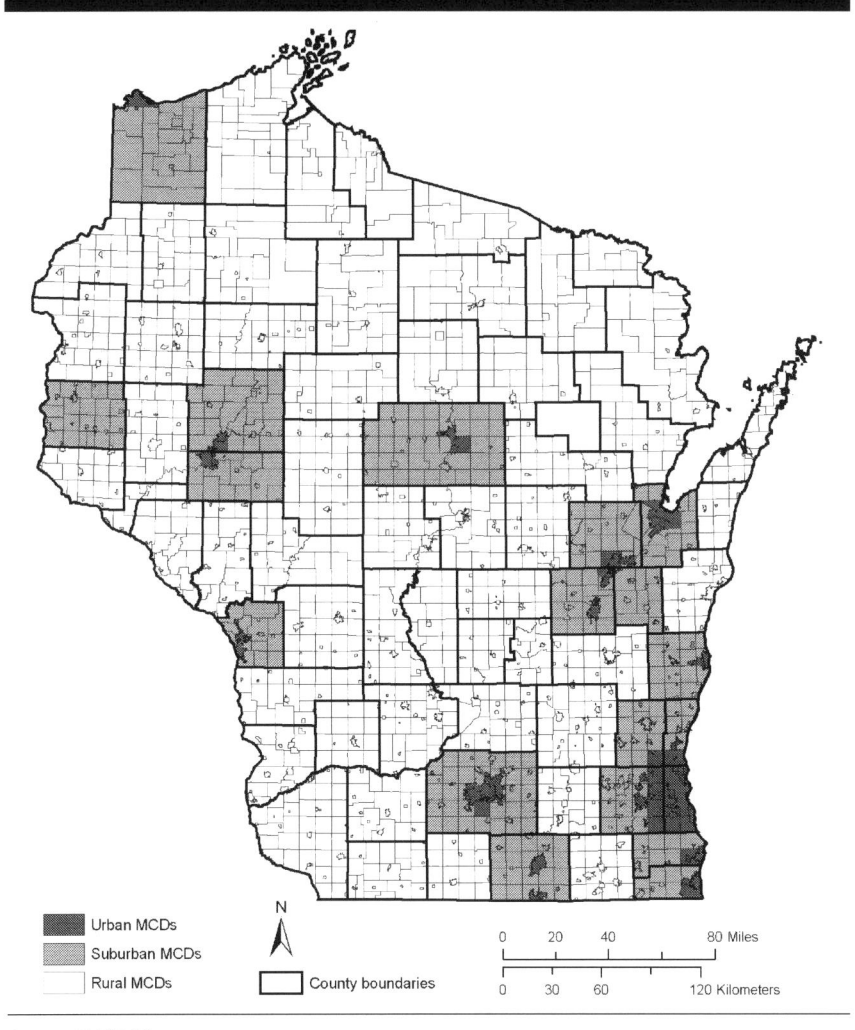

- Urban MCDs
- Suburban MCDs
- Rural MCDs
- County boundaries

Source: Chi (2012).

may offset each other when the local changes are aggregated from small areas to larger ones. The scale effect, as this phenomenon is known (Fotheringham & Wong, 1991), would be more obvious in an urban area, which has one or a few counties divided into several MCDs. An example from the existing literature is research revealing that highway expansion/construction may benefit neighborhoods a few blocks away from the work but might be unpleasant to those in the neighborhoods nearby (Chi & Parisi, 2011). Airport expansion is a similar situation, with the work benefiting areas not too far away but being unpleasant in nearby areas. In both cases, the neighborhoods that are not immediate would experience less population loss and potentially higher population growth than the immediate neighborhoods, but *in the county as a whole,* the total population change would not be affected much by the internal migration due to these situations. Using MCDs instead of counties or census tracts as the unit of measure can show such subtle changes in the associations of various variables with population change and provide insight for policy makers in the affected neighborhoods.

1.3.4 Population Change in Wisconsin

In our case study, population change in terms of population counts as reported by the U.S. Census Bureau is the response variable (or dependent variable) and is expressed as the natural log of population in a census year over the population ten years earlier. For example, the measure of the growth rate from 2000 to 2010 is the natural log of the 2010 population divided by the 2000 population. This measure of population change helps achieve a normal "bell-shaped" distribution; makes interpreting the population change rate easier (growth is shown by a positive value, decline is shown by a negative value, and no change at all is shown by zero); and accounts for initial population size (Chi, 2009). The population data for this case study are provided by decennial U.S. Census Bureau censuses from 1970 to 2010.

Figure 1.4 shows population change in Wisconsin in four time periods: 1970–1980, 1980–1990, 1990–2000, and 2000–2010. From 1970 to 1980, relatively high population growth occurred in rural and suburban areas. The 1970s marked a rural renaissance for the first time in Wisconsin, also called "turnaround migration" by

TABLE 1.1 ● **Descriptive statistics of population change at the MCD level in Wisconsin**

	All	Rural MCDs	Suburban MCDs	Urban MCDs
1970–1980	0.141 (0.193)	0.134 (0.185)	0.165 (0.205)	0.117 (0.248)
1980–1990	0.013 (0.122)	0.001 (0.117)	0.038 (0.128)	0.063 (0.128)
1990–2000	0.101 (0.152)	0.091 (0.145)	0.131 (0.171)	0.106 (0.154)
2000–2010	0.036 (0.139)	0.018 (0.126)	0.090 (0.167)	0.061 (0.105)
Number of MCDs (*n*)	1,837	1,334	417	86

Note: The numbers in each cell represent the average population change rate at the MCD level. Standard deviations are in parentheses.

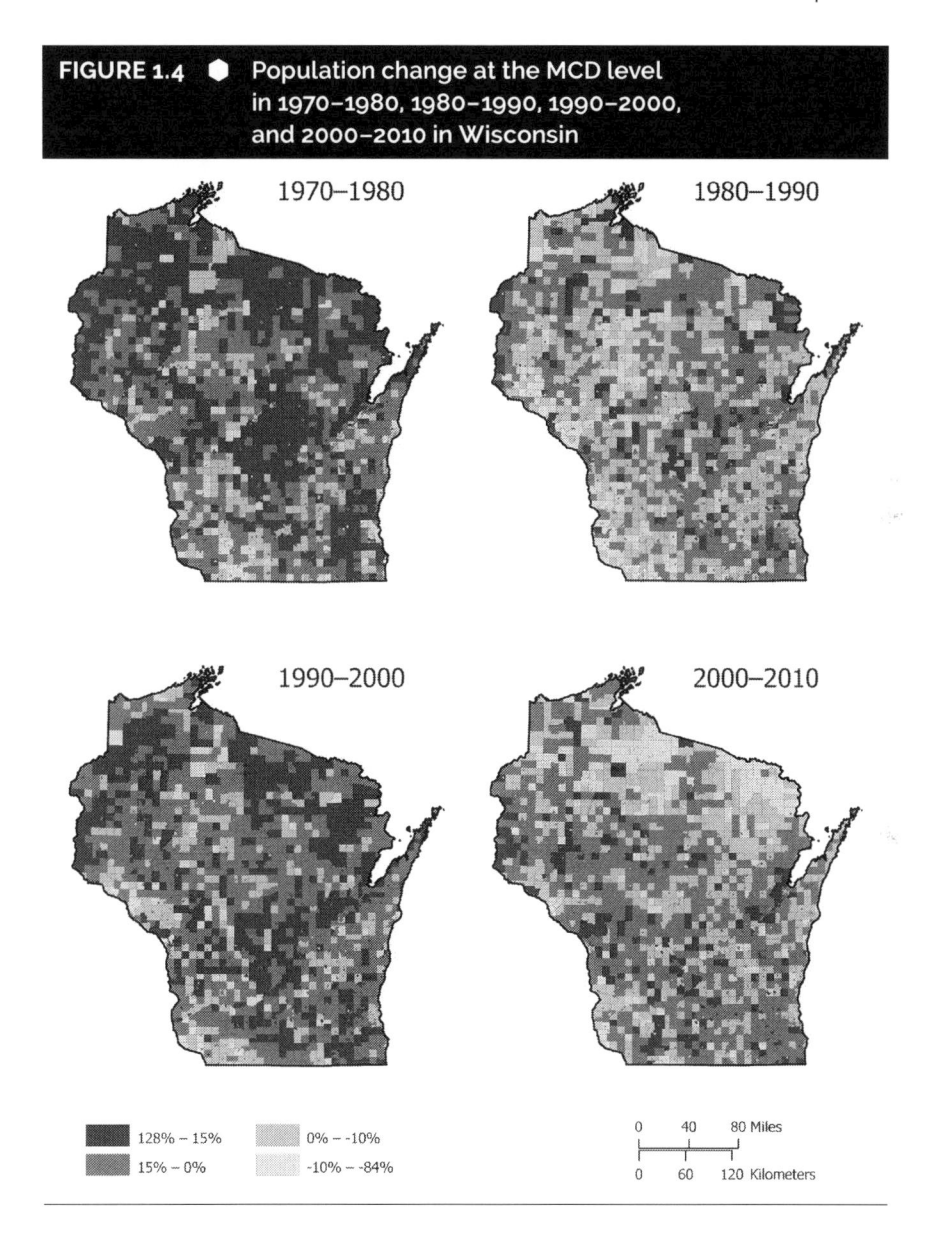

FIGURE 1.4 ● Population change at the MCD level in 1970–1980, 1980–1990, 1990–2000, and 2000–2010 in Wisconsin

1970–1980

1980–1990

1990–2000

2000–2010

128% – 15%
15% – 0%
0% – -10%
-10% – -84%

0 40 80 Miles
0 60 120 Kilometers

rural demographers, as natural amenities and employment opportunities attracted migrants to the amenity-rich rural areas (Johnson, 1999). During this time, rural and suburban MCDs experienced higher population growth rates than urban MCDs: the average population growth rate was 13.4 percent for rural MCDs, 16.5 percent for suburban MCDs, and 11.7 percent for urban MCDs (Table 1.1).

From 1980 to 1990, a majority of MCDs experienced population decline; it was the slowest growth decade in the history of Wisconsin. The population redistribution pattern was renewed metropolitan growth, mainly due to economic disruptions such as the farm debt crisis, deindustrialization (which downsized the manufacturing), and urban revival (which stopped people migrating to rural areas). In this decade, the average population growth rate in urban MCDs (6.3 percent) was much higher than that in suburban MCDs (3.8 percent), which was much higher than that in rural MCDs (0.1 percent).

From 1990 to 2000, rural areas rebounded as an improved economy and the areas' natural amenities attracted retirees. Relatively high population growth occurred in northern Wisconsin, central Wisconsin, and some suburban areas. The population growth rate of rural MCDs (9.1 percent) was similar to that of urban MCDs (10.6 percent), and the average population growth rate in suburban MCDs (13.1 percent) was relatively higher than those in rural and urban MCDs.

From 2000 to 2010, the population redistribution pattern was selective deconcentration; technological innovations in communications and transportation, companioned with the economic crisis that occurred in 2008, made migration more selective. It appears that population growth occurred mostly in suburban areas. The average population growth rate of MCDs from 2000 to 2010 in Wisconsin was 3.6 percent. The growth rate varies spatially along the urban-rural continuum: the average population growth rate was 1.8 percent in rural MCDs, 9 percent in suburban MCDs, and 6.1 percent in urban MCDs.

1.4 STRUCTURE OF THE BOOK

Throughout this book, each spatial regression method is introduced in two components. First, we explain what the method is and when we can or should use it by connecting it to a few social science research topics. Mathematical formulas and symbols are kept to a minimum. Second, we use three social science examples to demonstrate how to use the method and what the results can tell us. The primary example, which is the same research and data for most methods discussed in the book, examines the association between population growth from 1970 to 2010 in 1,837 Wisconsin MCDs and its relevant factors based on a geographically referenced longitudinal data set. The second example relates migration from 1995 to 2000 to individual, household, and community characteristics in Wisconsin. The third example examines poverty in association with demographic characteristics and socioeconomic conditions from 2000 to 2010 at the county level in the contiguous United States. Readers can apply our research procedures to their research at various levels of units of analysis, such as countries, regions, counties, census tracts, metro/nonmetro areas, neighborhoods, communities, block groups, and others.

This book is composed of eight chapters divided into thirty sections. Chapter 1 has provided a brief summary of spatial social science theories and thinking as well as introductions to spatial effects and the primary data example used throughout this book. Chapter 2 addresses some important concepts and issues of spatial regression models and methods, including exploratory data analysis, neighborhood structure and spatial weight matrix, spatial dependence and heterogeneity, and exploratory spatial data analysis.

Chapter 3 introduces spatial regression models dealing with spatial dependence, including spatial lag models and spatial error models. Advanced spatial regression models dealing with spatial dependence, including spatial error models with spatially lagged responses, spatial cross-regressive models, and multilevel linear regression models, are introduced in Chapter 4. Chapter 5 introduces spatial regression models and methods dealing with spatial heterogeneity, including aspatial regression models, spatial regime models, and geographically weighted regression. Although both this chapter and Chapter 2 are recommended to be read in full, Chapters 3 to 5, which each introduce one method, are recommended to be read consecutively but do not have to be—readers can go to the method of interest directly.

Chapter 6 discusses extended spatial regime models and approaches for dealing with both spatial dependence and spatial heterogeneity in spatial regression analysis. Chapter 7 introduces some more advanced spatial regression models, including spatio-temporal regression models, spatial regression forecasting models, and geographically weighted regression for forecasting. A general procedure for studying social science phenomena with the spatial dimension in mind is suggested in Chapter 8 using the poverty data example and R code.

Study Questions

1. Which social science disciplines have a spatial aspect? How? To what extent?
2. What are spatial effect, spatial data analysis, geographic analysis, and spatial analysis?
3. What is the difference between spatial data analysis and geographic analysis?
4. What is the difference between spatial analysis and spatial data analysis?
5. What are the four types of spatial data analysis? What are they mainly used for?
6. How is the spatial dimension of population change addressed in related disciplines?
7. For your area of research, are spatial concepts and/or theories used? If so, what are they?
8. For your area of research, how do empirical studies typically address the spatial dimension?

2

EXPLORATORY SPATIAL DATA ANALYSIS

LEARNING OBJECTIVES

- Review exploratory data analysis methods.
- Understand the concept and different types of neighborhood structure.
- Understand why and when to use spatial weight matrices and how to choose which spatial weight matrices to use.
- Distinguish spatial autocorrelation, spatial dependence, and spatial heterogeneity.
- Understand the statistics for measuring global and local spatial association.
- Familiarize yourself with methods for visualizing spatial data.

In this chapter, we introduce some basic but important concepts and issues related to spatial regression models as well as methods for preliminary analysis before conducting spatial regression analysis. Section 2.1 briefly summarizes exploratory data analysis, which is generally familiar to social scientists. Section 2.2 addresses neighborhood structures and spatial weight matrices, two key components of spatial data analysis. Section 2.3 discusses the concepts of spatial autocorrelation, dependence, and heterogeneity. Section 2.4 introduces exploratory spatial data analysis techniques. The use of these techniques is demonstrated by analyzing the data example of population growth in Wisconsin at the minor civil division (MCD) level as described in Chapter 1.

2.1 EXPLORATORY DATA ANALYSIS

2.1.1 The Methods

Data analysis using statistical methods frequently begins with exploratory data analysis (EDA), which provides a background of the data set to be investigated without formal statistical inference. Common practices in EDA include

- summarizing the distribution of the data graphically,
- describing the distribution of the data using summary statistics, and
- relating variables to each other using graphics or statistics.

Typically, it is informative to conduct exploratory data analysis before fitting regression models.

EDA helps researchers get familiar with and gain understanding of the data, and it also provides clues to choosing the more appropriate statistical methods to use for inference. EDA is recommended as the first thing to do before fitting any regression models.

During EDA, it is common to examine the distributions of response and explanatory variables and the variables' interrelations. Aspects to examine during EDA may include

- whether the variables show normal distributions,
- whether the response and each exploratory variable have a linear relation, and
- whether the explanatory variables have low correlations among themselves.

If EDA reveals that the distributions are not normal or that variable relations are not linear, the next step might be to transform the variables or create new variables such as higher-order terms and interaction terms (Fox, 1997). If EDA reveals high correlations among the explanatory variables, know that this might lead to unstable estimation and statistical inference due to multicollinearity (Baller, Anselin, Messner, Deane, & Hawkins, 2001). A remedy for this problem is to apply principal component or factor analysis to the explanatory variables with high correlations and create new explanatory variables.

EDA has been used in many, if not most, quantitative social science research works. EDA has also been covered in many statistical textbooks and introductory statistical classes. Readers are referred to existing textbooks and journal articles for details on EDA (e.g., Agresti & Finlay, 2009; Fox, 2008; Moore, 2010). This section mainly provides EDA for the explanatory variables of the population change example that are used for spatial regression analysis throughout the rest of this book.

2.1.2 Data Example

Population change is affected by a variety of factors that fall into the broad realm of five dimensions: demographic characteristics, socioeconomic conditions, transportation accessibility, natural amenities, and land use and development. In a Wisconsin study, Chi (2009, 2010a) identified and collected data for thirty-eight explanatory variables that are related to population growth. These explanatory variables fall into the five dimensions as follows:

- *Demographic characteristics:* previous population growth, population density, percent young, percent old, percent Blacks, and percent Hispanics

- *Socioeconomic conditions:* unemployment rate, income, crime rate, percent population with high school education, percent population with bachelor's degree, percent college population, percent female-headed families with children, percent nonmovers, percent housing units using public water, percent seasonal housing units, median house value, county seat status, percent workers in retail industry, and percent workers in agriculture industry

- *Transportation accessibility:* proximity to central cities, proximity to airports, proximity to major highways, highway density, travel time to work, and public transportation

- *Natural amenities:* percent forest coverage, percent water coverage, percent wetland coverage, percent public land coverage, lengths of lakeshore/riverbank/coastline, golf courses, and viewsheds

- *Land use and development:* water, wetland, slope, tax-exempt lands, and built-up lands

Data for these explanatory variables are from a variety of sources. Demographic and socioeconomic data come from the U.S. Census Bureau, the Federal Bureau of Investigation, and the *State of Wisconsin Blue Books*. The transportation infrastructure data come from the National Atlas of the United States, the Wisconsin Department of Transportation, the Wisconsin Bureau of Aeronautics, and the Department of Civil and Environmental Engineering of the University of Wisconsin–Madison. Data on the geophysical factors and natural amenity characteristics come from the U.S. Geological Survey, the Wisconsin Department of Natural Resources, and the Environmental Remote Sensing Center and the Land Information & Computer Graphics Facility of the University of Wisconsin–Madison. These primary and secondary data generate the explanatory variables at the MCD level. Refer to Chi (2010a, Table 1) for the explanatory variables and their corresponding data sources.

Although these many explanatory variables are useful for rigorously studying population change, for the illustrative purpose of our primary data example, we use only a few explanatory variables for three reasons. First, with the large number of explanatory variables, there could be a multicollinearity problem. Second, the large number of explanatory variables would not be easily interpreted and compared across different model specifications. Third, the purpose of this book is to illustrate the use of spatial regression models, not to investigate a research problem that would require a thorough consideration of the explanatory variables.

There are at least three approaches for achieving a small number of explanatory variables:

- We could take a theory-based approach and select the explanatory variables based on their conceptual or theoretical importance.
- We could take an automated variable selection approach such as backward elimination, forward selection, or stepwise regression.
- We could use principal component or factor analysis to reduce the data dimension.

These approaches are discussed in detail in Chapter 8. While each approach has its strengths and limitations, for this case study example, we use a combination of the theory-based approach and modified backward elimination to retain a small number of explanatory variables that not only are representative of the large dimension of population change's explanatory variables but also are statistically significant. We do this in two steps.

First, we select two explanatory variables from each of the first four population change components (demographic characteristics, socioeconomic conditions, transportation infrastructure, and natural amenities) based on Pearson's correlation analysis. The two explanatory variables selected are those that have the highest Pearson's correlation (in terms of the absolute value) with population change. We also include two additional explanatory variables in the first step: one is population growth in the previous decade, as previous growth is always an important factor of population change, and the other is the land developability index that represents the percentage of lands available for further development. The rationale for including the two additional explanatory variables is discussed further in the following subsections.

After Pearson's correlation analysis, ten explanatory variables are selected: *previous growth* (population growth rate from 1990 to 2000); *old* (the percentage of the old population [age sixty-five and older] in 2000); *high school* (the percentage of the population [age twenty-five and older] with high school degrees in 2000); *income* (median household income in 2000); *unemployment* (unemployment rate in 2000); *highway density* (main highway density, in miles per mile squared, including limited-access highways, principal highways, and secondary or through highways); *airport* (proximity to the nearest major commercial airport, i.e., the inverse distance from the centroid of an MCD to its nearest major commercial airport); *forest* (the percentage of forest coverage); *public lands* (the percentage of public lands, including national and state forests, parks, trails, wildlife refuges, and fishery areas); and *land developability* (the percentage of land available for development).

Second, we fit a standard linear regression model via ordinary least squares (OLS) estimation with the selected ten variables as explanatory variables. We then exclude statistically insignificant explanatory variables (at the $\alpha = .05$ level) and retain only the statistically significant explanatory variables, which are as follows:

- Previous growth (population growth rate from 1990 to 2000)
- Old (the percentage of the old population [age sixty-five and older] in 2000)
- Unemployment (unemployment rate in 2000)
- Airport (proximity to the nearest major commercial airport)
- Forest (the percentage of forest coverage)
- Land developability (the percentage of land available for development)

These six explanatory variables are used for data analysis throughout the remainder of this book. Their importance in affecting population change is reviewed and their descriptive statistics are provided in the subsections that follow.

2.1.2.1 Explanatory Variable 1: Previous Growth (Population Growth Rate From 1990 to 2000)

Population change in a unit of geography is often influenced by the trend of its previous change. Each unit of geography has its unique characteristics that promote population growth or population decline; the influence could last for some time. For instance, a place with a high in-migration rate is likely an attractive place; thus, a high in-migration rate in the past is a predictor of more migrants in the future, as the past migrants provide information and support to potential new migrants (Haug, 2008). This has been acknowledged in many demographic studies using time-series analysis and small-area population forecasting (e.g., Chi, 2009). The cohort component method of population forecasting, for example, uses information from previous time periods of fertility, mortality, and migration all by age-sex-race cohorts (Smith, Tayman, & Swanson, 2013). Previous population change has often been accounted for in regression analysis of population change.

In the example in this book, the population change rate from 1990 to 2000 is used as an explanatory variable of population change from 2000 to 2010. As discussed previously, in the 1990s, Wisconsin experienced rural rebound due to the fact that an improved economy attracted job seekers and natural amenities attracted retirees. Relatively high population growth occurred in northern Wisconsin, central Wisconsin, and some suburban areas. Overall, the MCDs had an average 10 percent growth rate, with a standard deviation (SD) of 15 percent (Table 2.1). The growth rate, however, varied spatially along the urban-rural continuum: 9 percent (SD: 15 percent) in rural MCDs, 13 percent (SD: 17 percent) in suburban MCDs, and 11 percent (SD: 15 percent) in urban MCDs. It should be noted that although the average growth rate was higher in urban MCDs than in rural MCDs, the gaps were lower than in the previous decade: the average growth rate in 1980 to 1990 was 0.1 percent in rural MCDs and 6.3 percent in urban MCDs.

2.1.2.2 Explanatory Variable 2: Old (the Percentage of the Old Population [Age Sixty-Five and Older] in 2000)

Research has shown that age and mobility have a strong nonlinear relation (Shaw, 1975; Shryock, 1964). Ages zero to four have relatively high mobility, as children in this age range accompany their mobile parents. As age approaches fourteen to fifteen, mobility rates decline, as children this age are nearing the end of middle school and parents are therefore less likely to be mobile. As age approaches twenty-two, the mobility rate peaks rapidly, as this is around the time that young adults enter college, the workforce, or military service. After this age, mobility rates decline. This strong age-mobility relation can be explained by the human

TABLE 2.1 Descriptive statistics of explanatory variables at the MCD level in Wisconsin				
	All	Rural MCDs	Suburban MCDs	Urban MCDs
Previous growth (%)	10.1 (15.2)	9.1 (14.5)	13.1 (17.1)	10.6 (15.4)
Old (%)	14.4 (5.7)	15.4 (5.9)	11.2 (4.0)	13.8 (4.3)
Airport (km)	0.028 (0.041)	0.020 (0.015)	0.041 (0.047)	0.091 (0.013)
Unemployment (%)	4.4 (3.1)	4.8 (3.3)	3.4 (2.2)	3.4 (1.7)
Forest (%)	29.7 (22.8)	33.8 (23.2)	20.0 (18.5)	13.2 (10.3)
Land developability (%)	72.5 (19.2)	72.0 (18.7)	78.8 (16.2)	50.0 (21.3)
Number of MCDs (n)	1,837	1,334	417	86

Note: The numbers in each cell represent the average of each variable at the MCD level. Standard deviations are in parentheses.

capital model, which recognizes that migration benefits can only be realized over time (DaVanzo, 1981; Kennan & Walker, 2003). This model considers migration an investment: all else being equal, the young are more likely to move than the old because they receive higher returns on mobility (Kennan & Walker, 2003).

Age has been used in various ways when examining its influence on population change: median age (Johnson, 2001), age structure (Lutz, 1994), and the percentages of residents fifteen to twenty-four years old and sixty-five years and older (Humphrey, 1980; Humphrey & Sell, 1975). In the example of this book, we use the percentage of residents aged twelve to eighteen to represent mobility potential and the percentage of residents aged sixty-five and older to represent the portion of the population "left behind" as the younger population moves away. The percentage of the old population (sixty-five and older) was retained after a variable selection process.

In our example, the old population was distributed mainly in three regions (Figure 2.1a): (1) the northern Wisconsin area, where rich natural amenities attracted retirees to these recreational counties (Chi & Marcouiller, 2011); (2) the central Wisconsin areas that are rural and remote from major cities; and (3) small villages and towns scattered throughout Wisconsin where "small-town living" and "sense of place" play large roles in in-migration (Stedman & Hammer, 2006). On average, the percentage of the old population was 14 percent with an SD of 6 percent for all MCDs in 2000 in Wisconsin (Table 2.1). That varied spatially along the urban-rural continuum: 15 percent in rural MCDs, 11 percent in suburban MCDs, and 14 percent in urban MCDs.

28 Spatial Regression Models for the Social Sciences

FIGURE 2.1 ● Independent variables

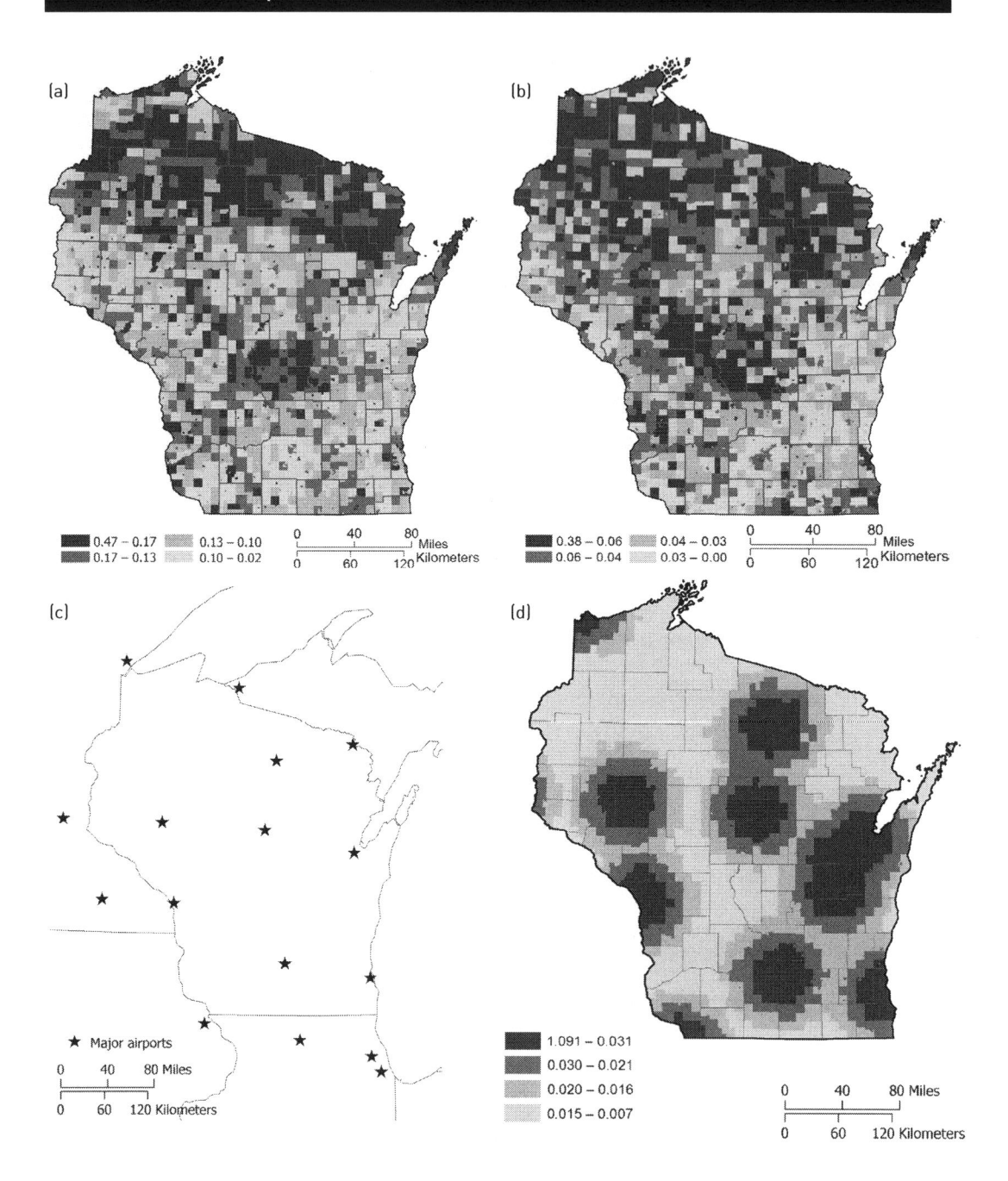

(a)

■ 0.47 – 0.17   ■ 0.13 – 0.10
■ 0.17 – 0.13   ■ 0.10 – 0.02

(b)

■ 0.38 – 0.06   ■ 0.04 – 0.03
■ 0.06 – 0.04   ■ 0.03 – 0.00

(c)

★ Major airports

(d)

■ 1.091 – 0.031
■ 0.030 – 0.021
■ 0.020 – 0.016
■ 0.015 – 0.007

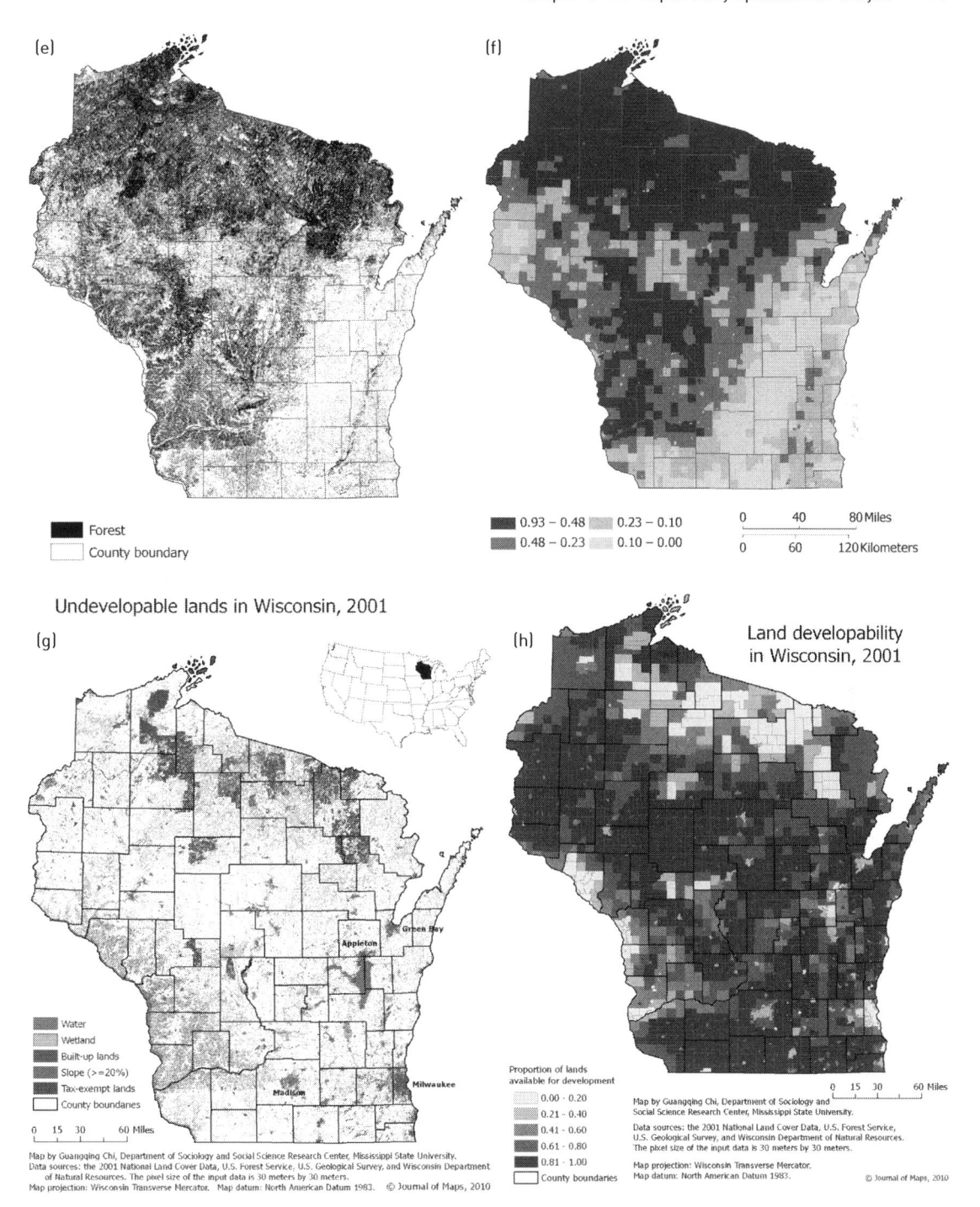

Chapter 2 ■ Exploratory Spatial Data Analysis 29

(e)

(f)

■ Forest
☐ County boundary

■ 0.93 – 0.48   ■ 0.23 – 0.10
■ 0.48 – 0.23   ☐ 0.10 – 0.00

Undevelopable lands in Wisconsin, 2001

(g)

■ Water
■ Wetland
■ Built-up lands
■ Slope (>=20%)
■ Tax-exempt lands
☐ County boundaries

(h) Land developability in Wisconsin, 2001

Proportion of lands available for development
☐ 0.00 – 0.20
☐ 0.21 – 0.40
■ 0.41 – 0.60
■ 0.61 – 0.80
■ 0.81 – 1.00
☐ County boundaries

Source: Chi (2010b).

Note: (a) The proportion of old population (sixty-five years and older) at the minor civil division (MCD) level in 2000 in Wisconsin, (b) the unemployment rate at the MCD level in 2000 in Wisconsin, (c) locations of major commercial airports in Wisconsin and neighboring states, (d) proximity to major commercial airports at the MCD level in Wisconsin and neighboring states, (e) forest coverage in Wisconsin, (f) the proportion of forest coverage in Wisconsin, (g) undevelopable land as of 2001 in Wisconsin, and (h) the proportion of land available for development at the MCD level as of 2001 in Wisconsin

2.1.2.3 Explanatory Variable 3: Unemployment (Unemployment Rate in 2000)

Economic forces have often been considered dominating factors in stimulating migration and population change. Migration flows from areas that have few economic opportunities to areas that have many opportunities, and by doing so, it balances population size and economic opportunities at aggregate levels (Frisbie & Poston, 1975). One of the most important economic factors that affect population redistribution (at least for persons of working age) appears to be employment (Treyz, Rickman, Hunt, & Greenwood, 1993).

Increased availability of local employment opportunities can create population growth due to the stimulation of household labor use and its effect on household incomes (Fuguitt & Beale, 1996). Empirical studies on regional development often explore the relation between residential choices and employment location decisions, especially in the literature examining the causal relationship between employment and population change (Henry, Barkley, & Bao, 1997). Carlino and Mills (1987) argue that performance of the economy in times of a functional market is what determines the causality between employment and population change; they contend that in times of well-performing markets, jobs follow people, whereas in times of poor-performing markets, people follow jobs. Many studies consider employment changes and population changes endogenous (e.g., Boarnet, 1994a, 1994b).

In our example, the high unemployment rate was distributed mainly in the northern Wisconsin area that has a higher retiree population, in the central Wisconsin area that is remote and rural, and in the southeast Wisconsin MCDs that are close to the Chicago area (Figure 2.1b). On average, the unemployment rate was 4.4 percent with an SD of 3.1 percent for all MCDs in 2000 in Wisconsin. That varied spatially along the urban-rural continuum: 4.8 percent in rural MCDs, 3.4 percent in suburban MCDs, and 3.4 percent in urban MCDs (Table 2.1).

2.1.2.4 Explanatory Variable 4: Airport (Proximity to the Nearest Major Commercial Airport)

A large body of literature discusses the impact of airports on economic growth and development (Goetz, 1992; Goetz & Sutton, 1997). Airports can have direct and indirect impacts on employment and economic growth (Kasarda & Lindsay, 2011). For example, airports create direct job opportunities, such as jobs in airport management and airline operations, as well as indirect job opportunities, such as jobs at in-airport vendors and near-the-airport hotels. Airports may also attract firms to the area that value fast delivery or easy travel, and they may entice migrants who appreciate long-distance travel made simple.

Airports make long-distance travel more convenient than surface transportation methods such as highways and railways. They reduce distance limits on social, economic, and city interactions (Irwin & Kasarda, 1991) and link cities, creating a nationwide or even worldwide economic region out of otherwise isolated economic regions (Brueckner, 2003). Most studies of airport impacts have been conducted in metropolitan areas and have found that airports promote both population growth and economic growth. Irwin and Kasarda (1991), for example, found that an airline network causes rather than is caused by employment growth. Brueckner (2003) and Green (2007) used passenger boardings to measure airline service and found that good airline service helps promote urban economic growth. Although some airport studies have been conducted in rural areas, the findings are mixed. Rasker, Gude, Gude, and Noort (2009), for instance, found that in high-amenity rural areas, airport access promotes economic development, whereas Isserman, Feser, and Warren (2009) found that where economic development is concerned, the distance to major airports is a rather unimportant factor in rural areas.

The sixteen airports selected for the example used throughout this book are commercial service airports in Wisconsin as well as those in neighboring states but close to Wisconsin (Figure 2.1c). We measure proximity to airports as a function of the inverse distance (in kilometers) from an MCD to its nearest airport (Figure 2.1d).

On average, the proximity to major commercial airports was 0.028 with an SD of 0.041 for all MCDs in 2000 in Wisconsin (Table 2.1). That varied spatially along the urban-rural continuum: 0.02 in rural MCDs, 0.041 in suburban MCDs, and 0.091 in urban MCDs. The proximity to major commercial airports is correlated with urban status, as urban areas are more likely to have airports than rural areas.

2.1.2.5 Explanatory Variable 5: Forest (the Percentage of Forest Coverage)

A growing body of literature suggests that natural amenities (idyllic landscapes, open spaces, forests, bodies of water, pleasant climates, etc.) affect economic and sociodemographic change regionally. Several studies credit people's attraction to natural amenities for the post-1970 "turnaround migration" in the United States (Brown et al., 1997; Fuguitt & Brown, 1990; Johnson & Beale, 1994). Other work identifies natural amenities as latent inputs to the production of goods and services in rural regions (Graves, 1979, 1980, 1983; Marcouiller, 1998). In addition, the equilibrium theory argues that differences in amenities (and not differences in economic opportunities) are the main determinants of migration (Graves, 1979, 1983; Graves & Linneman, 1979). Life-cycle literature suggests there are important relations between demographics and amenities—specifically that as people get older, regional amenities increase in importance (Clark & Hunter, 1992). Some say that economic development is in a postindustrial or postconsumer phase that makes quality of life and amenities important determinants of population change due to increased affluence, transportation infrastructure development, active regional competitiveness, globalization, and environmental awareness and sensitivity (Freudenburg, 1992; Galston & Baehler, 1995). Many studies consider forest to be a type of natural amenity (e.g., Fuguitt, Brown, & Beale, 1989; Johnson, 2001; Kim, Marcouiller, & Deller, 2005; Marcouiller, Clendenning, & Kedzior, 2002; Marcouiller, Kim, & Deller, 2004). For the example used in this book, forest, which is measured by the percentage of forest coverage in each MCD, was selected for the final list of explanatory variables.

The majority of forest is concentrated in northern Wisconsin and in the west to the Wisconsin River (Figure 2.1e). We measure forest by the percentage of forest coverage in each MCD (Figure 2.1f). On average, the percentage of forest coverage is 30 percent with an SD of 23 percent for all MCDs in 2000 in Wisconsin. That varied spatially along the urban-rural continuum: 34 percent in rural MCDs, 20 percent in suburban MCDs, and 13 percent in urban MCDs (Table 2.1).

2.1.2.6 Explanatory Variable 6: Land Developability (the Percentage of Land Available and Suitable for Development)

Information on land developability can help predict the direction of future land development and therefore be a predictor of population growth and redistribution. Land developability, or the percentage of land available and suitable for development, is generated based on water, wetlands, slope (>20 percent), public lands, and built-up lands, which are all considered undevelopable (Figure 2.1g). Two approaches are commonly used to study the associations of land developability factors with migration and population redistribution. One approach uses the factors individually in regression analysis. Doing so, however, may double- or triple-count some land covers—for example, a single area could fall under both national park (public lands) and water and therefore be double-counted in regression analysis. The other approach employs factor analysis or other statistics-based weighted aggregation methods to aggregate the explanatory variables into one or more indices representing the overall land use status (Kim et al., 2005). Such indices, however, are unable to provide an accurate estimate of the amount of developable lands.

In this book, we use the land developability index of Chi (2010b), which was developed using spatial overlay. Spatial overlay is a set of methods used for integrating information into one data layer from multiple geographic data layers that share all or part of the same area. Using spatial overlay methods to generate land developability is more accurate than using other methods (Chi, 2010b). Therefore, throughout this book, we use this land developability index to represent land development potential. For our Wisconsin example, the index generation began by overlaying the data layers of water, wetlands, slope (>20 percent), public lands, and built-up lands to create one layer that represented the undevelopable lands in Wisconsin. This layer was overlaid with a geographic MCD layer to create a new single layer to show the undevelopable land data at the MCD level. Then the percentage of undevelopable land was calculated for each MCD. In the final step, the percentage of undevelopable land was subtracted from 1 to generate the land developability index for Wisconsin.

Figure 2.1h shows the land developability in the Wisconsin MCDs in 2001. The numbers represent the percentages of developable lands in each MCD. Higher numbers (darker shading*) indicate higher percentages of developable lands, and smaller numbers (lighter shading*) indicate lower percentages of developable lands. Figure 2.1h reveals that there is potential for development in MCDs from roughly the northwest to the southeast corner and in MCDs from the northeast peninsula to the southwest corner of the state, with some isolated MCDs as exceptions. There is not much land available for further development in urbanized areas of metropolitan counties (such as Milwaukee and Madison), northern natural-resource-rich counties, or southwestern MCDs along the Mississippi and Wisconsin Rivers; many of the MCDs in these areas have less than 40 percent developable lands. On average, land developability was 73 percent with an SD of 19 percent for all MCDs in 2000 in Wisconsin (Table 2.1). That varied spatially along the urban-rural continuum: 72 percent in rural MCDs, 79 percent in suburban MCDs, and 50 percent in urban MCDs.

2.2. NEIGHBORHOOD STRUCTURE AND SPATIAL WEIGHT MATRIX

2.2.1 What Is a Neighborhood Structure?

To conduct exploratory spatial data analysis (ESDA) and spatial regression modeling, it is often necessary to specify a neighborhood structure for each areal unit (i.e., a unit

---

*Full-color shading of Figure 2.1h uses dark and light green, as can be seen at study.sagepub.com/research methods/quantitative-statistical-research/chi

of geography for analysis such as a census tract or county) comprising its neighboring areal units on a lattice (Anselin, 1988b). Neighborhood structure, as the name suggests, specifies the neighbors for each areal unit on a spatial lattice in the study area. Neighborhood structure is an important concept in, and is required for, areal data analysis such as quantifying spatial autocorrelation in the response variable or regression errors and accounting for spatial dependence using spatial regression models.

> Conducting exploratory spatial data analysis and spatial regression often involves the specification of a neighborhood structure for each areal unit that comprises its neighboring units on a lattice.

A neighborhood structure can be one of two types:

- contiguity based or
- distance based.

A contiguity-based neighborhood structure is constructed on the basis of whether two areal units "touch" each other. On a regular grid, a neighborhood structure is relatively straightforward to specify. For example, the "rook's case" contiguity neighborhood structure specifies neighbors as areal units with shared boundaries (Figure 2.2a). The neighbors are also the closest in terms of distance between the centroids of the two areal units. The "queen's case" contiguity neighborhood structure specifies neighbors as areal units with shared boundaries or vertices (Figure 2.2b). Higher-order neighborhood structures are defined analogously or considered as first-, second-, or higher-order neighbors of neighbors.

In general, a distance-based neighborhood structure is constructed on the basis of a specified number of nearest neighbors or a specified distance to potential

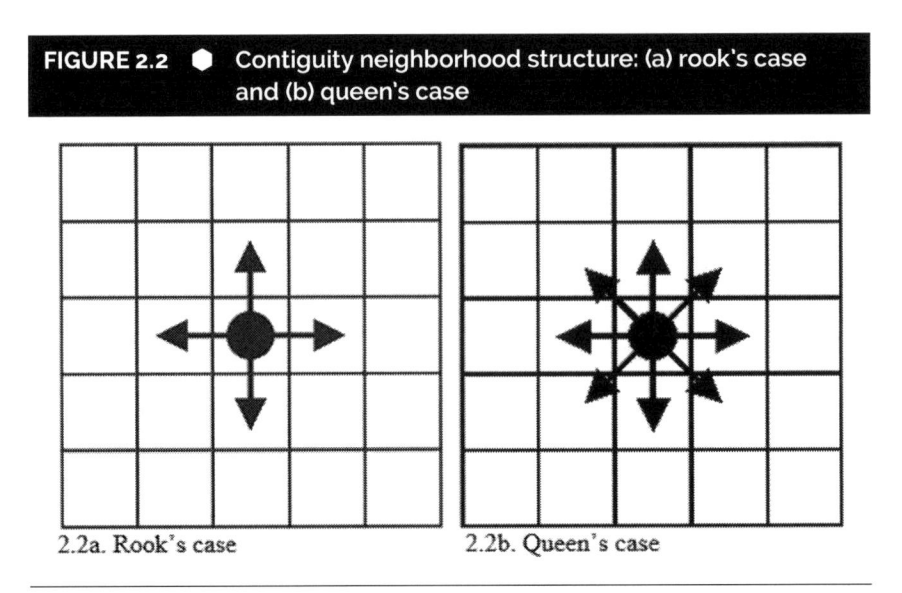

FIGURE 2.2 ● Contiguity neighborhood structure: (a) rook's case and (b) queen's case

2.2a. Rook's case

2.2b. Queen's case

neighbors. For instance, we could construct a neighborhood structure in which each areal unit has a certain number of nearest neighbors, or we could construct a neighborhood structure in which all the areal units that have centroids within a defined distance band from each other are neighbors.

The spatial areal data that we deal with in social science research are typically on *irregular* spatial lattices. For example, states, counties, MCDs, census tracts, and other census geographies all have irregular spatial shapes. When we build neighborhood structures for these irregular geographic units, we use the same rules as for the regular grids. Let's use MCDs, the geographic unit of this book's data example, to describe neighborhood structures for an irregular spatial lattice. In a rook's case contiguity neighborhood structure, an MCD's neighbors are the MCDs with shared border lines. In a queen's case contiguity neighborhood structure, an MCD's neighbors are the MCDs with shared border lines or vertices. In a distance-based neighborhood structure based on a specified number of neighbors (say five), an MCD's neighbors are the five nearest MCDs as measured by the distance between the centroids of MCDs. In a distance-based neighborhood structure based on a specified distance (say 20 miles), an MCD's neighbors are the MCDs that are within 20 miles of the MCD as measured by the distance between the centroids of MCDs.

> Spatial areal data in social science research typically are on spatial lattices that are irregular.

2.2.2 What Is a Spatial Weight Matrix?

A neighborhood structure itself is not enough for spatial data analysis; instead, we need to *quantify* the neighborhood structure to make it operational in ESDA and spatial regression modeling. We do this through spatial weight matrices. A **spatial weight matrix** comprises spatial weights that each relates a variable (the response variable or regression errors) at one areal unit to the variable at neighboring areal units according to a prespecified neighborhood structure.

> **Spatial weight matrix** comprises a **spatial weight** that relates a variable at one areal unit to that same variable at a neighboring unit per a specified neighborhood structure.

Both neighborhood structures and spatial weight matrices play important roles in ESDA and spatial regression modeling. While the terms are often used interchangeably in the existing spatial social science research, they refer to different things: the former is more like a concept (or basic foundation, or map of where you need to go), and the latter is more like an operation (or detailed procedure, or directions of how to get there). The following paragraphs illustrate the conversion from a neighborhood structure to a spatial weight matrix.

Say we have a regular lattice with four rows by four columns for a total of sixteen areal units (or cells) (Figure 2.3). We label the cells from 1 to 16. Let's consider

FIGURE 2.3 ● A 4 × 4 lattice

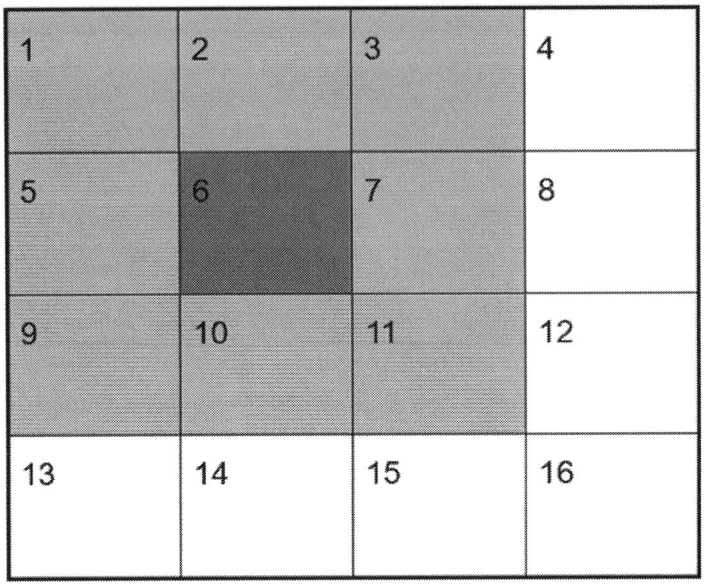

1	2	3	4
5	6	7	8
9	10	11	12
13	14	15	16

cell 6 to be our areal unit of interest. Applying the first-order queen's contiguity neighborhood structure, cell 6 has eight neighbors: cells 1, 2, 3, 5, 7, 9, 10, and 11. We can do this for all cells.

Now let's put each cell in its own row and each cell in its own column; we now have rows from 1 to 16 and columns from 1 to 16. The possible neighbors of the cells in rows 1 to 16 could be the cells in columns 1 to 16. We now have a 16 × 16 matrix (Figure 2.4). The neighbors for the cells in rows 1 to 16 are labeled with a "1" in the corresponding columns. For example, in row 6, there is a "1" in columns 1, 2, 3, 5, 7, 9, 10, and 11 to indicate that these are the neighbors for cell 6. The total number of neighbors for each cell is labeled on the right.

The number of neighbors is not the same for all cells, which results in larger weight sums for some cells and smaller weight sums for others. A common way to deal with this is to standardize each row of a spatial weight matrix by dividing each cell by the sum of that row (Figure 2.5). Applying a row-standardized spatial weight matrix in ESDA and spatial regression modeling results in the weighted average attribute of neighbors, which makes the interpretation more meaningful and easier to understand (Anselin, 1992). For the remainder of this book, all spatial weight matrices are row standardized.

FIGURE 2.4 ● A 16 × 16 spatial weight matrix without row standardization

FIGURE 2.5 ● A 16 × 16 spatial weight matrix with row standardization

In the example described above, the neighbors of an areal unit are weighted equally—this is called a fixed spatial weight matrix. The often-used fixed weight matrices include rook's and queen's contiguity weight matrices, the *k*-nearest neighbor weight matrices, and the general distance weight matrices. In all three types of weight matrices, each neighbor, far or near, large or small in size, provides the same weight.

> The neighbors of an areal unit are weighted equally in a fixed spatial weight matrix but differently in a variable spatial weight matrix.

The neighbors of an areal unit could be weighted differently—this is called a variable spatial weight matrix; such a matrix can be constructed on the basis of a function or a variable. Here we provide four examples. First, we could weight the neighbors based on the distances from their centroids to the centroid of an areal unit and use an inverse distance function to give the nearer neighbors more weight than the farther ones (equation [2.1]). We could further use a squared (or higher-order) inverse distance function to approximate the gravity model of spatial interaction (equation [2.2]). Let d_{ij} denote the distance between areal unit i and areal unit j and let δ denote a threshold distance. The weight between areal units i and j is the inverse of d_{ij} if the distance is within δ and 0 otherwise. That is,

$$w_{ij} = \frac{1}{d_{ij}} \text{ if } d_{ij} \text{ is within distance } \delta \ (d_{ij} < \delta); \ 0 \text{ otherwise} \quad (2.1)$$

More generally, the weight between areal units i and j could be the inverse of d_{ij} to the power of $\gamma \geq 0$, up to distance δ:

$$w_{ij} = \left(\frac{1}{d_{ij}}\right)^{\gamma} \text{ if } d_{ij} \text{ is within distance } \delta \ (d_{ij} < \delta); \ 0 \text{ otherwise} \quad (2.2)$$

Second, we could weight the neighbors based on the lengths of boundaries that they share with an areal unit (equation [2.3]). This provides more weight to the neighbors that have a longer border with an areal unit. Let l_{ij} denote the length of the common border between areal unit i and areal unit j and let l_i denote the perimeter of areal unit i. The weight between areal units i and j is l_{ij} over l_i, raised to the power of $\tau \geq 0$. That is,

$$w_{ij} = \left(\frac{l_{ij}}{l_i}\right)^{\tau} \quad (2.3)$$

Third, we could weight the neighbors based on a combination of the lengths of boundaries shared with an areal unit and the distances to this areal unit (equation [2.4]). This weight considers both the distance effect and the length effect. The orders (τ and γ) of the weight could be defined as appropriate.

$$w_{ij} = \frac{\left(l_{ij}/l_i\right)^{\tau}}{d_{ij}^{\gamma}} \qquad (2.4)$$

Fourth, more complex spatial weight matrices can be created on the basis of theories and assumptions, such as actual travel distance or time (Boarnet, Chalermpong, & Geho, 2005) and economic distance (Case, Rosen, & Hines, 1993).

2.2.3 Why Should We Use a Spatial Weight Matrix?

Now we know how to construct a neighborhood structure and specify a corresponding spatial weight matrix. But why should we use a spatial weight matrix? One main reason is that a spatial weight matrix is needed to conduct ESDA and fit spatial regression models. Suppose we have a data set with n observations. For a standard linear regression with $p - 1$ predictor variables, there are p regression coefficients. In addition, we assume that the errors are independently and identically distributed (often referred to as *i.i.d.*) with mean zero and a constant variance. However, if the errors are spatially dependent, we need to account for the spatial dependence. If we have one unique spatial dependence parameter for each observation (or unit), we would have *more* parameters ($p + 1 + n$) than the sample size n and the regression procedure could not be carried out. One way to get around this problem is to specify a neighborhood structure via a spatial weight matrix (with a small set of parameters) and apply them to all areal units. In this case, we would construct a spatial weight matrix that corresponds to the neighborhood structure so that we can express the resulting variance-covariance matrix of the response variables (or regression errors) as a function of a small number of estimable parameters relative to the sample size (Anselin, 2002).

Conducting exploratory spatial data analysis and fitting spatial regression models often involve a spatial weight matrix.

2.2.4 Which Spatial Weight Matrix Should We Use?

Though it is understood that spatial weight matrices are necessary for ESDA and spatial regression modeling and though the literature on the creation of spatial weight matrices is large (for a literature review, please see Getis & Aldstadt, 2004), there is limited theory available regarding how to select which spatial weight matrix to use. Some select a spatial weight matrix without much justification or further evaluation, while others compare several spatial weight matrices before selecting one (Anselin, 2002; Boarnet et al., 2005; Timmins, Hunter, Cattet, & Stenhouse, 2013). In recent years, Aldstadt and Getis (2006) have developed a multidirectional optimal ecotope-based algorithm (AMOEBA) that helps to identify the optimal spatial weight matrix, whereas Zhu, Huang, and Reyes (2010) have proposed a

Using a spatial weight matrix guided by existing theories or relevant studies in your field is prudent.

regularization method to select an appropriate spatial weight matrix by shrinking the autoregressive coefficients of the unimportant orders of neighbors to zero.

It is practical and acceptable for researchers to use a specific spatial weight matrix that has been suggested by existing theories or relevant studies. However, when no theoretical guidance or prior research exists to assist the researcher in selecting an appropriate spatial weight matrix, we suggest starting with a suitable set of spatial weight matrices or the AMOEBA method, fitting models with each spatial weight matrix individually, and selecting the matrix that captures the maximum spatial dependence in model residuals.

A spatial weight matrix corresponding to high spatial autocorrelation and high statistical significance in the response variable may be considered more appropriate for exploratory spatial data analysis, whereas a spatial weight matrix corresponding to high spatial dependence in model residuals and high statistical significance may be considered more appropriate for spatial regression modeling.

Chi (2010a) has proposed a relatively comprehensive approach to selecting an appropriate spatial weight matrix for areal data analysis. For ESDA purposes, it is appropriate to choose a spatial weight matrix that achieves high spatial autocorrelation in combination with a high level of statistical significance, often measured by Moran's I statistic based on the response variable. In addition, a z-score (the test for the significance of Moran's I statistic) is computed as the ratio of Moran's I statistic and the corresponding standard error. The p-values can be calculated based on a normal approximation. For spatial regression models, an appropriate spatial weight matrix is the one that captures high spatial dependence in the model residuals in combination with a high level of statistical significance. For instance, for fitting a spatial lag model, select the spatial weight matrix that encompasses the highest spatial dependence of the response variable. For fitting a spatial error model, select the spatial weight matrix that captures the highest spatial dependence of the residuals from a standard linear regression model fit. The spatial error model with spatially lagged responses needs two spatial weight matrices—one for the spatial lag dependence and the other for the spatial error dependence; the selection of the former can be based on the spatial dependence of the response variable, and the selection of the latter can be based on that of the residuals after fitting a spatial lag model. The selection of an appropriate spatial weight matrix is further discussed in chapters addressing the specific spatial regression models. However, it appears to remain an open research question about how to properly or even optimally specify a spatial weight matrix.

2.2.5 Issues With Spatial Weight Matrices and Solutions

In practice, specifying a spatial weight matrix poses at least two potential challenges (Anselin, 2002). One is that the weight may be affected by the topological quality of the geographic information system (GIS) data. For example, imprecise polygons and vertices in GIS may erroneously result in areal units without neighbors ("islands"). Another challenge is that some of the distance-based spatial weight matrices require threshold values, which are often difficult to determine, especially in cases of strong spatial heterogeneity. Small threshold values might result in too many areal units without neighbors, and large threshold values might result in a neighborhood that is too large. The threshold value problem is especially pronounced with census subcounty units, as they are often delineated according to population size and can be highly irregular. Also, using distance-based spatial weight matrices tends to result in too few neighbors in rural areas and too many neighbors in urban areas. One solution to this problem is to use the k-nearest neighborhood structure (Anselin, 2002). Our data example in Section 2.4 uses this neighborhood structure to resolve this problem. As is explained in that section, among forty different types of spatial weight matrices, using the 4-nearest neighbor weight matrix results in the highest spatial autocorrelation of population change and using the 5-nearest neighbor weight matrix results in the highest spatial autocorrelation of the residuals from a standard linear regression fit.

2.2.6 Data Example

The data example is illustrated in Section 2.4.5 along with the data example for ESDA.

2.3 SPATIAL AUTOCORRELATION, DEPENDENCE, AND HETEROGENEITY

In existing social science research using spatial regression models, three terms are often used to describe spatial effects (Getis, 2008):

- Spatial autocorrelation
- Spatial dependence
- Spatial heterogeneity

The distinction among them, especially between spatial autocorrelation and spatial dependence, is not unanimously agreed upon. Researchers from different fields understand and use these terms differently. For example, Anselin (1988a) and Voss (2007) distinguish spatial autocorrelation from spatial dependence and argue that the former is an indicator of the latter (as well as possibly of spatial heterogeneity). More often, *spatial autocorrelation* and *spatial dependence* are used interchangeably in the existing literature.

To understand the differences between the three terms more comprehensively, we reviewed several books written by geographers, statisticians, and regional scientists (Anselin, 1988b; Cressie, 1993; Isaaks & Srivastava, 1989; O'Sullivan & Unwin, 2010; Schabenberger & Gotway, 2005) and many journal articles dealing with spatial regression models (published in journals such as *Journal of Regional Science, Journal of Economic Geography, Urban Studies, American Journal of Agricultural Economics,* and others). We found that spatial autocorrelation is used more often for ESDA while spatial dependence and spatial heterogeneity are used more often in spatial regression modeling. We follow this understanding for the purposes of this book. The following paragraphs describe each of the three spatial effects.

> **Autocorrelation** is the correlation of a variable with itself at different time points or spatial locations.
>
> **Spatial autocorrelation** refers to the correlation of the same attribute between two locations.

Autocorrelation, as the name suggests, is the correlation of a variable with itself. Therefore, **spatial autocorrelation** (also known as *spatial interaction, local interaction,* or *small-scale spatial variation*) refers to the correlation between the same attribute at two locations (Schabenberger & Gotway, 2005). Spatial autocorrelation defined loosely is a similarity or dissimilarity measure between the attribute values of two locations that are spatially nearby. In other words, in positive spatial autocorrelation, locations with high or low attribute values tend to cluster in space, and in negative spatial autocorrelation, locations tend to be surrounded by neighbors with very different attribute values. Various indexes can be used to measure spatial autocorrelation. Probably the most well known is **Moran's *I*** statistic (Moran, 1948), which measures the degree of linear association between an attribute at a given location and the weighted average of the attribute at its neighboring locations. Moran's *I* statistic is discussed in further detail in Section 2.4.

> **Moran's *I*** is a measure of similarity between neighboring areal units, or spatial autocorrelation.

Conceptually, spatial autocorrelation is a form of spatial dependence; however, in this book, we reserve the former for ESDA of one variable at a time and the latter for spatial regression modeling. In the context of regression modeling, we want to know if there is spatial dependence in the response variable and/or in the model residuals. If there is spatial dependence, how can we account for it in the model to improve the model's overall performance? It should be noted that an indication of spatial autocorrelation of the response variable (and/or explanatory variables) from the ESDA does not necessarily indicate the need to specify spatial dependence in the model, as the spatial dependence in the response variable may be adequately captured by that in the explanatory variables. The issues related to spatial dependence as well as the relevant models are covered in Chapters 3 and 4.

> **Spatial heterogeneity** refers to differences in a spatial region in the mean, variance, or spatial covariance (or spatial correlation) structures.

Spatial heterogeneity (also known as *spatial structure, nonstationarity,* or *large-scale global trends*) refers to differences in a spatial region in the mean, variance, spatial covariance (or spatial correlation) structures and/or spatial autocorrelation (LeSage, 1999). In contrast, spatial homogeneity (also known as *stationarity*) requires both the mean and the variance of an attribute to be constant across space and requires that correlation of the attribute at any two locations depends upon the lag distance between the two locations (but not the actual locations) (Bailey & Gatrell, 1995). Spatial heterogeneity can be modeled by data partition methods, spatial regime models, and geographically weighted regression, which are addressed in Chapter 5.

It should be noted that statisticians, especially geostatisticians, use different terms to refer to spatial effects. For instance, spatial effects may be broken down into large-scale variation, small-scale variation, microscale variation, and measurement error (Cressie, 1993). The large-scale variation can be viewed as spatial heterogeneity in the mean and the small-scale and microscale variations as spatial dependence. For the purposes of this book, we use *spatial autocorrelation* for ESDA and we use *spatial dependence* and *spatial heterogeneity* for spatial regression modeling.

2.4 EXPLORATORY SPATIAL DATA ANALYSIS

EDA, as discussed in Section 2.1, provides a summary of data using graphics or summary statistics but does not specifically address possible spatial patterns, whereas ESDA is a critical additional step to the exploratory analysis of spatial data. A specific goal of ESDA is to display and summarize data from the spatial perspective, which helps suggest potential models to formulate and statistical methods to apply for inference. **ESDA** often involves

- visualization of the spatial patterns exhibited by the data,
- identification of spatial clusters and spatial outliers, and
- diagnosis of any misspecifications of spatial aspects of the statistical models.

Exploratory spatial data analysis (ESDA) displays and summarizes data spatially, helping researchers choose potential models and statistical methods.

All of this assists in better specifying regression models (Anselin, 1996; Baller et al., 2001). In this book, we discuss ESDA in the context of examining the spatial patterns of data for spatial regression.

2.4.1 Visualizing Spatial Data

The initial step in ESDA often involves spatially visualizing the data of interest. Doing so allows potential spatial patterns of the data to be identified, as human eyes are good at recognizing spatial patterns from graphical presentations of data. Visualizing spatial data is often one of the major components in cartography and introductory GIS courses. Software packages focusing on geographic analysis such as ArcGIS and MapInfo provide a variety of tools for visualizing spatial data. In addition, software packages focusing on spatial data analysis such as R and GeoDa also provide basic functions for visualizing spatial data before other ESDA and spatial regression modeling. Spatial data visualization is covered in books such as *Making Maps* (Krygier & Wood, 2005) and in GIS tutorials such as *Getting to Know ArcGIS Desktop* (Law & Collins, 2015). Readers are referred to these and other related resources for instruction on visualizing spatial data; in this book we focus on the "analysis" part.

> Mapping variables or residuals visually displays possible spatial patterns in an exploratory spatial data analysis.

For graphics in ESDA, mapping variables or error terms provides visual displays of possible spatial patterns. However, most maps do not quantify how strong a possible spatial pattern is or indicate whether it is statistically significant. In this regard, statistical measures and formal tests can be helpful. The strength and statistical significance of spatial autocorrelation can be measured both globally and locally—the global measures are for detecting spatial dependence across the study area and the local measures are for detecting local spatial heterogeneity. In this section, we discuss several well-known statistics:

- Moran's *I* statistic (global)
- Geary's *c* statistic (global)
- Local indicator of spatial association (LISA)
    - Local Moran's *I* statistic
    - Local Geary's *c* statistic
    - *G* statistic (local)

2.4.2 Moran's *I* Statistic

Let n denote the total number of areal units on a lattice and y_i denote the value of an attribute at areal unit i, for $i = 1, \ldots n$. Moran's *I* statistic (Moran, 1950) is defined as

$$I = \left(\frac{n}{\sum_{i=1}^{n}\sum_{j=1}^{n} w_{ij}} \right) \frac{\sum_{i=1}^{n}\sum_{j=1}^{n} w_{ij}(y_i - \overline{y})(y_j - \overline{y})}{\sum_{i=1}^{n}(y_i - \overline{y})^2} \quad (2.5)$$

where

$i, j = 1, \ldots, n$ index the n areal units,

w_{ij} is a spatial weight between areal units i and j, and

$\bar{y}$ is the average value of the attribute y_i at all areal units.

Moran's I is a measure of the strength of spatial autocorrelation—in other words, a measure of similarity between neighboring areal units. When the attributes are more similar (or dissimilar) between two neighbors, Moran's I statistic tends to be a larger positive (or negative) value. When the relation between two neighbors is weaker, however, Moran's I statistic is closer to 0. Thus, Moran's I statistic bears similarity to a Pearson's correlation that measures the strength of a linear relation between the two variables y and Wy, where $y = (y_1, \ldots, y_n)^T$ is an n-dimensional vector of the attributes and $W = [w_{ij}]^n_{i,j=1}$ is an n-by-n spatial weight matrix (Anselin, 1995). It can be also interpreted as the slope of the regression of the attribute on the weighted average (Pacheco & Tyrrell, 2002). A Moran scatterplot can be used to illustrate spatial autocorrelation visually: the weighted average on the vertical axis is plotted against the attribute on the horizontal axis (Anselin, 1995). For randomly distributed data, that is, under the assumption of no spatial autocorrelation, the expectation of I is

$$E(I) = -\frac{1}{n-1} \quad (2.6)$$

which gets closer to 0 as the sample size n increases (Cliff & Ord, 1981, p. 42).

For a large sample size n, the theoretical bound for Moran's I falls between −1 and 1 (Anselin, 1995; Cliff & Ord, 1973; Moran, 1948). For positively correlated data with similar neighbors, I is between 0 and 1. The stronger the positive spatial autocorrelation is, the closer I is to 1. A typical positive spatial pattern features spatial clustering of high values with high values or low values with low values. For negatively correlated data with dissimilar neighbors, I is between −1 and 0. The stronger the negative spatial autocorrelation is, the closer I is to −1. Checkerboard patterns are typical, indicating negative association among neighbors. Some researchers (e.g., Schabenberger & Gotway, 2005) prefer not to mention the (−1, 1) range but rather interpret the strength of spatial autocorrelation based on $(I − E[I])$.

> The theoretical bound for Moran's I falls between −1 and 1 for a large sample size n.

Furthermore, the statistical significance of spatial autocorrelation can be tested by a z-test statistic:

$$z = \frac{I - E(I)}{\sqrt{Var(I)}} \tag{2.7}$$

where the expectation of I is given in equation (2.6) under the assumption of no spatial autocorrelation and the variance of I can be approximated. The p-value of the test can be obtained via permutation tests, Monte Carlo tests, or normal approximation tests based on the asymptotic distribution of I (Cliff & Ord, 1981, p. 21; Schabenberger & Gotway, 2005, p. 22).

2.4.3 Geary's c Statistic

Geary's c statistic (Geary, 1954) is defined as

$$c = \left(\frac{n-1}{2 \sum_{i=1}^{n} \sum_{j=1}^{n} w_{ij}} \right) \frac{\sum_{i=1}^{n} \sum_{j=1}^{n} w_{ij}(y_i - y_j)^2}{\sum_{i=1}^{n} (y_i - \bar{y})^2} \tag{2.8}$$

where

$i, j = 1, \ldots, n$ index the n areal units,

w_{ij} is a spatial weight between areal units i and j, and

$\bar{y}$ is the average value of the attribute y_i at all areal units.

> **Geary's c is a measure of dissimilarity between neighboring areal units, or spatial autocorrelation.**

Geary's c is another measure of spatial autocorrelation and similarity between neighboring areal units. The value of c will always be positive because of the squared term in the numerator. Under the assumption of no spatial dependence, the expectation of c is 1:

$$E(c) = 1 \tag{2.9}$$

When the neighbors have similar values, Geary's c will be closer to 0 (Cliff & Ord, 1981). Thus, for spatially positively correlated data, c is closer to 0. For randomly distributed data, the numerator is not all that different from the denominator and hence c is close to 1. For spatially negatively correlated data, c will be larger than 1 (Griffith, 1987).

Both Moran's I and Geary's c are suitable for binary data, normal data, and in general any kind of quantitative data (Upton & Fingleton, 1985). But generally, Moran's I is more powerful than Geary's c, except in the case of spatial binary data.

2.4.4 Local Indicator of Spatial Association (LISA)

Although global measures such as Moran's *I* statistic and Geary's *c* statistic can detect spatial patterns and diagnose spatial autocorrelation, they do so only globally, as each of them provides a single statistic for the entire study area. Moran's *I* and Geary's *c* are useful for analyzing data that are relatively homogeneous in a region, but computing a single Moran's *I* or Geary's *c* value for data across a region with several spatial regimes may not prove as informative (Anselin, 1996). For example, if a Moran scatterplot shows both positive and negative spatial autocorrelation, indicating different spatial regimes and thus local instability, then a global indicator of spatial autocorrelation such as Moran's *I* may be too crude a measure of the actual spatial autocorrelation (Anselin, 1996). One solution in this type of instance is to develop local indicators of spatial association (LISA), such as local Moran's *I* (Anselin, 1995; Cliff & Ord, 1973, 1981), *G* and *G** statistics (Ord & Getis, 1995), and *K* statistic (Getis, 1984; Ord & Getis, 1995). In other words, global measures can be used to quantify overall spatial dependence, but local measures are needed to detect spatial heterogeneity. **LISA** can help researchers (Schabenberger & Gotway, 2005)

- assess the assumptions of stationarity such as constant variance in space,
- detect local regions of nonstationarity such as spatial clusters or "hotspots" (areal units with excessively high values) and "coldspots" or "pockets" (areal units with unusually low values),
- identify distances beyond which spatial association is weak or no more, and
- identify outliers or different spatial regimes.

LISA can take on the form of localized Moran's *I* statistic, localized Geary's *c* statistic, and *G* statistic, among others.

> To evaluate the local variation in spatial patterns (spatial heterogeneity), a localized statistic for measuring spatial dependence, or **Local Indicator of Spacial Association (LISA)**, can be used.

2.3.4.1 Local Moran's *I* Statistic

A special case of LISA is a local version of the Moran's *I* statistic defined as (Anselin, 1995)

$$I_i = (y_i - \bar{y}) \sum_{j=1, j \neq i}^{n} w_{ij}(y_j - \bar{y}) \qquad (2.10)$$

For ease of interpretation, the weight w_{ij} can be row standardized.

Local Moran's *I* measures similarity between the *i*th areal unit and its neighbors.

Local Moran's *I* is a measure of similarity between the *i*th areal unit and its neighbors. Interpretation and tests based on a local Moran's *I* are analogous to the global Moran's *I*. The difference, however, is that Moran's *I* statistic is a global measure of spatial autocorrelation and spatial pattern in an entire study area, while local Moran's *I* focuses on one areal unit at a time and measures the association between the observation y_j and all other observations based on the spatial weight matrix.[1]

2.3.4.2 Local Geary's *c* Statistic

Similarly, a special case of LISA through a local version of the Geary's *c* statistic is defined as (Anselin, 1995)

$$c_i = \sum_{j=1, j \neq i}^{n} w_{ij} \left(y_i - y_j \right)^2 \quad (2.11)$$

Interpretation and tests based on a local Geary's *c* are analogous to the global Geary's *c*. The difference, however, is that Geary's *c* statistic is a global measure of spatial autocorrelation and spatial pattern in an entire study area, while local Geary's *c* focuses on one areal unit at a time and measures the association between the observation y_i and the observations y_j in the neighborhood.

2.3.4.3 *G* Statistic

Local spatial dependence can also be measured by the *G* statistic, which was developed by Getis and Ord (1996). There are several versions (and thus formulations) of *G* statistics; the most often used one is specified as

$$G_i = \frac{\sum_j w_{ij(d)} y_j}{\sum_j y_j} \quad (2.12)$$

where

$i, j = 1, \ldots, n$ index the n areal units,

y_j is the value of the attribute at areal unit *j*, and

$w_{ij(d)}$ is a spatial weight between areal units *i* and *j* with 1 for all those within a threshold distance *d* but 0 for those outside of the threshold distance *d*.

---

[1] Spatial weight matrices that we use typically have thresholds. For example, in the *k*-nearest neighbor spatial weight matrices, a certain number of observations are selected as neighbors. In the general distance or inverse distance spatial weight matrices, a threshold distance is usually defined so that only observations falling within that distance are neighbors.

The numerator is the summation of attributes of all areal units within a threshold distance d and the denominator is the sum of attributions of all areal units. Therefore, the G_i statistic can be interpreted as the proportion of the sum of attributes of all areal units that are within the distance d of areal unit i. The **G statistic** is a measure of the concentration (or lack of concentration) of the sum of the attributes in the study area (Getis, 1995). As a side note, the attribute of areal unit i could be accounted for in either both the nominator and the denominator or neither of them, resulting in two different versions of G statistics. The expectation of G_i statistic is given as

> **G statistic** is a measure of the concentration (or lack of concentration) of the sum of the study area's attributes.

$$E(G_i) = \frac{\sum_{j}^{n} w_{ij}(d)}{n-1} \quad (2.13)$$

2.4.5 Data Example

This section illustrates ESDA by using population change from 2000 to 2010, the response variable in our Wisconsin case study, as an example. First, we visually examined the distribution of population change from 2000 to 2010 as presented in the lower right panel of Figure 1.4. Spatial dependence of population change is plausible, as the data seem to exhibit a spatial pattern. In addition, the assumption of independent errors may not be appropriate in a standard linear regression model. From the graphical display of the data distribution (Figure 1.4), though, it is unclear whether the spatial dependence is statistically significant, and even if it is, it is not obvious whether the spatial dependence can be explained by the spatial patterns in the explanatory variables.

To explore the spatial autocorrelation of the data, we tested the significance of Moran's I statistic using multiple spatial weight matrices, including the rook's and queen's case contiguity weight matrices with order 1 and order 2; the k-nearest neighbor weight matrices with k ranging from 3 to 8; and the general distance weight matrix and the inverse distance weight matrices with power 1 or power 2, from 0 to 100 miles at 10-mile increments based on the distance between the centroids of MCDs (Table 2.2). The results reveal that the magnitudes of the Moran's I statistics are not particularly high, with the 4-nearest neighbor weight matrix having the highest value ($I = 0.21$). The z-score test statistic for the significance of Moran's I is computed as the ratio of Moran's I and the corresponding standard error. The p-values are computed using a normal approximation and are all less than .001, which is strong evidence of spatial autocorrelation in population change in the 2000s in the Wisconsin MCDs based on all forty spatial weight matrices.

TABLE 2.2 ● Moran's *I* statistic of population change from 2000 to 2010 by forty spatial weight matrices

Spatial weight matrix	Moran's *I*	Spatial weight matrix	Moran's *I*
Queen's contiguity, order 1	0.199***	Inverse distance, 10 miles, power 1	0.188***
Queen's contiguity, order 2	0.149***	Inverse distance, 10 miles, power 2	0.191***
Rook's contiguity, order 1	0.199***	Inverse distance, 20 miles, power 1	0.159***
Rook's contiguity, order 2	0.164***	Inverse distance, 20 miles, power 2	0.173***
3-nearest neighbors	0.197***	Inverse distance, 30 miles, power 1	0.133***
4-nearest neighbors	0.210***	Inverse distance, 30 miles, power 2	0.160***
5-nearest neighbors	0.207***	Inverse distance, 40 miles, power 1	0.111***
6-nearest neighbors	0.205***	Inverse distance, 40 miles, power 2	0.150***
7-nearest neighbors	0.204***	Inverse distance, 50 miles, power 1	0.096***
8-nearest neighbors	0.200***	Inverse distance, 50 miles, power 2	0.142***
General distance, 10 miles	0.194***	Inverse distance, 60 miles, power 1	0.083***
General distance, 20 miles	0.151***	Inverse distance, 60 miles, power 2	0.136***
General distance, 30 miles	0.112***	Inverse distance, 70 miles, power 1	0.074***
General distance, 40 miles	0.083***	Inverse distance, 70 miles, power 2	0.132***
General distance, 50 miles	0.063***	Inverse distance, 80 miles, power 1	0.067***
General distance, 60 miles	0.048***	Inverse distance, 80 miles, power 2	0.128***
General distance, 70 miles	0.038***	Inverse distance, 90 miles, power 1	0.062***
General distance, 80 miles	0.031***	Inverse distance, 90 miles, power 2	0.125***
General distance, 90 miles	0.029***	Inverse distance, 100 miles, power 1	0.058***
General distance, 100 miles	0.026***	Inverse distance, 100 miles, power 2	0.123***

***$p \leq .001$.

The Moran scatterplot shown in Figure 2.6 illustrates population growth from 2000 to 2010 for the MCDs (*x*-axis) in relation to the average population growth for the neighbors, weighted by the 4-nearest neighbor weight matrix (*y*-axis). MCDs with population growth that are surrounded by MCDs with population growth are indicated in the upper right quadrant of the scatterplot. There are more of these MCDs than there are of MCDs with population decline that are surrounded by MCDs with population decline (lower left quadrant), MCDs with population growth that are surrounded by MCDs with population decline (lower right quadrant), and MCDs with population decline that are surrounded by MCDs with population growth (upper left quadrant). The scatterplot regression line slope is 0.21, indicating considerable positive spatial dependence of population growth from 2000 to 2010. Population change exhibits spatial autocorrelation. The reasons for spatial autocorrelation of population have been addressed by both spatial-explicit theories and spatial-implicit theories, as discussed in Section 1.3.1. Population growth in one geographic unit can be shown to be autocorrelated with its neighboring units.

Figure 2.7 displays the local spatial dependence of population change from 2000 to 2010 for the Wisconsin MCDs by high-high (high-growth MCDs that are surrounded by high-growth MCDs), low-low (low-growth MCDs that are surrounded by low-growth MCDs), low-high (low-growth MCDs that are surrounded by high-growth MCDs), and high-low (high-growth MCDs that are surrounded by low-growth MCDs), showing only MCDs with a local Moran's I statistic significant at the $\alpha = .05$ level based on a randomization procedure. High-high MCDs are mainly located in suburbs of major cities (such as Madison, Milwaukee, Green Bay, Appleton, and Minneapolis–St. Paul), whereas low-low MCDs are mainly in northern Wisconsin. Most of the low-high MCDs are neighbors of the hotspot (growth-growth) MCDs, whereas high-low MCDs are neighbors of coldspot (decline-decline) MCDs.

FIGURE 2.6 ● Moran scatterplot of population change at the minor civil division (MCD) level from 2000 to 2010 in Wisconsin

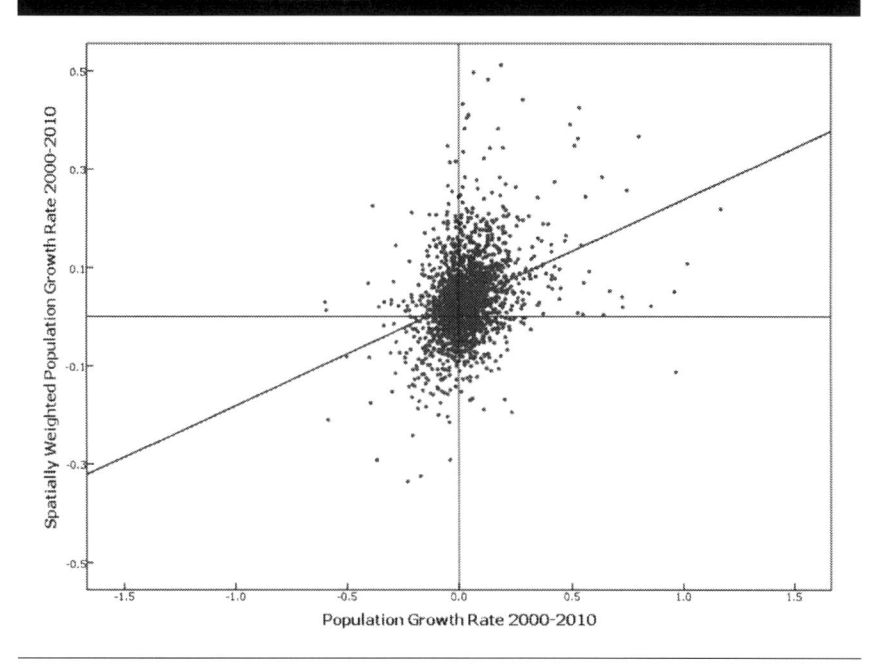

FIGURE 2.7 ● **LISA of population change at the minor civil division (MCD) level from 2000 to 2010 in Wisconsin**

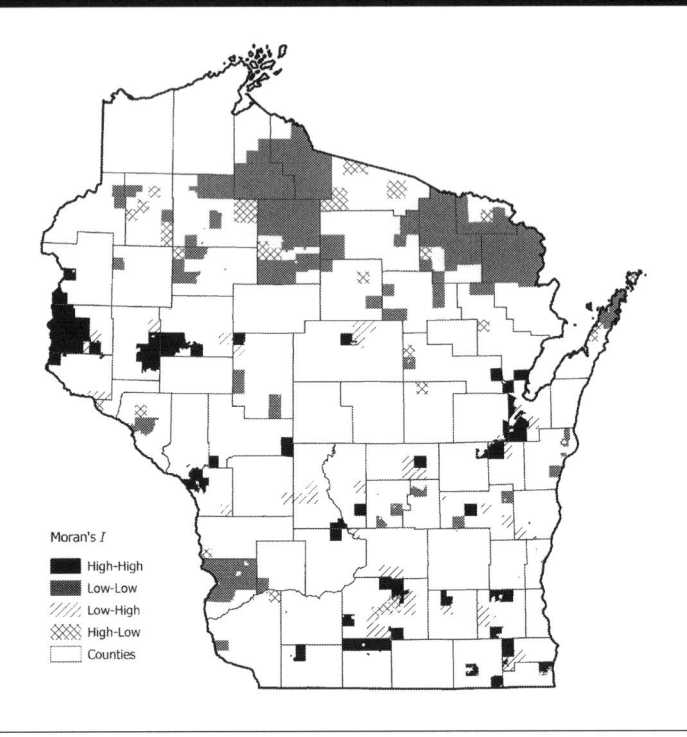

Moran's I
- High-High
- Low-Low
- Low-High
- High-Low
- Counties

We further provided Moran's I statistics for all explanatory variables (online Appendix B.1) and identified in bold their corresponding spatial weight matrices that capture the maximum spatial autocorrelation companioned with a high level of statistical significance. This will help us select a more suitable spatial weight matrix in spatial regression modeling in the later chapters of this book.

For each of the six explanatory variables (*previous growth, old, unemployment, airport, forest,* and *land developability*), we calculated Moran's I statistic based on the forty spatial weight matrices as used for the response variable. It should be noted that we purposefully use forty spatial weight matrices in this book to demonstrate the importance of selecting an appropriate spatial weight matrix in ESDA and spatial regression modeling—the results change when different spatial weight matrices are used. We suggest readers consider a set of spatial weight matrices that suits their subject matter.

The spatial dependence of each of the six explanatory variables is statistically significant based on any of the forty spatial weight matrices. The more appropriate spatial weight matrices are determined to be the 4-nearest neighbor weight matrix for *previous growth,* the first-order rook's contiguity weight matrix for *old,* the 5-nearest neighbor weight matrix for *unemployment,* the 3-nearest neighbor weight matrix for *airport,* the first-order rook's contiguity weight matrix for *forest,* and the first-order queen's contiguity weight matrix for *land developability.*

Study Questions

1. What goals does exploratory spatial data analysis aim to achieve?

2. What is a neighborhood structure? What types of neighborhood structures are there? What are the differences between contiguity-based and distance-based neighborhood structures?

3. What is a spatial weight matrix? What is the difference between a fixed and a variable spatial weight matrix?

4. What is the difference between a neighborhood structure and a spatial weight matrix?

5. When do we need a spatial weight matrix?

6. How do we choose an appropriate spatial weight matrix?

7. What are the issues with and corresponding solutions for using spatial weight matrices?

8. What are spatial autocorrelation, spatial dependence, and spatial heterogeneity? What are their differences?

9. What statistics can be used to measure spatial autocorrelation? How do we interpret a Moran's I statistic and a Geary's c statistic?

10. What statistics can be used to measure local spatial association? How do we interpret a local Moran's I and a G statistic?

11. In your area of research, which spatial weight matrices are typically used?

12. Which spatial weight matrix would you use in your research? How will you choose an appropriate one?

3

MODELS DEALING WITH SPATIAL DEPENDENCE

LEARNING OBJECTIVES

- Understand why and when to account for spatial dependence and how to interpret the diagnostics for spatial dependence in standard linear regression.
- Understand when and how to fit a spatial lag model, interpret the spatial lag effect, and use appropriate diagnostics to assess the model.
- Understand when and how to fit a spatial error model, interpret the spatial error effect, and use appropriate diagnostics to assess the model.
- Identify appropriate spatial weight matrices to use in a spatial lag model or a spatial error model.
- Describe the cautions about using a spatial lag model and a spatial error model.
- Choose between a spatial lag model and a spatial error model in fitting to data.

In Chapters 1 and 2, we introduced basic concepts and methods of exploratory spatial data analysis. When we conduct exploratory spatial data analysis, we might find that spatial autocorrelation (or dependence) and/or spatial heterogeneity are present in the response variable and/or explanatory variables. As a common practice, we fit standard linear regression models to examine the relations between explanatory variables and the response variable, and we might find spatial dependence and/or spatial heterogeneity in the residuals after the model fit.

If there is spatial dependence and/or spatial heterogeneity in a response variable or residuals, should we, and how do we, account for them? In this and Chapter 4, we introduce models dealing with spatial dependence. In Chapter 5, we introduce models dealing with spatial heterogeneity.

In this chapter, we start with standard linear regression models (Section 3.1) and discuss how to diagnose spatial dependence and, if it exists, how we can account for it. We then introduce two often-used basic spatial regression models—spatial lag models (Section 3.2) and spatial error models (Section 3.3).

Each of the three sections is illustrated with a data example examining population change from 1990 to 2010 at the minor civil division (MCD) level in Wisconsin. More advanced models dealing with spatial dependence are introduced in Chapter 4.

3.1 STANDARD LINEAR REGRESSION AND DIAGNOSTICS FOR SPATIAL DEPENDENCE

3.1.1 Standard Linear Regression

Standard linear regression models assuming independent errors are familiar to social scientists. As a common practice, standard linear regression models are often fitted before considering more advanced models. Here we briefly review such models with the main purpose of diagnosing possible spatial dependence and thus building the grounds for using spatial regression models.

To begin, a standard linear regression model expressed in matrix notation is

$$Y = X\beta + \varepsilon \tag{3.1}$$

where

Y is an n-by-1 vector of n observations on the response variable,

X is an n-by-p design matrix with a vector of n ones in the first column for the intercept and $p - 1$ (n-by-1) vectors of explanatory variables in the remaining columns,

β is a p-by-1 vector of regression coefficients, and

ε is an n-by-1 vector of n error terms that are independently and identically distributed as normal distribution with mean 0 and a constant variance.

The vector of regression coefficients β can be estimated by the ordinary least squares (OLS) method such that the total squared difference between the observed and the expected values of the response variable, $(Y - X\beta)^T(Y - X\beta)$, is minimized with respect to β. The OLS estimate of β is thus based on the data Y and the design matrix X and provides an estimate of the relations between the response variable Y and the $p - 1$ explanatory variables in the design matrix X.

For drawing statistical inference about the unknown vector β such as hypothesis testing and constructing confidence intervals, however, model assumptions are needed. A standard linear regression model generally assumes that the error terms have mean zero and are independently, identically, and normally distributed (e.g., Draper & Smith, 1998; Fox, 1997; Greene, 2000). That is, in equation (3.1), the model is linear in the sense that the regression coefficients enter the model linearly via addition, subtraction, or multiplication but not division, exponentiation, or other nonlinear forms. Furthermore, it is assumed that the errors are independent and follow a normal distribution with mean zero and a constant variance. Under these assumptions, the OLS estimate of β is unbiased, normal, and statistically efficient in the sense that the variance of the OLS estimate is minimized among all linear unbiased estimators. Alternatively, maximum likelihood estimation (MLE) can be used to provide the parameter estimates that make the data most probable in terms of a likelihood function (Millar, 2011). For the standard linear regression, the OLS estimates and the MLEs for the regression coefficients β are the same.

> In a standard linear regression model, the error terms are assumed to have mean zero and are independently, identically, and normally distributed.

When these model assumptions are not adequately met, however, the subsequent statistical inference of the parameters in the standard linear regression model may not be appropriate or reliable. In particular, if the errors are spatially dependent, the OLS estimate of β can still be unbiased and normal but is no longer efficient. Alternative models and estimation procedures (e.g., generalized least squares) that take into account spatial dependence would generally be more efficient. Thus, it is important to perform model diagnostics that examine whether the model assumptions are reasonably met.

Diagnostics for standard linear regression models are often based on residuals, which are the differences between the observed and model-fitted values of the response variable. Residual analysis is often performed by examining patterns in various residual plots. Certain distinct patterns in the residuals may suggest departure from model assumptions and indicate nonlinear relations, unequal variances, and/or nonnormality. Testing for nonlinear relations helps reveal anisotropy and nonstationarity (Bailey & Gatrell, 1995; Graaff, Florax, Nijkamp, & Reggiani,

> Standard linear regression model diagnostics are often based on residuals—the differences between the response variable's observed values and model-fitted values.

2001). Unequal variances, or heteroscedasticity, can be revealed with tests such as the Breusch-Pagan test (Breusch & Pagan, 1979) or the Koenker-Bassett test (Koenker & Bassett, 1982). Nonnormality can be revealed using tests such as the Jarque-Bera test (Bera & Jarque, 1980), which has an asymptotic chi-squared distribution with two degrees of freedom. If there is clear evidence of departure from any of the model assumptions, remedial measures should be considered.

A common remedial measure is the transformation of the response variable and/or the explanatory variables to better conform to the assumptions of linearity, equal variance, and normality. For example, the response variable is examined and possibly transformed to have an approximate normal distribution. For each explanatory variable, linearity against the response variable is examined and possibly corrected via transformation. Although not a model assumption, multicollinearity occurs when some of the explanatory variables are highly correlated. Multicollinearity can be concerning, as the estimated coefficients may be unreliable, and thus is often examined as a part of the model diagnostics, such as via a variance inflation factor (Allison, 1999) or a multicollinearity condition number[1] (Anselin, 2005).

3.1.2 Diagnostics for Spatial Dependence

From the spatial regression perspective, we are particularly interested in the independence assumption of the errors, which could be violated due to spatial dependence. If there is clear evidence of spatial dependence, standard linear regression fitting may no longer be appropriate. For example, the standard errors of the regression coefficients may be overestimated (or underestimated), indicating an overstatement (or understatement) of the significance of relations (Baller et al., 2001; Doreian, 1980; Loftin & Ward, 1983). Tools for diagnosing spatial dependence, particularly spatial autocorrelation, include Moran's I plot[2] and Moran's I statistic of the residuals (Baller et al., 2001; Cliff & Ord, 1972; Hepple, 1998; Loftin & Ward, 1983).

If the errors are diagnosed to be spatially dependent, a common remedial measure is to expand the standard linear regression models to spatial linear regression models, types of which we introduce in Sections 3.2 and 3.3. Most of these spatial

> If the residuals of standard linear regression models show clear spatial dependence, such model fitting may no longer be appropriate.

---

[1] A multicollinearity condition number is not a test statistic but a diagnostic of the regression stability due to multicollinearity. A condition number over 30 typically suggests potential issues due to multicollinearity.

[2] Moran's I plot of errors can also detect if there are any outliers. Outliers are not necessarily "bad," and further exploration of the outliers might provide interesting findings. Practically, we can code the outliers as one explanatory variable, where the outliers are represented as 1 and the others as 0. If the coefficient significantly differs from zero, there is evidence that these are "real" outliers. In spatial data analysis, outliers detected by a Moran scatterplot may indicate possible problems with the specification of the spatial weight matrix or with the spatial scale at which the observations are recorded (Anselin, 1996). Outliers should be studied carefully before being discarded (Mur & Lauridsen, 2007).

regression models consider spatial lag dependence and/or spatial error dependence, two basic types of spatial dependence.

The appropriateness of a spatial regression model with respect to spatial lag dependence and spatial error dependence can be partly indicated by

- the Lagrange multiplier (LM) test (Bera & Yoon, 1993) and
- the robust LM test.

The **LM test** statistic follows a chi-squared distribution with one degree of freedom under the null hypothesis of no spatial dependence and can be used to reveal spatial dependence in the form of an omitted spatially lagged dependent variable and/or spatial error dependence (Anselin, 1988a). When the lag dependence and error dependence are both found to be statistically significant using the LM test, a **robust LM test** can reveal further spatial dependence (Baltagi & Yang, 2013). The robust LM test can be used to diagnose spatial lag dependence in the presence of spatial error dependence and to diagnose spatial error dependence in the presence of a spatially lagged dependent variable (Anselin, Bera, Florax, & Yoon, 1996). MLE can be used to estimate the parameters in the appropriate spatial regression model indicated by the robust LM test.

LM test and the **robust LM test** can help indicate the appropriateness of a spatial regression model with respect to spatial lag dependence and spatial error dependence.

3.1.3 Model Evaluation

For a given data set, various linear regression models can be specified. Measures of model fit have often been used to evaluate the goodness of model fitting to data and to compare different models. In quantitative social science research that uses standard linear regression, it is common practice to specify multiple candidate models and select the best-fitting model to use for drawing inference and discussing results in a scientific context. Social scientists have traditionally used R^2 and adjusted R^2 as the measures of fit of standard linear regression models. In this chapter, we discuss alternative measures of fit, including the likelihood ratio test (LRT), Akaike's information criterion (AIC) (Akaike, 1973), and Schwartz's Bayesian information criterion (BIC) (Schwartz, 1978), when addressing spatial regression models.

3.1.4 When Do We Need to Account for Spatial Dependence?

So far, we have learned the diagnostics for spatial dependence in the response variable and explanatory variables as well as for spatial dependence in the model residuals. The question is, should we always account for spatial dependence when it is diagnosed? From a statistical perspective, whether a spatial regression model is needed is based on the indication of spatial dependence among the standard linear

The need for a spatial regression model is based on the spatial dependence indicated among the standard linear regression residuals.

regression residuals rather than that from the observations of the response variable or explanatory variables. The observations of the response variable or explanatory variables may exhibit spatial dependence—in other words, one or more of the variables may exhibit a spatial pattern from one place to another; however, the spatial dependence of a variable itself does not necessitate a spatial regression model because the spatial dependence of the response variable might be explained by the possible spatial dependence of other explanatory variables.

For instance, we know that infrastructure investment is a strong predictor of economic output such as employment growth at aggregated levels (Boarnet, 1997). We fit a standard linear regression model in which employment growth is a function of infrastructure investment in a certain time period at a certain geographic level. If employment growth exhibits strong spatial autocorrelation, that does not necessitate a spatial regression model—infrastructure investment might exhibit similar spatial autocorrelation. The spatial autocorrelation of infrastructure investment may be able to explain most of the spatial autocorrelation of employment growth, making the standard linear regression residuals not autocorrelated in space. In this case, a spatial regression model is not needed for the analysis. However, the spatial autocorrelation of infrastructure investment may not be able to explain most of the spatial autocorrelation of employment growth, making the standard linear regression residuals spatially autocorrelated. In this situation, a spatial regression model is desirable to account for the spatial autocorrelation in the model errors.

3.1.5 Data Example

3.1.5.1 Population Change and Its Explanatory Variables

As discussed in Section 2.4, throughout this book, we use the data example of population change in Wisconsin from 2000 to 2010 and its relation with its explanatory variables to demonstrate the use of various spatial regression models. In this section, we fit a standard linear regression model on the example data set as the starting point for explaining when and what kind of spatial regression models are needed.

Table 3.1 shows the MLEs of the regression coefficients, their standard errors, and the level of significance indicated by p-values for testing whether the true regression coefficient is zero. The intercept is estimated to be 0.077 with a standard error of 0.019. In general, however, its significance is not of particular interest, as it concerns the expected response variable (here, population change) when all the explanatory variables are held at zero. All explanatory variables are statistically significant at the $\alpha = .05$ level in explaining population change from 2000 to 2010.

TABLE 3.1 ● Standard linear regression results by maximum likelihood estimation

Variable	Coefficient	SE
Intercept	0.077***	0.019
Previous growth	0.071***	0.021
Old	−0.335***	0.060
Unemployment	−0.279*	0.109
Airport	0.161*	0.079
Forest	−0.086***	0.015
Land developability	0.046**	0.018
Diagnostics for spatial dependence		
Moran's *I* for residuals	0.119***	
LM test for lag	76.189***	
LM test for error	57.038***	
Robust LM test for lag	43.806***	
Robust LM test for error	24.655***	
Measures of fit		
Log-likelihood	1,108.98	
AIC	−2,203.95	
BIC	−2,165.34	

Note: 4-nearest neighbor weight matrix is used for diagnosing spatial dependence. LM = Lagrange multiplier; AIC = Akaike's information criterion; BIC = Schwartz's Bayesian information criterion; SE = standard error.

*Significant at the α = .05 level. **Significant at the α = .01 level.***Significant at the α = .001 level.

A more nuanced approach to interpret the *p*-values is based on the strength of the evidence. Roughly speaking, when a *p*-value is less than .001 (***), between .001 and .01 (**), between .01 and .05 (*), between .05 and .10, or greater than .10, we consider the evidence against the null hypothesis to be very strong, strong, moderate, weak, or none, respectively. We recommend this approach to supplement the interpretation of *p*-values based on significance testing.

There is very strong evidence that population change has a positive relation with *previous growth*; each additional 1 percent of previous growth is associated with 0.07 percent of population change in 2000 to 2010, with all the other explanatory variables held constant. Population change in a unit of geography is often influenced by the trend of its previous population change. Population growth (or decline) in the past is affected by its growth mechanism and areal characteristics (Chi, 2012), and the effect could continue into the current time period. This has been acknowledged in many demographic studies conducting time-series analysis and population forecasting (e.g., Chi, 2009).

There is very strong evidence that population change has a negative relation with *old*, the percentage of the old population (sixty-five and older); each additional percentage of the old population is associated with 0.34 percent of population decline in 2000 to 2010. This finding is consistent with those from previous studies that found that places with high percentages of old populations are more likely to experience population decline (e.g., Humphrey, 1980). This is due to at least two reasons. One, the older population has a higher mortality rate than the younger population, which contributes to higher mortality in places with higher percentages of old populations than in places with lower percentages of old populations (i.e., higher percentages of young populations). Two, the older population members are "stayers" but the younger population members are "movers" (Chi & Voss, 2005); places with higher percentages of old populations may have this higher old population as a result of their loss of the young population due to their unattractiveness (e.g., rurality) to the younger population.

There is moderate evidence that population change has a negative relation with *unemployment*; each additional 1 percent of unemployment is associated with 0.28 percent of population decline in 2000 to 2010, with all the other explanatory variables held constant. This finding is consistent with findings from previous research that argue employment is one of the most important determinants affecting migration decision making (DaVanzo, 1981). Increased availability of local employment opportunities can attract migrants due to the stimulation of household labor use and its effect on household incomes.

There is moderate evidence that population change has a positive relation with *airport;* each additional unit in proximity to airport (measured as the inverse distance) is associated with 16.1 percent of population growth in 2000 to 2010, with all the other explanatory variables held constant. This finding is also consistent with findings from previous research, which found airports play an important role in promoting economic growth and development. Compared with highways and railways, airports provide more convenient long-distance travel and thus attract migrants who appreciate this convenience. Airports also increase intercity agglomeration (Kasarda & Lindsay, 2011) because air travel reduces distance limits on economic and social interactions (Irwin & Kasarda, 1991), linking cities, increasing distant cities' interactions, and integrating individual economic regions into a nationwide or worldwide economic region (Brueckner, 2003). Thus, airports promote population change (Zipf, 1946).

There is very strong evidence that population change has a negative relation to *forest;* each additional 1 percent of forest coverage is associated with 0.09 percent of population decline in 2000 to 2010, with all the other explanatory variables held constant. Although forests are a natural amenity and might be pleasant to people, forests do not, in and of themselves, have much recreational value. Forests become attractive only when they are accessed through managed recreational areas, such as parks, trails, wildlife refuges, and fishing areas. This finding can be partially supported by McGranahan (2008), who found that a moderate amount of forest coverage promotes population growth at the county level but too much forest does not.

Finally, there is strong evidence that population change has a positive relation with *land developability;* each additional 1 percent of land available for development is associated with 0.05 percent of population growth in 2000 to 2010, with all the other explanatory variables held constant. The development is limited by the availability of lands for conversion and development. The higher the land developability is, the higher the potential of the development, which would lead to growth and development (Chi, 2010b).

3.1.5.2 Model Diagnostics Using Standard Linear Regression Residuals

While the results from the standard linear regression model sound reasonable, we now ask, is the model specification adequate? If not, the model-fitting results can be unreliable. The standard linear regression model has several assumptions, including linearity, independence, normality, and equal variance. While it is important to examine each of them, in this book, we focus on the independence assumption as it relates to why we need spatial regression models.

After fitting the standard linear regression model, we examined whether the residuals indicate that the errors are spatially dependent. We calculated Moran's *I* statistics of the residuals based on the forty spatial weight matrices as introduced in Section 2.2. Residuals of the standard linear regression model exhibit statistically significant spatial dependence with strong evidence based on any of the forty spatial weight matrices (online Appendix B.2). The evidence of spatial dependence was the strongest based on the 4-nearest neighbor weight matrix. The distribution of residuals based on the 4-nearest neighbor weight matrix is also illustrated in Figure 3.1, which shows clear

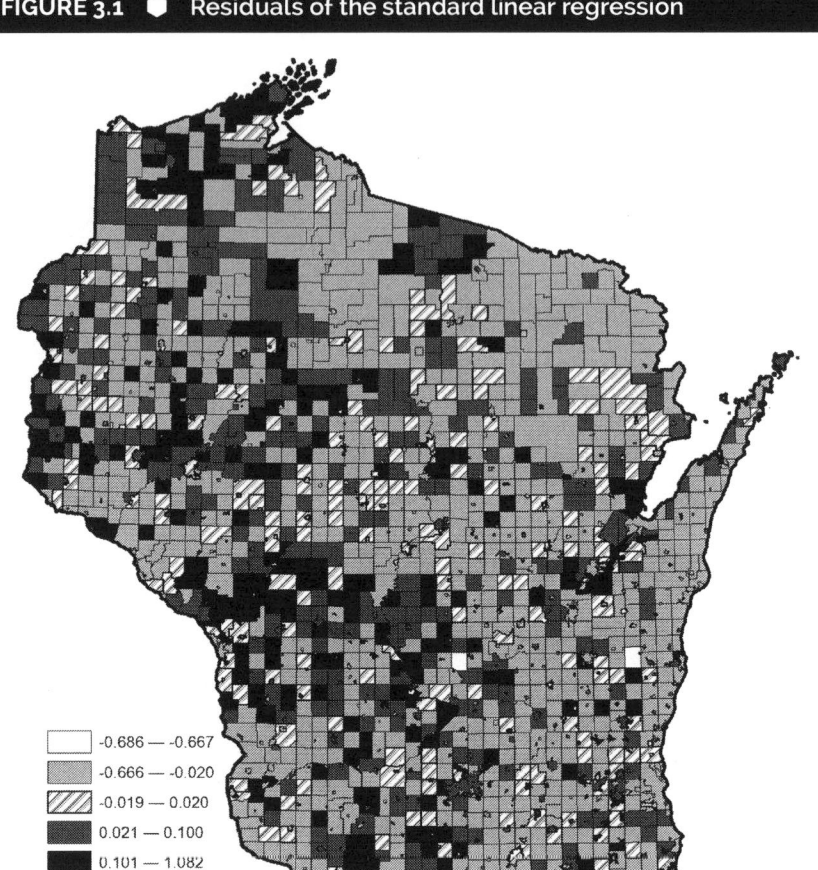

FIGURE 3.1 ● Residuals of the standard linear regression

- ☐ -0.686 — -0.667
- ▨ -0.666 — -0.020
- ▩ -0.019 — 0.020
- ▤ 0.021 — 0.100
- ■ 0.101 — 1.082

evidence of residual clusters. For example, high and positive residuals were clustered along I-94 from Minneapolis to Eau Claire and Warsau and along I-90 from La Crosse to Madison; high and negative residuals were distributed throughout many towns in Wisconsin.

Although we know from these results that there is spatial dependence, we do not know yet how to go about modeling the spatial dependence or what type of spatial dependence it is. To explore this, we may use LM tests for lag dependence and error dependence. Based on the 4-nearest neighbor weight matrix, both the spatial lag dependence and spatial error dependence are statistically significant with strong evidence (Table 3.1; online Appendix B.2). We further use the robust LM tests for lag dependence and error dependence to compare them. Based on the 4-nearest neighbor weight matrix, again, the spatial lag dependence and spatial error dependence are statistically significant with strong evidence in addition to the type of spatial dependence. This suggests that we should include both spatial lag dependence and spatial error dependence in the model.

3.2 SPATIAL LAG MODELS

In Section 3.1, we reviewed standard linear regression models. If there is clear evidence that the residuals are spatially dependent, the spatial dependence should be accounted for. One way to do so is via spatial linear regression models. A spatial linear regression model can be considered a generalization of a standard linear regression model in that spatial models allow and explicitly account for spatial dependence in the error term (Anselin, 1988b). The usual regression coefficients of the explanatory variables (β) and the variance of the error term (σ^2) are the model parameters. The spatial regression models that are most commonly used also have a spatial dependence parameter (ρ) measuring the strength of the spatial dependence. Both a variance weight matrix (D) and a spatial weight matrix (W) corresponding to a neighborhood structure are specified before the model is fitted. Although more complicated spatial dependence models are possible, the focus in this chapter is restricted to models with only one spatial dependence parameter. We start with spatial lag models in this section.

Spatial regression models allow and explicitly account for spatial dependence in the error term.

3.2.1 What Is a Spatial Lag Model?

A **spatial lag model** relates a response variable and a set of explanatory variables via regression as in standard linear regression (Anselin & Bera, 1998). In addition, the response variable is autoregressed on spatially lagged response variables. A spatial lag model is specified as

$$Y = X\beta + \rho WY + \varepsilon \qquad (3.2)$$

where

Y is an n-by-1 vector of response variables,

X is an n-by-p design matrix of explanatory variables,

β is a p-by-1 vector of regression coefficients,

ρ is a scalar spatial lag parameter,

W is an n-by-n spatial weight matrix, and

ε is an n-by-1 vector of error terms that are normally and independently but not necessarily identically distributed.

*A **spatial lag model** relates explanatory variables and a response variable as in a standard linear regression model, except the response variable is autoregressed on spatially lagged response variables.*

WY denotes a spatially lagged variable because it is a weighted average of the neighborhood response variables.

When $\rho = 0$, the spatial lag model (equation [3.2]) is reduced to the standard linear regression model (equation [3.1]). That is, the standard linear regression model (equation [3.1]) is nested in the more advanced spatial lag model (equation [3.2]). Since Y denotes the response variable and W denotes the spatial weight matrix, WY (also known as *autocovariate* or *autoregressor*) denotes a spatially lagged variable in the sense that it is a weighted average of the response variables in the neighborhood. Thus, the spatial lag model (equation [3.2]) builds a relation between the response variable in an areal unit with a weighted average of the response variables at neighboring areal units. To do this, we need to

> A spatial lag model relates the response variable in one areal unit with a weighted average of the neighboring areal units' response variables.

- identify the neighbors by defining a neighborhood structure and
- provide weights to the neighbors.

Both are featured in the spatial weight matrix, W.

3.2.2 Model Fitting via Maximum Likelihood

For spatial linear regression model fitting, OLS estimation is limited because it does not directly account for spatial dependence in the data. An alternative approach for estimation and inference is based on maximum likelihood. While these two estimations are often discussed with more rigorous mathematical statistics in other textbooks, here we aim to contrast them intuitively.

> **OLS estimation** chooses the model fitting that has resulted in the least squares of errors.

The **OLS estimation,** as the name suggests, selects a set of regression coefficients that results in the least squares of errors (i.e., the difference between the observed and fitted values of the response variable) among all possible sets of regression coefficients. When we fit regression by OLS within a software package, say Stata or SPSS, the output provides the set of parameter estimates that makes the sum of squared errors the smallest. The **MLE method,** also as the name suggests, selects the set of parameter estimates (including the coefficients and spatial parameters) that results in the maximum likelihood (i.e., the largest probability) of the observed data (Millar, 2011). For the MLE, the likelihood of observed data is a function of the parameters. Intuitively, there could be an infinite number of combinations of the parameters, and each set results in a likelihood value. Among all the likelihood values, we want the parameters that make the data most probable with the highest likelihood. The resulting parameters are called maximum likelihood estimates.

> **MLE method** chooses the set of parameter estimates that has resulted in the maximum likelihood of the observed data.

In the likelihood inference framework, the often-used measures of the goodness of the model fit include maximum log-likelihood value, Akaike's information criterion (AIC) (Akaike, 1973), and Schwartz's Bayesian information criterion (BIC) (Schwartz, 1978). Nested models (simpler models reduced from another more complex model after constraining certain parameters in the complex model) can be compared by a likelihood ratio test (LRT). For nonnested models, AIC and BIC are often used; they measure the model fitting to the data but penalize overly complex models. Models having a smaller AIC or a smaller BIC are considered the better models in the sense of model fitting balanced with model parsimony.

3.2.3 Model Diagnostics

There are several model diagnostics to perform when fitting a spatial lag model. One set of diagnostics is performed after fitting a standard linear regression model. It includes diagnostics for possible multicollinearity among explanatory variables, possible heteroscedasticity by the Breusch-Pagan test (Breusch & Pagan, 1979), and the spatial Breusch-Pagan test, among others.

Another set of diagnostics is for detecting possibly remaining spatial dependence after accounting for spatial lag dependence through the spatial lag model. The possibly remaining spatial lag dependence can be diagnosed by an LRT, and the possibly remaining spatial error dependence can be diagnosed by the LM and robust LM tests. It can happen that two different models fit the data about equally well, as there may not be enough information in the data to pinpoint what the "true" model is (as if a true model exists).

3.2.4 When Is a Spatial Lag Model Needed?

When we want to explain (or model) a response variable, we usually start with a standard linear regression model. If the OLS residuals provide clear evidence that the errors have spatial lag dependence, that is, if the OLS residuals can be explained by the weighted average of the response variables in the neighborhood, a spatial lag model would be appropriate to examine the response variable.

It should be noted that whether a spatial lag model is needed is based on the indication of spatial dependence among the OLS residuals rather than the observations of the response variable. The observations of the response variable may display spatial dependence; in other words, the response variable may exhibit a spatial pattern from one place to another. However, the spatial dependence of the response variable itself does not necessitate a spatial lag model because the spatial dependence of the response variable might be explained by the possible spatial dependence of its explanatory variables. This was discussed in an example in Section 3.1.

The necessity of a spatial lag model is indicated by the spatial dependence among the OLS residuals.

3.2.5 Which Spatial Weight Matrix to Use in a Spatial Lag Model?

Different spatial weight matrices will result in different parameter estimates.

To fit a spatial lag model, a spatial weight matrix needs to be prespecified. However, there are many types of spatial weight matrices with different specifications. The use of different spatial weight matrices will result in different parameter estimates (β and ρ). One practical question arises regarding which spatial weight matrix to use when fitting a spatial lag model. As addressed in Section 2.2, if there are theories or previous studies suggesting an appropriate spatial weight matrix for the phenomenon under study, adopting the suggested spatial weight matrix is recommended.

If there are no such theories or previous studies, which often happens when the line of research has not seen much spatial regression analysis, a data-driven approach can be considered to select an appropriate spatial weight matrix. One approach is to fit the spatial lag model with a variety of spatial weight matrices and select the one that encompasses the highest spatial dependence of the response variable in combination with a high level of statistical significance (Chi & Zhu, 2008). Alternatively, one may use an information criterion, such as AIC or BIC, to compare the fit of the models under different spatial weight matrices. Other approaches are possible and continue to be developed. By and large, it appears to remain an open research question as to how to properly or even optimally specify the spatial weight matrix.

How to properly and optimally specify a spatial weight matrix remains an open research question.

3.2.6 Cautions About Spatial Lag Models

Cautionary note 1: The spatial lag effect can be either positive or negative. The spatial lag effect is not necessarily always positive. A negative spatial lag effect is also possible. A positive spatial lag effect is sometimes called a *spread effect* and a negative spatial lag effect is called a *backwash effect* in growth pole theory (Perroux, 1955). For example, the growth and development in a central city might draw resources from the surrounding areas, which leads to a decline in the surrounding areas; this is a negative or backwash effect.

Cautionary note 2: Interpretation of a statistically significant spatial lag coefficient is not always straightforward. Although strong spatial dependence may be indicated by a statistically significant spatial lag term, that spatial lag term may also indicate a mismatch of the spatial scales between the one at which the phenomenon is studied and the one at which it is measured. This is part of the scale effect of the modifiable areal unit problem (MAUP) (Fotheringham & Wong, 1991; Robinson, 1950). The MAUP should be carefully considered, although it is familiar to most scientists who deal with spatial analysis.

Cautionary note 3: The expectation of Y *is not* Xβ *unless* ρ = 0. This imposes difficulty on the interpretation of β. Because of the autoregressive term ρWY on the right-hand side of equation (3.2), the expectation of the response variable Y involves Xβ and ρW. Thus, the usual interpretation of the regression coefficients β no longer holds and it is not straightforward to tease apart the associations due to the explanatory variables and those due to the autoregressors WY.

3.2.7 Data Example

Many social science phenomena could potentially exhibit spatial lag effects and thus could be modeled by spatial lag models. Examples include housing prices, population growth, employment growth, crime, and many others.

For instance, population growth is found to exhibit spatial lag effects (also called *spatial spillover effects* or *spatial diffusion effects*) (Hudson, 1972). A place's growth likely leads to growth in its surrounding areas: in a situation where a place experiences population growth that causes housing prices to increase, some residents leave for neighboring places with lower housing prices until the prices reach equilibrium; in a situation where a place experiences population decline that causes housing prices to decrease, some residents from neighboring places will move into this place until the prices reach equilibrium.

To illustrate the use of a spatial lag model, we use our example that examines population growth from 2000 to 2010 and its relation to its explanatory variables at the MCD level in Wisconsin. We expect that the explanatory variables cannot sufficiently explain population growth and that spatial lag dependence might exist in the standard linear regression model residuals. We further apply a spatial lag model to account for the spatial lag dependence.

According to the standard linear regression (via OLS estimation) results (Table 3.1; online Appendix B.2), the residuals exhibit statistically significant spatial dependence based on any of the forty spatial weight matrices. The LM and robust LM tests indicate that the standard linear regression residuals exhibit both spatial lag and spatial error dependence. In this section, we focus on the spatial lag dependence and apply spatial lag models to deal with it.

As discussed previously in this chapter, the use of different spatial weight matrices could result in different model parameter estimates. For illustration purposes, we fit spatial lag models with all forty spatial weight matrices in this chapter. Online Appendix B.3 shows that the parameter for the spatial lag effect and the regression coefficients for the explanatory variables vary when the spatial lag model is fitted with different spatial weight matrices. Because of this variation, it is recommended to select an appropriate spatial weight matrix and justify it when fitting spatial lag models, although some existing studies select a spatial weight matrix without such justifications.

As discussed previously, it remains an open research question as to how to properly or even optimally specify the spatial weight matrix. Here we use two approaches for illustrative purposes:

- One based on the spatial dependence of the response variable
- One based on information criteria

Based on the former, the more appropriate spatial weight matrix to choose is the one that captures the maximum spatial dependence of the response variable companioned with a high level of statistical significance. According to Table 2.2, population growth from 2000 to 2010 (the response variable) has the highest Moran's I value based on the 4-nearest neighbor weight matrix among forty spatial weight matrices. Using this weight matrix, we fit a spatial lag model. Comparing the results (Table 3.2; model 6 of online Appendix B.3) to the standard linear regression results (Table 3.1), the spatial lag model is better fitted to data balanced with model parsimony based on the fact that the AIC and BIC values are smaller in the spatial lag model than those in the standard linear regression model. Therefore, the spatial lag model is deemed better than the standard linear regression model for interpreting the association of the explanatory variables with population growth. The clusters of residuals (Figure 3.2) are fewer and less obvious than those of the standard linear regression residuals (Figure 3.1).

TABLE 3.2 ● Spatial lag model results based on the 4-nearest neighbor weight matrix

	Model 6
Intercept	0.060**
Previous growth	0.053**
Old	−0.262***
Unemployment	−0.245*
Airport	0.113

	Model 6
Forest	−0.064***
Land developability	0.036*
Spatial lag	0.248***
Measures of fit	
Log-likelihood	1,142.03
AIC	−2,268.05
BIC	−2,223.92

Note: AIC = Akaike's information criterion; BIC = Schwartz's Bayesian information criterion.

*Significant at the α = .05 level. **Significant at the α = .01 level. ***Significant at the α = .001 level.

FIGURE 3.2 Residuals of the spatial lag model based on the 4-nearest neighbor weight matrix

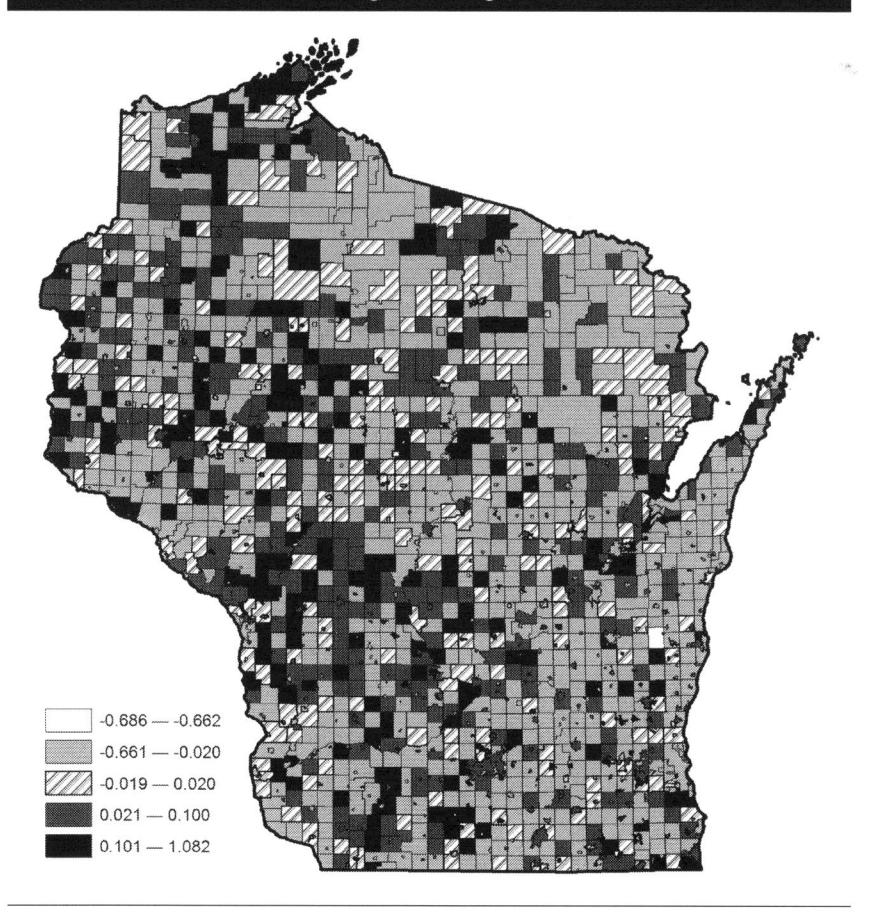

−0.686 — −0.662
−0.661 — −0.020
−0.019 — 0.020
0.021 — 0.100
0.101 — 1.082

Overall, the coefficient magnitudes (in terms of the absolute value) of the explanatory variables in the spatial lag model are smaller than those in the standard linear regression model. The statistical significance of the coefficients does not change much except that the proximity to airports becomes statistically insignificant at the $\alpha = .05$ level. Each additional 1 percent of previous population growth is associated with 0.05 percent of population growth in 2000 to 2010, with all the other explanatory variables held constant. Each additional 1 percent of old population is associated with 0.26 percent of population decline in 2000 to 2010, with all the other explanatory variables held constant. Each additional 1 percent of unemployment rate is associated with 0.25 percent of population decline in 2000 to 2010, with all the other explanatory variables held constant. Each additional 1 percent of forest coverage is associated with 0.06 percent of population decline in 2000 to 2010, with all the other explanatory variables held constant. Each additional 1 percent of land available for development is associated with 0.04 percent of population growth in 2000 to 2010, with all the other explanatory variables held constant. The interpretation of the association between these explanatory variables and the response variable is not as straightforward as the standard linear regression (see cautionary note 3 in Section 3.2.6).

The spatial lag effect is positive and statistically significant. The spatial lag effect comes from the spatially lagged population change in 2000 to 2010. Each MCD gains 0.25 percent for each percentage point of weighted population growth in its neighbors. Recall that the 4-nearest neighbor weight matrix is the one used for fitting the spatial lag model. Thus, the spatially lagged population change is measured as the average of the 4-nearest neighbors' population change in 2000 to 2010. If each of the four neighbors gains 1 percent of population growth, the spatial lag effect is associated with 0.25 percent population growth in the MCD, with all the explanatory variables held constant. The 0.25 percent growth does not originate from "organic" growth but evolves as a "gift" from its neighbors.

Based on the information criteria approach, the more appropriate spatial weight matrix to choose is the one that provides the best model fitting to data balanced with model parsimony, which can be detected by AIC or BIC. According to online Appendix B.3, the spatial lag model is best fit to data balanced with model parsimony based on the 20-mile general distance weight matrix among forty matrices (Table 3.3; model 12 of online Appendix B.3). There appears to be less clustering of residuals (Figure 3.3) than that of the spatial lag model residuals based on the 4-nearest neighbor weight matrix (Figure 3.2) and obviously less than that of

TABLE 3.3 ● Spatial lag model results based on the 20-mile general distance weight matrix

	Model 12
Intercept	0.024
Previous growth	0.047*
Old	−0.186**
Unemployment	−0.236*
Airport	0.086
Forest	−0.028
Land developability	0.039*
Spatial lag	0.617***
Measures of fit	
Log-likelihood	1,167.01
AIC	−2,318.02
BIC	−2,273.89

Note: AIC = Akaike's information criterion; BIC = Schwartz's Bayesian information criterion.
*Significant at the $\alpha = .05$ level. **Significant at the $\alpha = .01$ level. ***Significant at the $\alpha = .001$ level.

the standard linear regression residuals (Figure 3.1). The coefficient magnitudes (in terms of the absolute value) of the explanatory variables in model 12 are all smaller than those of model 6, correspondingly, except *intercept, land developability,* and *spatial lag*. The coefficient of the spatial lag increases from 0.248 in model 6 to 0.617 in model 12.

What are plausible reasons for the spatial lag effect? It may partly be explained by the improvement of the transportation network and tools, which integrate nearby places together. Tobler's (1970) first law of geography states that everything relates to each other, but the nearer ones do more so than the more distant ones. Location theory sees transportation infrastructure as a facilitator of population flows (Chi, 2010a). With improved transportation infrastructure, people gain more autonomy in choosing their home MCD. When housing prices increase in an MCD due to population growth, residents move to neighboring MCDs with lower housing prices until the prices reach equilibrium, and vice versa.

According to online Appendix B.3, applying a different spatial weight matrix to the spatial lag model results in a different set of coefficients. To illustrate this point, we

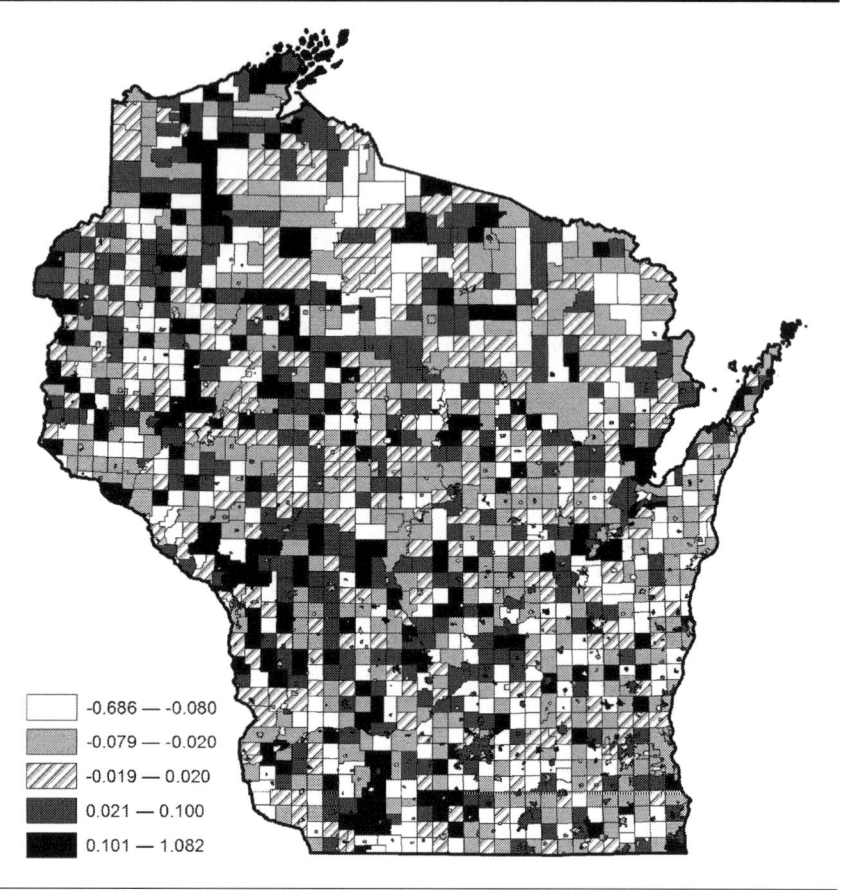

FIGURE 3.3 ● Residuals of the spatial lag model based on the 20-mile general distance weight matrix

-0.686 — -0.080
-0.079 — -0.020
-0.019 — 0.020
0.021 — 0.100
0.101 — 1.082

select *land developability* as an example and graph its coefficients based on each of the forty spatial weight matrices in Figure 3.4. The coefficients of *land developability* fall between 0.03 and 0.05. The general distance weight matrices based on 90 and 100 miles produce the highest coefficient (= 0.049). The 4-nearest neighbor weight matrix produces the lowest coefficient (= 0.036). There is a clear pattern that the coefficients increase from 10 miles to 100 miles based on the general distance weight matrices.

3.3 SPATIAL ERROR MODELS

3.3.1 What Is a Spatial Error Model?

Spatial dependence is accounted for in a **spatial error model** by an error term and an associated spatially lagged error term.

Besides a spatial lag model, a **spatial error model** is the other type of spatial regression model that is often used in the social sciences. A spatial error model accounts

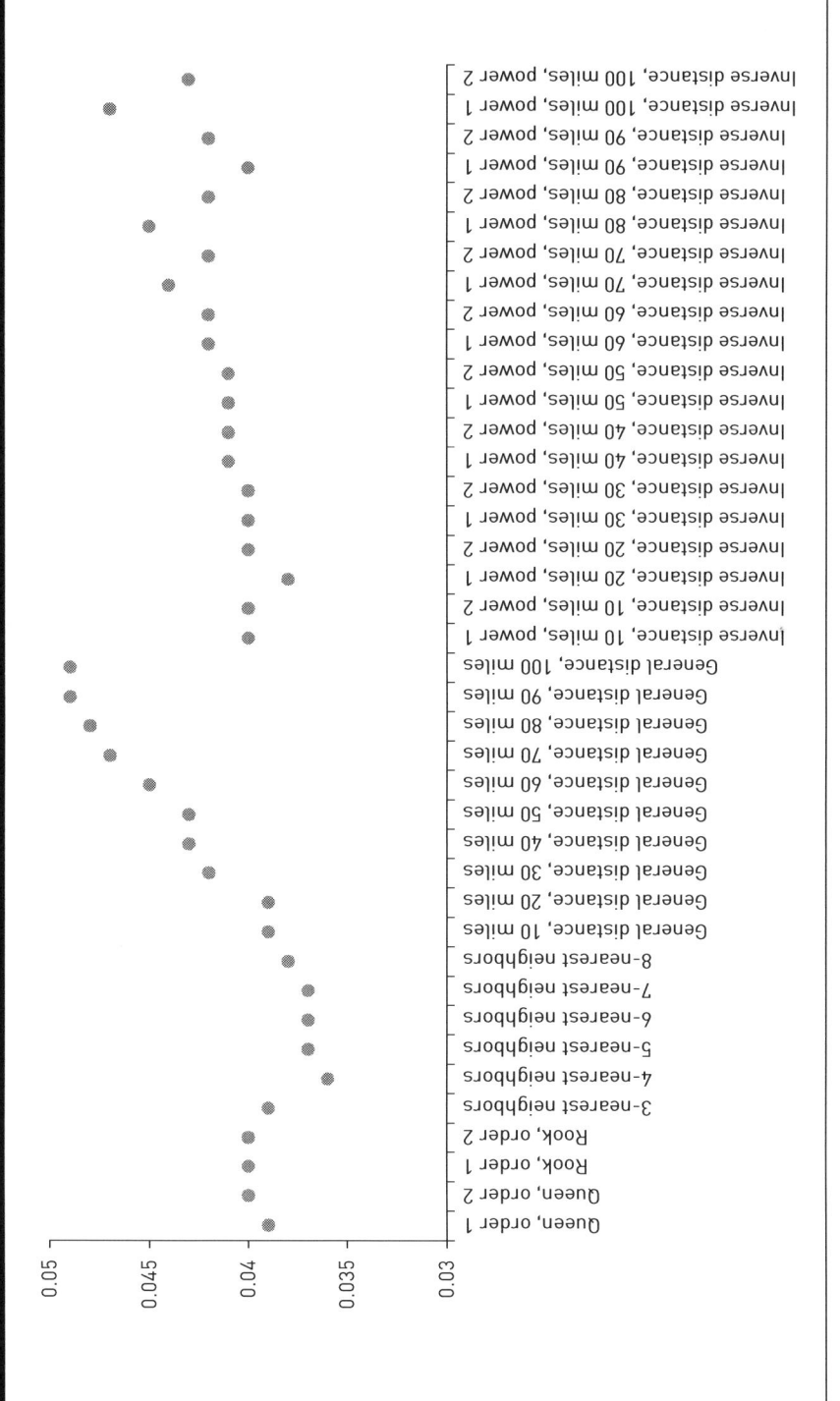

FIGURE 3.4 ● Coefficient estimates of land developability in spatial lag models

for spatial dependence by an error term and an associated spatially lagged error term (Anselin & Bera, 1998). A spatial error model is specified as

$$Y = X\beta + u, \; u = \rho W u + \varepsilon \qquad (3.3)$$

where

Y is an n-by-1 vector of response variables,

X is an n-by-p design matrix of explanatory variables,

β is a p-by-1 vector of regression coefficients,

u is an n-by-1 vector of error terms,

ρ is a scalar spatial error parameter,

W is an n-by-n spatial weight matrix, and

ε is an n-by-1 vector of error terms that are normally and independently but not necessarily identically distributed.

When $\rho = 0$, the spatial lag model (equation [3.3]) is reduced to the standard linear regression model (equation [3.1]). That is, the standard linear regression model (equation [3.1]) is nested in the more advanced spatial lag model (equation [3.3]). Unlike for the spatial lag model, for the spatial error model the expectation of Y is $X\beta$ and the interpretation of β is more straightforward.

Wu is a spatially lagged error term because it is a weighted average of the neighborhood error terms.

Since u is a vector of error terms and W denotes a spatial weight matrix, Wu is a spatially lagged error term in the sense that it is a weighted average of the error terms in the neighborhood. Just as in a spatial lag model where the spatial dependence is modeled by the response variable (Y) and the associated spatially lagged variable (WY), in a spatial error model, the spatial dependence is modeled by the relation between an error term (u) and the associated spatially lagged error term (Wu). The spatial error model is sometimes referred to as the *simultaneous spatial autoregressive model*.

3.3.2 Model Fitting via Maximum Likelihood

As with spatial lag models, the parameters of spatial error models are estimated and inferred via maximum likelihood; the OLS estimation as used in standard linear regression models does not directly account for spatial dependence in the model. Model fitting to data balanced with model parsimony can be measured by AIC and BIC. Refer to Section 3.2 for details.

3.3.3 Model Diagnostics

Similar to the diagnostics for a spatial lag model, there are several sets of model diagnostics to perform when fitting a spatial error model:

- The first sets of diagnostics are those performed after fitting a standard linear regression model, including diagnostics for possible multicollinearity, heteroscedasticity, and others.

- Another set of diagnostics is to detect possibly remaining spatial dependence after accounting for spatial dependence through the spatial error model.

The measures of model fitting to data include maximum log-likelihood value, AIC, and BIC. Refer to Section 3.2 for details.

3.3.4 When Is a Spatial Error Model Needed?

The question now becomes, when do we need a spatial error model? Generally, there are two situations in which an analysis would benefit from spatial error modeling. The first, which is the most often referenced justification, is when spatial error dependence exists (Anselin & Bera, 1998). A spatial error model is considered when the standard linear regression residuals exhibit spatial dependence in the residuals; this can be diagnosed by the LM test and robust LM test for errors. Essentially, after we fit a standard linear regression model, we could diagnose whether the regression residuals exhibit spatial error dependence on the basis of a number of spatial weight matrices. If the LM test and robust LM test indicate clear evidence of spatial dependence in the residuals, a spatial error model would be appropriate and often is deemed more appropriate than the standard linear regression model in inferring about the relation between the response variable and explanatory variables. The measures of goodness of model fit, such as AIC and BIC, could be compared to determine whether the spatial error model is superior to the standard linear regression model in terms of model fitting to data balanced with model parsimony.

The second situation in which a spatial error model might be appropriate is when the researchers suspect the standard linear regression residuals are spatially correlated, especially when the phenomenon of study is a spatial one and when some potentially important explanatory variables are not included in the model. A statistically significant spatial dependence parameter indicates spatial dependence in

> In a spatial error model, spatial dependence in errors indicated by a statistically significant spatial dependence parameter may be due to key explanatory variables that are not included in the model.

errors, which is sometimes due to key explanatory variables that are not included in the model (Anselin & Bera, 1998). Conceptually, a spatial error model helps account for explanatory variables that could have strong additional associations with the response variable but are not included in the model.

One school of thought is that the exclusion of spatial error dependence when it exists is not as serious as the exclusion of spatial lag dependence (Anselin & Bera, 1998). The main argument is that if spatial error dependence exists, the standard linear regression estimates become inefficient, but they are still unbiased, whereas if spatial lag dependence exists, the standard linear regression estimates become inconsistent and biased.

3.3.5 Which Spatial Weight Matrix to Use in a Spatial Error Model?

In a spatial error model, a spatial weight matrix needs to be specified. Again, many types of spatial weight matrices with different specifications could be potentially useful. The use of different spatial weight matrices will result in different parameter estimates for β and ρ. Which spatial weight matrix is to be used for a spatial error model? Similar to spatial lag models, there are at least two approaches to select an appropriate spatial weight matrix for fitting a spatial error model. The first approach is based on theoretical concepts or findings of previous studies.

If such related concepts or studies do not exist, we could adopt a data-driven approach, which is the second approach. After we fit the standard linear regression model, we could examine the spatial dependence in the residuals, which can be measured by Moran's I statistic based on a variety of spatial weight matrices. The spatial weight matrix that we deem as more appropriate is the one that captures the maximum spatial dependence of the standard linear regression residuals companioned with a high level of statistical significance (Chi & Zhu, 2008). Alternatively, we may use an information criterion, such as AIC or BIC, to compare the fit of the models under different spatial weight matrices. Other approaches are possible and continue to be developed. By and large, as we mentioned in Section 3.2, it remains an open research question as to how to properly or even optimally specify the spatial weight matrix.

3.3.6 Spatial Lag Models or Spatial Error Models?

Now we have learned both spatial lag models and spatial error models. The next question is, which one is to be used if the diagnostics indicate spatial dependence? The literature offers at least two approaches:

- a data-driven approach and
- a theory-based approach.

The data-driven approach fits a spatial lag model and tests for lack of spatial error dependence and then fits a spatial error model and tests for lack of spatial lag dependence. The data-driven approach was found by Voss and Chi (2006), in a study examining population growth, to be helpful in determining the better model specification to account for spatial dependence. The theory-based approach makes the question of whether to use a spatial lag model or a spatial error model based on substantive grounds (Doreian, 1980). Both approaches are used for spatial regression; however, researchers tend to prefer the data-driven method when data rather than theoretical concerns are what motivate spatial data analysis (Anselin, 2002, 2003).

3.3.7 Spatial Models: SAR, CAR, and SMA

Areal data analysis can be conducted using different models (or processes). A frequently used one in the existing social science literature is the **simultaneous autoregressive (SAR) model**. In a SAR model, the relations among the response variables at all locations are explained simultaneously and the spatial effects are considered to be endogenous (Anselin, 2003; Cressie, 1993). Another popular process is the **conditional autoregressive (CAR) model**. In CAR models, the distribution of a response variable (or regression error) at one location is specified by conditioning on the values of its neighbors, and the neighbors' spatial effect is considered to be exogenous (Anselin, 2003; Cressie, 1993). It should be noted that the spatial lag model, spatial error model, and other spatial regression models introduced in the rest of this book are specified using the SAR model.

Areal data analysis can be conducted using **simultaneous autoregressive** models, **conditional autoregressive** models, or **spatial moving average** models.

Model specification is the key distinction between the SAR and CAR models (Cressie, 1993). Statistics literature and other disciplines often employ CAR models, while spatial econometrics and spatial regression models for social scientists favor SAR models. The interpretation of the spatial autocorrelation coefficients in SAR models is similar to that of the standard linear regression coefficients and is common for social scientists, thus making SAR models seem more natural for social scientists. The two models are related, however, as SAR models may be represented by higher-order CAR models (Cressie, 1993).

In addition, areal data can be analyzed using the **spatial moving average (SMA) model**, which models the error process by a linear combination of white noises at neighboring locations, akin to the moving average models in time series.

3.3.8 Data Example

To illustrate the use of spatial error models, we use our example that examines population growth from 2000 to 2010 and its relation to its explanatory variables at the MCD level in Wisconsin. We expect that the explanatory variables do not sufficiently explain population growth and that spatial dependence might exist in the error term of the standard linear regression model. We further apply a spatial error model to account for the spatial error dependence.

According to the standard linear regression results (Table 3.1; online Appendix B.2), the standard linear regression residuals exhibit statistically significant spatial dependence based on any of the forty spatial weight matrices. The LM and robust LM tests indicate that the standard linear regression residuals exhibit both spatial lag and spatial error dependence. In this section, we focus on the spatial error dependence and apply a spatial error model to account for it.

As discussed previously in this chapter, the use of different spatial weight matrices could result in different model parameter estimates. An appropriate spatial weight matrix to choose is the one that captures the maximum spatial dependence of the standard linear regression residuals companioned with a high level of statistical significance. Alternatively, we could use AIC or BIC to compare the fit of the models under different spatial weight matrices. Both approaches were demonstrated for selecting a more appropriate spatial lag model in Section 3.2. For purposes of simplicity, we use the first approach in this section. Based on online Appendix B.2, the standard linear regression model residuals have the highest Moran's I value based on the 4-nearest neighbor weight matrix among forty spatial weight matrices. Thus, the 4-nearest neighbor weight matrix is selected for fitting a spatial error model; the results are presented in Table 3.4.

Overall, the coefficient magnitudes and the significance of the explanatory variables in the spatial error model are similar to those in the standard linear regression model and the spatial lag model based on the 4-nearest neighbor weight matrix. Proximity to airports becomes statistically insignificant at the $\alpha = .05$ level, though. Each additional 1 percent of previous population growth is associated with 0.05 percent of population growth in 2000 to 2010, with all the other explanatory variables held constant. Each additional 1 percent of old population is associated with 0.26 percent of population decline in 2000 to 2010, with all the other explanatory variables held constant. Each additional 1 percent of unemployment rate is associated with 0.28 percent of population decline in 2000 to 2010, with all the other explanatory variables held constant. Each additional 1 percent of forest coverage is associated with 0.09 percent of population decline in 2000 to 2010, with all

TABLE 3.4 ● Spatial error model results

	Coefficient	SE
Intercept	0.078***	0.020
Previous growth	0.046*	0.021
Old	−0.261***	0.060
Unemployment	−0.276*	0.109
Airport	0.106	0.086
Forest	−0.089***	0.017
Land developability	0.037*	0.018
Spatial error	0.237***	0.031
Measures of fit		
Log-likelihood	1,147.10	
AIC	−2,280.21	
BIC	−2,241.60	

Note: 4-nearest neighbor weight matrix is used here. AIC = Akaike's information criterion; BIC = Schwartz's Bayesian information criterion; SE = standard error.

*Significant at the $\alpha = .05$ level. ***Significant at the $\alpha = .001$ level.

the other explanatory variables held constant. Each additional 1 percent of land available for development is associated with 0.04 percent of population growth in 2000 to 2010, with all the other explanatory variables held constant. Comparing the results of the spatial error model to the spatial lag model based on the 4-nearest neighbor weight matrix (Table 3.2), the spatial error model is slightly better fitted to data balanced with model parsimony based on the fact that the AIC and BIC values are smaller in the spatial error model than in the spatial lag model. The estimated regression coefficients of *intercept, old,* and *land developability* in the spatial error model are larger than those in the spatial lag model, while the estimated regression coefficients of *previous growth, unemployment, airport,* and *forest* in the former are smaller than their counterparts in the latter.

Comparing these results to the standard linear regression results (Table 3.1), the spatial error model is revealed to be better fitted to data balanced with model parsimony based on the fact that the AIC and BIC values are smaller in the spatial error model than those in the standard linear regression model. Therefore, the spatial error model is deemed better than the standard linear regression model for interpreting the explanatory variables' associations with population growth.

The spatial error effect is positive and statistically significant, which may be attributed to not including some important explanatory variables in the model. The spatial error term is slightly smaller than the spatial lag term of the spatial lag model based on the 4-nearest neighbor weight matrix (Table 3.2). The inclusion of the spatial error effects assists in accounting for those variables. The interpretation of the spatial error effects, however, is not as straightforward as that of the spatial lag effects, because the spatial dependence is among the unobserved error terms, not the observable response variable. The distribution of the spatial error model residuals (Figure 3.5) suggests that there remain clusters of residuals along I-90 from La Crosse to Madison and some areas in the Northwoods. This demands further examination of the spatial dependence in advanced models, which are introduced in Chapter 4.

FIGURE 3.5 ● **Residuals of the spatial error model based on the 4-nearest neighbor weight matrix**

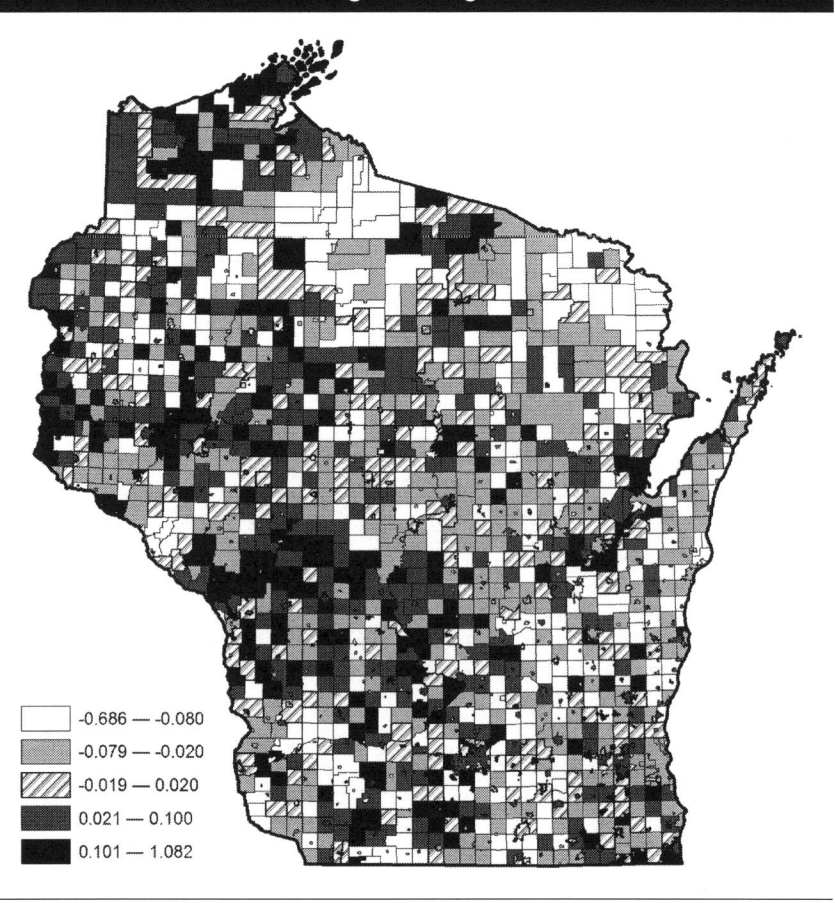

Study Questions

1. What are the assumptions of a standard linear regression model for fitting to data? And which one is related to spatial dependence?

2. What tools do we use to diagnose spatial dependence in the model residuals?

3. When do we need to account for spatial dependence?

4. What is the difference between the ordinary least squares (OLS) estimation and the maximum likelihood estimation (MLE)?

5. What is a spatial lag model? What is a spatial error model?

6. How do we fit a spatial lag model? How do we fit a spatial error model?

7. How do we interpret the spatial lag effect and the spatial error effect?

8. Which spatial weight matrix do we use in a spatial lag model or a spatial error model?

9. What should we be cautious about when using a spatial lag model or a spatial error model?

10. How do we choose between a spatial lag model and a spatial error model?

11. For your research, is a data-driven approach or a theory-driven approach more appropriate in selecting a spatial weight matrix and choosing an appropriate spatial regression model?

12. By using a spatial lag model or a spatial error model, how might the interpretation of the results help you make a (spatial) theoretical contribution to your area of research?

4

ADVANCED MODELS DEALING WITH SPATIAL DEPENDENCE

LEARNING OBJECTIVES

- Understand when and how to fit a spatial error model with spatially lagged responses, interpret the spatial lag effect and the spatial error effect, and use appropriate diagnostics to assess the model.

- Understand when and how to fit a spatial cross-regressive model, interpret the effect of the spatially lagged explanatory variables, and use appropriate diagnostics to assess the model.

- Identify appropriate spatial weight matrices to use in a spatial error model with spatially lagged responses and a spatial cross-regressive model.

- Understand when and how to fit a multilevel linear regression model and interpret the effects at two levels, the reliability estimates, and within- and across-group variances.

- Describe the cautions in fitting a multilevel linear regression model.

In Chapter 3, we introduced spatial lag models and spatial error models, the two often-used basic spatial regression models that deal with spatial dependence. They control for spatial lag dependence and spatial error dependence, respectively. But what if both spatial lag and spatial error dependence exist? What if there is spatial lag dependence among the explanatory variables? What if the spatial dependence comes from aggregated geographic levels while conducting individual-level analysis? In this chapter, we introduce three corresponding models:

- spatial error models with spatially lagged responses (Section 4.1),
- spatial cross-regressive models (Section 4.2), and
- multilevel linear regression models (Section 4.3).

The first two sections are illustrated with a data example examining population change from 1970 to 2010 at the minor civil division (MCD) level in Wisconsin. The third section is illustrated with a data example modeling migration from 1995 to 2000 in Wisconsin.

4.1 SPATIAL ERROR MODELS WITH SPATIALLY LAGGED RESPONSES

4.1.1 What Is a Spatial Error Model With Spatially Lagged Responses?

Spatial error model with spatially lagged responses (SEMSLR) is a spatial error model that includes spatially lagged response variables.

A **spatial error model with spatially lagged responses (SEMSLR)**, according to its name, is a spatial error model that includes spatially lagged response variables. It is different from a spatial lag model or a spatial error model in which only one of the two types of spatial dependence (i.e., spatial lag dependence or spatial error dependence) is considered. Both spatial lag dependence and spatial error dependence are considered in an SEMSLR, which is also referred to as a *spatial error model with lag dependence* (Chi, 2010a). An SEMSLR is specified as

$$Y = X\beta + \theta W_1 Y + u, \quad u = \rho W_2 u + \varepsilon \quad (4.1)$$

where

Y is an n-by-1 vector of observations on the response variable,

X is an n-by-p design matrix with a vector of n ones in the first column for the intercept and $p - 1$ vectors (n-by-1) of explanatory variables in the remaining columns,

β is a p-by-1 vector of regression coefficients,

θ is a scalar coefficient for the spatially lagged response variables,

W_1 is an n-by-n spatial weight matrix for the response variables,

W_1Y is a spatially lagged response variable in the sense that it is a weighted average of the response variables in the neighborhood,

u is an n-by-1 vector of error terms,

ρ is a scalar coefficient for the spatially lagged error terms,

W_2 is an n-by-n spatial weight matrix for the error terms,

W_2u is a spatially lagged error term in the sense that it is a weighted average of the error terms in the neighborhood, and

ε is an n-by-1 vector of error terms that are normally and independently but not necessarily identically distributed.

The terms Y, X, β, and ε are denoted as in a standard linear regression model (equation [3.1] in Chapter 3), but the remainder of the terms in the model—W_1, W_2, θ, ρ, and u—are additional.

4.1.2 Why and When Is an SEMSLR Needed?

After we fit a standard linear regression model, sometimes the regression residuals exhibit spatial dependence. We could use some tests such as the Lagrange multiplier (LM) tests and robust LM tests to diagnose which type of dependence it is (Anselin et al., 1996). If it is lag dependence, a spatial lag model would be appropriate for the data modeling. If it is error dependence, a spatial error model would be appropriate for the data modeling. But what if both spatial lag dependence and spatial error dependence exist in the standard linear regression residuals?[1]

It is possible to model spatial lag and spatial error dependence simultaneously. This can be achieved through a **spatial autoregressive moving average (SARMA) model** (Anselin & Bera, 1998). While the SARMA model can be fitted in existing software packages, doing so is not straightforward. Moreover, it would be difficult to apply the SARMA methods while simultaneously dealing with spatial heterogeneity, the second type of spatial effects, which are addressed in Chapter 5. Therefore, in practice, we sometimes use an SEMSLR as an alternative to a SARMA model.

Modeling spatial lag and spatial error dependence simultaneously can be achieved through a **spatial autoregressive moving average (SARMA) model**.

4.1.3 Model Fitting

In an SEMSLR, the spatially lagged response variable is treated as an explanatory variable and modeled exogenously; the error term is modeled endogenously like in a

---

[1] It should be noted that in practice spatial lag dependence and spatial error dependence often appear together and cannot be easily separated.

spatial error model. In practice, we can first create a spatially lagged response variable and then treat it as an additional explanatory variable and fit a spatial error model.

As with spatial lag models and spatial error models, SEMSLRs are estimated and inferred via maximum likelihood. Model fitting to data balanced with model parsimony can be measured by Akaike's information criterion (AIC) and Schwartz's Bayesian information criterion (BIC). Refer to Sections 3.2 and 3.3 for details.

Similar to diagnostics for a spatial lag model, there are several sets of model diagnostics to perform when fitting SEMSLRs. The first sets of diagnostics are those performed after fitting a standard linear regression model, including diagnostics for possible multicollinearity, heteroscedasticity, and others. Another set of diagnostics is to detect possibly remaining spatial dependence after accounting for spatial dependence through the SEMSLR. The measures of model fitting to data include maximum log-likelihood value, AIC, and BIC. Refer to Sections 3.2 and 3.3 for details.

> The spatially lagged response variable in an SEMSLR is treated as an explanatory variable and is modeled exogenously, whereas the error term in an SEMSLR is modeled endogenously.

4.1.4 Which Spatial Weight Matrices Should Be Used in an SEMSLR?

Because an SEMSLR has two spatial dependence terms, we need two spatial weight matrices—one for the spatial lag term and the other for the spatial error term. As addressed in Sections 2.2 and 3.2, spatial weight matrices can be selected on the basis of theories if they exist. If there is no theory for guiding the selection of a spatial weight matrix for the phenomenon of study, data-driven approaches can be used. There are several data-driven approaches for selecting defensible spatial weight matrices.

> Appropriate spatial weight matrices can be selected on the basis of theories or by using data-driven approaches.

First, spatial weight matrices can be selected among many possible matrices by comparing the strength and statistical significance of spatial dependence using each matrix. In this approach, the selection of a spatial weight matrix for the spatial lag term is based on the spatial dependence of the response variable; the matrix that provides the highest spatial dependence of the response variable companioned with a high level of statistical significance is more appropriate. The selection of a spatial weight matrix for the spatial error term is based on the spatial dependence of the residuals after fitting spatial lag models; the matrix that provides the highest spatial dependence of the residuals companioned with a high level of statistical significance is more appropriate.

Second, Aldstadt and Getis (2006) have developed a procedure called *a multidirectional optimal ecotope-based algorithm* (AMOEBA) for identifying the optimal spatial weight matrix. Third, spatial weight matrices can be selected based on model fitting to data balanced with model parsimony, which is indicated by AIC or BIC. The spatial weight matrix that results in the "best" model according to AIC or BIC is the more appropriate spatial weight matrix (see Sections 2.2 and 3.2 for details). However, it should be noted that there does not exist a standard criterion for properly or even optimally specifying a spatial weight matrix; that remains an open research question.

Could we use the same spatial weight matrix for both the spatial lag and spatial error terms? This may be acceptable for an SEMSLR, but we prefer not to do so for a SARMA, because with SARMA models, using the same spatial weight matrix for both the spatial lag and spatial error terms results in statistical problems (Anselin & Bera, 1998). Because an SEMSLR is related to a SARMA model, we prefer to follow the above recommendation for the SARMA model.

4.1.5 Data Example

To illustrate the use of SEMSLRs, we use our example that examines population growth from 2000 to 2010 and its relation to the explanatory variables at the MCD level in Wisconsin. According to diagnostics for standard linear regression based on residuals (online Appendix B.2), both spatial lag dependence and spatial error dependence exist on the basis of LM tests and robust LM tests for lag dependence and error dependence. In Sections 3.2 and 3.3, we used a spatial lag model and a spatial error model to account for spatial lag dependence and spatial error dependence, respectively.

However, since both spatial lag dependence and spatial error dependence exist, it could make more sense to account for both simultaneously rather than one at a time. A model similar to a SARMA can be applied through an SEMSLR.

In practice, we first create a spatially lagged response variable and then add it as an explanatory variable to a spatial error model. For demonstration purposes, we select spatial weight matrices by comparing the strength and statistical significance of spatial dependence (a data-driven approach, as discussed previously). The 4-nearest neighbor weight matrix, which captures the maximum spatial dependence (based on Moran's *I* value) of population growth from 2000 to 2010 among forty spatial weight matrices (Table 2.2), is selected for creating a spatially lagged response variable. In other words, in equation (4.1), W_1 is represented by the 4-nearest neighbor weight matrix.

To select an appropriate spatial weight matrix for W_2, we fit a spatial lag model with the 4-nearest neighbor weight matrix and diagnose for spatial dependence in the remaining errors (Table 4.1). The LM test indicates that the 20-mile general distance weight matrix captures the maximum spatial dependence of the remaining errors companioned with a high level of statistical significance. Therefore, the 20-mile general distance weight matrix is selected to represent W_2.

TABLE 4.1 ● The selection of the second spatial weight matrix for an SEMSLR

Spatial weight matrix	Remaining spatial errors	Spatial weight matrix	Remaining spatial errors
Queen's contiguity, order 1	0.273	Inverse distance, 10 miles, power 1	1.420
Queen's contiguity, order 2	12.816***	Inverse distance, 10 miles, power 2	7.740**
Rook's contiguity, order 1	0.438	Inverse distance, 20 miles, power 1	11.085***
Rook's contiguity, order 2	14.260***	Inverse distance, 20 miles, power 2	2.281
3-nearest neighbors	32.915***	Inverse distance, 30 miles, power 1	16.303***
4-nearest neighbors	44.346***	Inverse distance, 30 miles, power 2	2.269
5-nearest neighbors	2.180	Inverse distance, 40 miles, power 1	17.162***
6-nearest neighbors	0.284	Inverse distance, 40 miles, power 2	2.716
7-nearest neighbors	2.734	Inverse distance, 50 miles, power 1	14.932***
8-nearest neighbors	7.004**	Inverse distance, 50 miles, power 2	3.223
General distance, 10 miles	6.605**	Inverse distance, 60 miles, power 1	10.952***
General distance, 20 miles	55.114***	Inverse distance, 60 miles, power 2	3.741
General distance, 30 miles	53.378***	Inverse distance, 70 miles, power 1	9.961**
General distance, 40 miles	42.888***	Inverse distance, 70 miles, power 2	4.094*
General distance, 50 miles	29.012***	Inverse distance, 80 miles, power 1	9.396**
General distance, 60 miles	14.291***	Inverse distance, 80 miles, power 2	4.357*
General distance, 70 miles	10.712***	Inverse distance, 90 miles, power 1	11.140***
General distance, 80 miles	9.238**	Inverse distance, 90 miles, power 2	4.508*
General distance, 90 miles	12.818***	Inverse distance, 100 miles, power 1	11.674***
General distance, 100 miles	14.145***	Inverse distance, 100 miles, power 2	4.703*

Note: The results are based on an LM test of the errors after running a spatial lag model with a 4-nearest neighbor weight matrix.

*Significant at the $\alpha = .05$ level. **Significant at the $\alpha = .01$ level. ***Significant at the $\alpha = .001$ level.

The SEMSLR regression results are presented in Table 4.2. The SEMSLR is better fitted to data balanced with model parsimony than are the standard linear regression model, the spatial lag model, and the spatial error model, based on the fact that the AIC and BIC values are smaller in the SEMSLR regression than in the other models. Therefore, the SEMSLR is deemed better than the standard linear regression model, spatial lag model, and spatial error model for interpreting the explanatory variables' associations with population growth. This is largely due to the fact that the SEMSLR accounts for both spatial lag and spatial error dependence. Also, the clusters of the SEMSLR model residuals (Figure 4.1) appear to be fewer and less obvious than those of the standard linear regression model (Figure 3.1), the spatial lag models (Figure 3.2 and Figure 3.3), and the spatial error model (Figure 3.4).

Overall, the magnitudes of the coefficient estimates and their significance in the SEMSLR are different from those in the standard linear regression model, spatial

TABLE 4.2 ● **The results of the spatial error model with spatially lagged responses (SEMSLR)**

Variable	Coefficient	SE
Constant	0.055**	0.021
Previous growth	0.034	0.021
Old	−0.188**	0.062
Unemployment	−0.277**	0.108
Airport	0.061	0.082
Forest	−0.059**	0.019
Land developability	0.033	0.018
Spatial lag	0.229***	0.043
Spatial error	0.475***	0.067
Measures of fit		
Log-likelihood	1,178.7	
AIC	−2,341.39	
BIC	−2,297.27	

Note: AIC = Akaike's information criterion; BIC = Schwartz's Bayesian information criterion; SE = standard error.

**Significant at the $\alpha = .01$ level. ***Significant at the $\alpha = .001$ level.

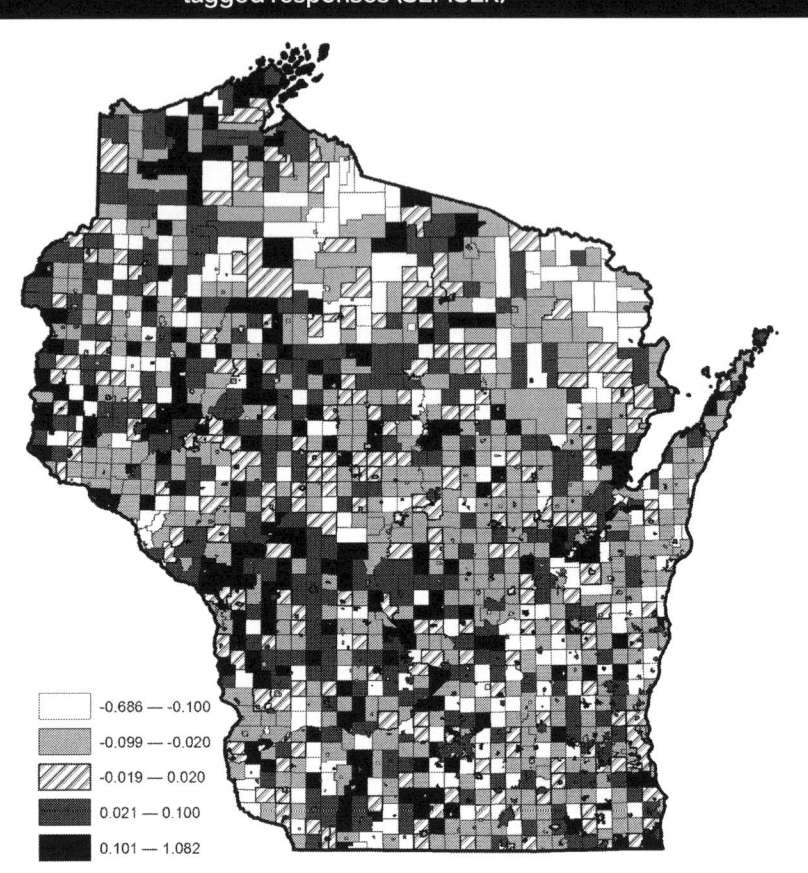

FIGURE 4.1 ● **Residuals of the spatial error model with spatially lagged responses (SEMSLR)**

Legend:
- -0.686 — -0.100
- -0.099 — -0.020
- -0.019 — 0.020
- 0.021 — 0.100
- 0.101 — 1.082

Note: The 4-nearest neighbor weight matrix is used for calculating the spatially lagged responses; the 20-mile general distance weight matrix is used for controlling for the spatial error dependence.

lag model, and spatial error model. Previous growth (in 1990–2000) and land developability become statistically insignificant in explaining population growth at the $p \leq .05$ level. Old, unemployment, and forest continue to have negative associations with population growth.

Both spatial lag and spatial error dependence have positive associations with population growth. The spatial lag effect comes from the spatially lagged population growth from 2000 to 2010, which is measured as the average of the 4-nearest neighbors. Each MCD gains 0.23 percent for each percentage point of weighted population growth in its neighbor MCDs with all the other explanatory variables held constant. The spatial error term helps account for explanatory variables that are excluded from the model but are important for explaining population growth.

4.2 SPATIAL CROSS-REGRESSIVE MODELS

4.2.1 What Is a Spatial Cross-Regressive Model?

A **spatial cross-regressive model** (Florax & Folmer, 1992) assumes a linear relation between the response variable and the explanatory variables and their associated spatially lagged explanatory variables. A spatial cross-regressive model is specified as

$$Y = X\beta + WX\theta + \varepsilon \qquad (4.2)$$

where

Spatial cross-regressive model assumes a linear relation between the response variable and the explanatory variables and their associated spatially lagged explanatory variables.

Y is an n-by-1 vector of observations on the response variable,

X is an n-by-p design matrix with a vector of n ones in the first column for the intercept and $p - 1$ vectors (n-by-1) of explanatory variables in the remaining columns,

β is a p-by-1 vector of regression coefficients,

W is an n-by-n spatial weight matrix,

WX is a n-by-p design matrix of spatially lagged explanatory variables in the sense that they are weighted averages of their corresponding explanatory variables in the neighborhood,

θ is a p-by-1 vector of coefficients for spatially lagged explanatory variables, and

ε is an n-by-1 vector of error terms that are independently and identically distributed as normal distribution with mean 0 and a constant variance.

The terms Y, X, β, and ε are denoted as in a standard linear regression model (equation [3.1]), but the remainder of the terms of the model—W and θ—are additional.

It should be noted that a spatial cross-regressive model is in the form of a standard linear regression model because the error terms are assumed to be independently and identically distributed. This model differs from the spatial regression models previously described in that there are endogenous spatial terms or parameters. The spatial parameters in a spatial cross-regressive model are not estimated endogenously but exogenously through the regression coefficients (β).

4.2.2 Model Fitting

A spatial cross-regressive model is estimated just like a standard linear regression model but includes spatially lagged explanatory variables (i.e., the weighted averages of the explanatory variables in the neighborhood). Once the spatially lagged explanatory

> A spatial cross-regressive model is estimated as a standard linear regression model but also includes the spatially lagged explanatory variables.

variables are created, they can be treated as explanatory variables to be included in a standard linear regression model. Refer to Anselin (1988b) and Florax and Folmer (1992) for details about the spatial cross-regressive model.

It should also be noted that not all spatially lagged explanatory variables need to be used in a spatial cross-regressive model. The spatially lagged explanatory variables can be selected and used as needed (i.e., when there is a reason to use them).

Because a spatial cross-regressive model is estimated just like a standard linear regression model, it can be estimated via either ordinary least squares (OLS) or maximum likelihood. Model fitting to data balanced with model parsimony can be measured via the AIC or BIC criteria. Refer to Chapter 3 for a detailed discussion of estimation.

Similar to diagnostics for other spatial regression models, there are usually two sets of model diagnostics to perform when fitting spatial cross-regressive models. The first sets of diagnostics are those performed after fitting a standard linear regression model, including diagnostics for nonlinear relations, unequal variances, and/or nonnormality. The second set of diagnostics is to detect possible spatial dependence in model residuals. Refer to Section 3.1 for details.

4.2.3 When Is a Spatial Cross-Regressive Model Needed?

The spatial cross-regressive model has been used in a limited number of studies (e.g., Boarnet et al., 2005; Fingleton & Lopez-Bazo, 2006) and has not received much attention in existing spatial regression studies. We believe, however, that a spatial cross-regressive model can be useful for the following scenarios:

- Conceptually or theoretically, one or more of the spatially lagged explanatory variables has associations with the response variable (scenario 1).
- One or more of the explanatory variables exhibits strong spatial dependence (scenario 2).

The data example at the end of this section, for example, indicates that the spatial cross-regressive model closely fits the data as well as the spatial error model does, although not as well as the spatial lag model and the SEMSLR. There could be other scenarios, yet to be discovered, under which a spatial cross-regressive model is useful for data modeling as well.

4.2.4 Which Spatial Weight Matrices Should Be Used in a Spatial Cross-Regressive Model?

As addressed previously, there are several approaches for selecting spatial weight matrices, but a universal approach does not seem to exist. Based on the model fitting to data approach, we could fit a spatial cross-regressive model with a range of spatial weight matrices for each variable and select the set of spatial weight matrices that results in the best model fitting to data. However, this approach would involve a large number of model fittings and might be time consuming.

Another approach for selecting appropriate spatial weight matrices for a spatial cross-regressive model is entirely based on the corresponding explanatory variables. We want a spatial weight matrix that can capture the maximum spatial dependence of an explanatory variable companioned with a high level of statistical significance. If we want to include more than one spatially lagged explanatory variable, we can select different (or the same) spatial weight matrices for each of them; the selection criterion would be based on which matrix captures the maximum spatial dependence of an explanatory variable companioned with a high level of statistical significance. There are no restrictions regarding whether the spatial weight matrices must be the same or different since a spatial cross-regressive model is estimated exogenously rather than endogenously.

4.2.5 Data Example

To illustrate the use of a spatial cross-regressive model, we continue to use the example that examines population growth from 2000 to 2010 and its relation to its explanatory variables at the MCD level in Wisconsin. The explanatory variables include *previous growth, old, unemployment, airport, forest*, and *land developability*. We argue that their spatially lagged explanatory variables have strong associations with population growth (scenario 1). For example, population growth in an MCD could be partially predicted by previous growth in neighbor MCDs because of the spillover effects and spread and backwash effects as discussed in Section 3.2. Population growth in an MCD could also be partially affected by economic conditions such as unemployment rate in its neighbors—a place with attractive socioeconomic conditions and opportunities attracts migrants not only into its territory but also into neighboring places.

We also expect that these explanatory variables exhibit strong spatial dependence (scenario 2). According to online Appendix B.1, these explanatory variables have strong spatial dependence (based on Moran's I value) companioned with a high level of statistical significance. The more appropriate spatial weight matrices are the 4-nearest neighbor weight matrix for *previous growth*, first-order rook's contiguity weight matrix for *old*, 5-nearest neighbor weight matrix for *unemployment*, 3-nearest neighbor weight matrix for *airport*, first-order rook's contiguity weight matrix for *forest*, and first-order queen's contiguity weight matrix for *land developability*. These spatial weight matrices are used to create corresponding spatially lagged explanatory variables. The explanatory variables as used in the standard linear regression model (Table 3.1) and their corresponding spatially lagged explanatory variables are used to refit a standard linear regression model; the results are presented in Table 4.3.

TABLE 4.3 ● The results of the spatial cross-regressive model fit based on the 4-nearest neighbor weight matrix

Variable	Coefficient	SE
Constant	0.063*	0.028
Previous growth	0.036	0.021
Old	−0.206**	0.065
Unemployment	−0.193	0.112
Airport	−0.012	0.108
Forest	−0.041	0.029
Land developability	0.013	0.021
Spatially lagged previous growth	0.161***	0.034
Spatially lagged old	−0.625***	0.107
Spatially lagged unemployment	0.096	0.216
Spatially lagged airport	294.312*	138.490
Spatially lagged forest	0.011	0.034
Spatially lagged land developability	0.084**	0.031
Diagnostics for spatial dependence		
Moran's *I* for residuals	0.100***	
LM test (lag)	45.894***	
LM test (error)	40.484***	
Robust LM test (lag)	9.319**	
Robust LM test (error)	3.909*	
Kelejian-Robinson test (error)	68.306***	
LM test (lag and error)	49.803***	

Variable	Coefficient	SE
Measures of fit		
Log-likelihood	1,148.48	
AIC	−2,270.96	
BIC	−2,199.26	

Note: AIC = Akaike's information criterion; BIC = Schwartz's Bayesian information criterion; LM = Lagrange multiplier; SE = standard error.

*Significant at the $\alpha = .05$ level. **Significant at the $\alpha = .01$ level. ***Significant at the $\alpha = .001$ level.

Comparing the results of this model to the standard linear regression results (Table 3.1), the spatial cross-regressive model is better fitted to data balanced with model parsimony based on the fact that the AIC and BIC values are smaller in the spatial cross-regressive model than those in the standard linear regression model. In addition, the spatial cross-regressive model closely fits the data as well as the spatial error models but not as well as the spatial lag models and the SEMSLR. The clusters of residuals (Figure 4.2) are slightly fewer and less obvious than those of the standard linear regression residuals (Figure 3.1). Therefore, the spatial cross-regressive model is deemed more appropriate for interpreting the explanatory variables' associations with population growth.

Within this model all explanatory variables, except *old*, become statistically insignificant in explaining population growth. In contrast, four of the six spatially lagged explanatory variables are statistically significant in explaining population growth. Every 1 percent of weighted average of previous growth in the neighborhood is associated with 0.16 percent population growth with all the other explanatory variables held constant. Every 1 percent of weighted average of the old population in the neighborhood is associated with 0.63 percent population decline with all the other explanatory variables held constant. Every 1 percent of weighted average of land developability in the neighborhood is associated with 0.08 percent population growth with all the other explanatory variables held constant. The weighted average of proximity to airports in the neighborhood also has a positive relation with population growth.

The diagnostics based on the spatial cross-regressive model residuals and on all forty spatial weight matrices are presented in online Appendix B.4. Moran's *I* statistics indicate that the model residuals (also illustrated in Figure 4.3) have small but statistically significant spatial dependence based on forty spatial weight matrices. The LM and robust LM tests suggest that the model has spatial lag and/or spatial error dependence, depending on the selection of spatial weight matrices. If we want to

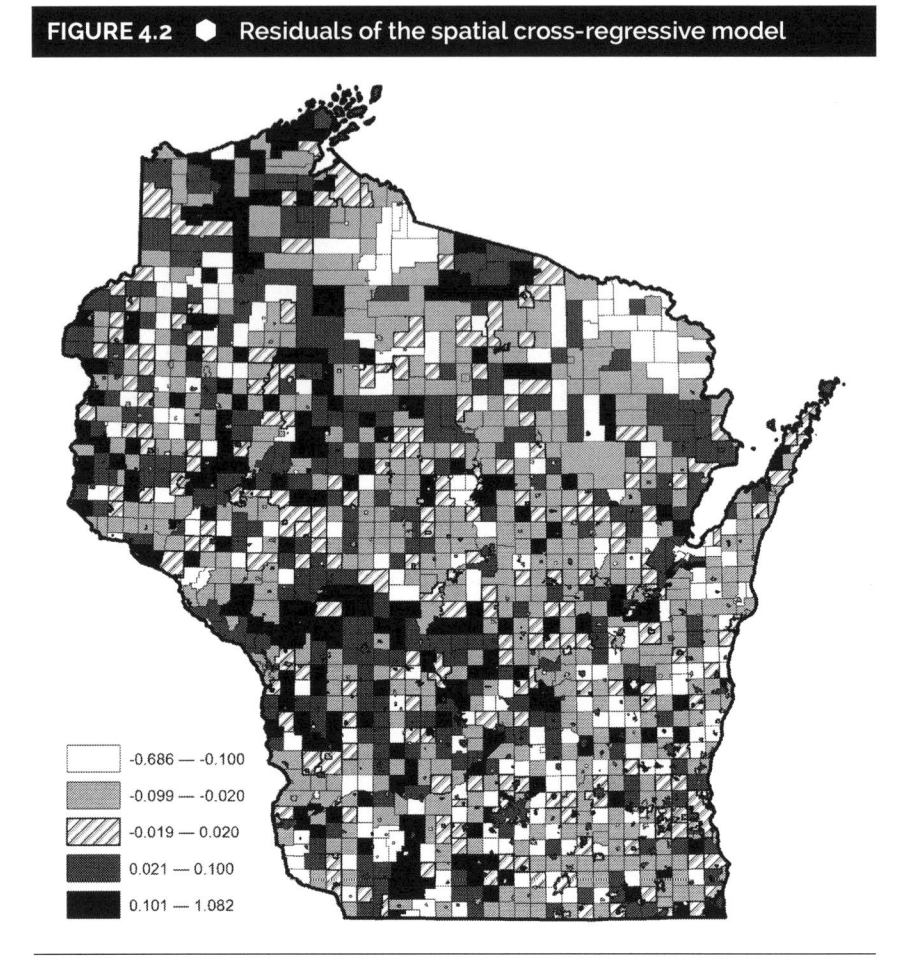

FIGURE 4.2 ● Residuals of the spatial cross-regressive model

-0.686 — -0.100
-0.099 — -0.020
-0.019 — 0.020
0.021 — 0.100
0.101 — 1.082

account for the spatial dependence, we could further use the spatial cross-regressive model in combination with a spatial lag model, a spatial error model, or an SEMSLR to model the data.

4.3 MULTILEVEL LINEAR REGRESSION

For many years, social scientists who used regression models conducted their research either at the individual level or at the aggregated level. The former is mostly based on each study subject and most likely this refers to each individual person. The latter is based on geographic levels such as counties, census tracts, MCDs, blocks, ZIP codes, and so on within the spatial context or based on aggregated time periods such as daily, weekly, monthly, quarterly, yearly, and so forth versus at an exact time point.

> Social scientists using regression models have often conducted research at the individual level or the aggregated level, but it is important to note that doing so makes the research vulnerable to the ecological fallacy and the scale effect of the modifiable areal unit problem.

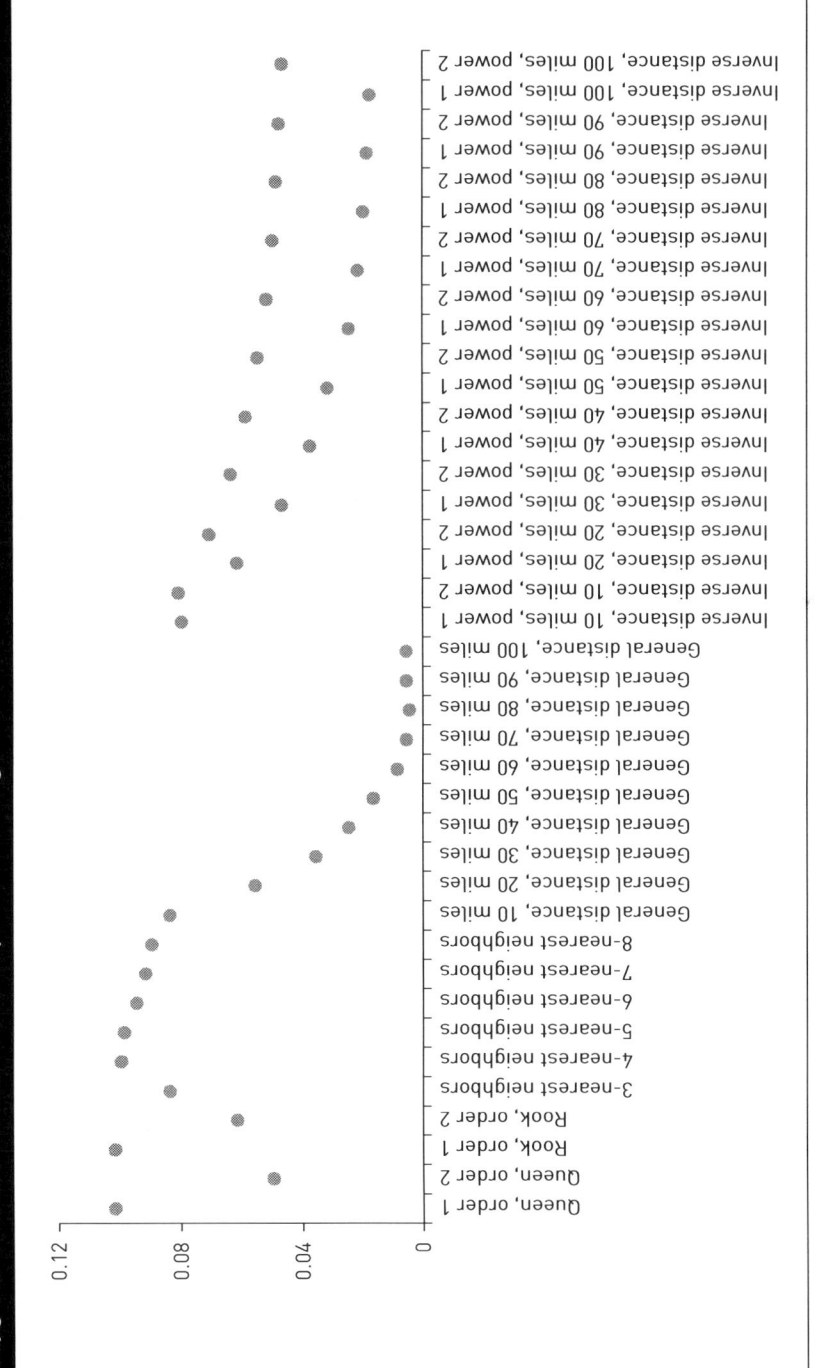

FIGURE 4.3 ● Moran's *I* statistics of the spatial cross-regressive model residuals

The limitation of conducting research at either the individual level or the aggregated level is that, for the most part, we can interpret the results only at their corresponding level and cannot apply them to the other level. This is related to the ecological fallacy (Robinson, 1950) and the scale effect of the modifiable areal unit problem (Green & Flowerdew, 1996).

> **Multilevel linear regression (MLR) models** address the limitation of not being able to interpret results at both levels by incorporating both individual-level and aggregated-level associations.

Multilevel linear regression (MLR) models were developed to address this limitation by incorporating both the individual-level associations and the aggregated-level associations (the latter are often geographic-level associations in the spatial regression context) (Raudenbush & Bryk, 2002). We are seeing rapidly increasing attention to MLR models in social science research (e.g., Alfes, Shantz, & Ritz, 2018; Amara & Jemmali, 2018; Bellani, Esping-Andersen, & Nedoluzhko, 2017; Bilecen & Cardona, 2018; Diez-Roux et al., 2017; Ekbrand & Hallerod, 2018; Evans, Williams, Onnela, & Subramanian, 2018; Heisig, Schaeffer, & Giesecke, 2017; Hsu, Chang, & Yip, 2017). The wide use of MLR by social scientists is due to a variety of reasons such as the following:

- Individual data are increasingly collected with geographic information aided by the availability of inexpensive mobile devices.
- Individual-level data can be more easily integrated with aggregated-level data due to the development of spatial analysis software packages.
- More advanced multilevel regression models have been developed to tackle a variety of individual-aggregated issues.

4.3.1 What Is an MLR Model?

Let's start with a standard linear regression model, with two explanatory variables, which can be specified as

$$Y_i = \beta_0 + X_{1i}\beta_1 + X_{2i}\beta_2 + \varepsilon_i$$
$$\varepsilon_i \sim N(0, \sigma^2)$$
(4.3)

where

i indexes the ith observation at the individual level for $i = 1, 2, \ldots, n$ and n is the number of observations;

Y_i is the ith response variable;

X_{1i} and X_{2i} are the ith covariates;

β_0, β_1, and β_2 are the intercept, regression coefficient for X_1, and regression coefficient for X_2, respectively; and

ε_i is an error term and the error terms are independently and identically distributed as normal distribution with mean 0 and a constant variance σ^2.

However, from the spatial perspective, the coefficients could conceivably differ across geographic units (such as counties, MCDs, school districts, etc.). For example, adding extracurricular activities in one school district may help increase school performance in that school district but may not be able to do so or to add as much in another school district. While such heterogeneity is not easily identified or corrected in a standard linear regression model, it can be addressed by adding second-level variables to explain the first-level coefficients as in a standard linear regression model. The following is a two-level regression model with an individual level (level 1) and an aggregated level (level 2).

The level 1 equation is specified as

$$Y_{ij} = \beta_{0j} + X_{1ij}\beta_{1j} + X_{2ij}\beta_{2j} + \varepsilon_{ij}$$
$$\varepsilon_{ij} \sim N(0, \sigma^2) \tag{4.4}$$

where i indexes the individuals and j indexes the geographic units.

At level 1, we still assume the error term (ε_{ij}) to be identically and independently distributed as normal distribution with mean 0 and variance σ^2. Notice, however, that the intercept and the coefficients are subscripted by j, which allows each geographic unit to have its own intercept and coefficients. We also assume that the regression coefficients are random variables with expectations, variances, and covariances as follows:

$$\begin{aligned} E(\beta_{0j}) &= \gamma_0, Var(\beta_{0j}) = \tau_{00} \\ E(\beta_{1j}) &= \gamma_1, Var(\beta_{1j}) = \tau_{11} \\ E(\beta_{2j}) &= \gamma_2, Var(\beta_{2j}) = \tau_{22} \\ Cov(\beta_{0j}, \beta_{1j}) &= \tau_{01} \\ Cov(\beta_{0j}, \beta_{2j}) &= \tau_{02} \\ Cov(\beta_{1j}, \beta_{2j}) &= \tau_{12} \end{aligned} \tag{4.5}$$

where

γ_0 is the expectation of the random intercept among aggregated units,

τ_{00} is the variance of the random intercept among aggregated units,

γ_1 is the expectation of the random coefficient for explanatory variable X_1 among aggregated units,

τ_{11} is the variance of the random coefficient for X_1 among aggregated units,

γ_2 is the expectation of the random coefficient for explanatory variable X_2 among aggregated units,

τ_{22} is the variance of the random coefficient for X_2 among aggregated units,

τ_{01} is the covariance between the random intercept and the random coefficient for X_1,

τ_{02} is the covariance between the random intercept and the random coefficient for X_2, and

τ_{12} is the covariance between the random coefficient for X_1 and the random coefficient for X_2.

The regression coefficients in equation (4.4) can vary greatly across the aggregated units, and they can be modeled by a set of level 2 equations. In particular, at level 2, we can model each regression coefficient from level 1 as a response variable, which can then be a function of explanatory variables at level 2.

> In an MLR model, the intercept and coefficients may vary greatly across aggregated units and can be modeled by a set of level 2 equations.

Let's suppose that we have two explanatory variables at level 2, Z_1 and Z_2; each regression coefficient from level 1 is assumed to be a function of Z_1 and Z_2. The level 2 equations are specified as

$$\begin{aligned}
\beta_{0j} &= \gamma_{00} + \gamma_{01} Z_{1j} + \gamma_{02} Z_{2j} + u_{0j} \\
u_{0j} &\sim N(0, \tau_{00}) \\
\beta_{1j} &= \gamma_{10} + \gamma_{11} Z_{1j} + \gamma_{12} Z_{2j} + u_{1j} \\
u_{1j} &\sim N(0, \tau_{11}) \\
\beta_{2j} &= \gamma_{20} + \gamma_{21} Z_{1j} + \gamma_{22} Z_{2j} + u_{2j} \\
u_{2j} &\sim N(0, \tau_{22})
\end{aligned} \quad (4.6)$$

We can also assume one or more of the coefficients (including the intercept) to not be affected by level 2 characteristics, and in that case, we assume them to be randomly distributed around the expectation of the random coefficient. For example, if the coefficients for X_1 are not affected by Z_1 and Z_2, the level 2 equations can be respecified as the same model in equation (4.6) except that

$$\beta_{1j} = \gamma_{10} + u_{1j} \quad (4.7)$$

4.3.2 MLR Model Diagnostics

A useful diagnostic for an MLR model is the reliability estimates of level 1 coefficients (Raudenbush & Bryk, 2002). The estimated variance of the coefficients for level 1 variables is divided into two portions—within groups and across groups. In other words, the ability of level 1 variables to explain the response variable is divided into two portions—within and across each aggregated unit of level 2. The estimated reliability is the proportion of the estimated across-group variance over the estimated within-group variance. If the across-group variance compared to the within-group variance is larger, then the reliability will be larger and the MLR level 1 coefficients will be more reliable.

The estimated reliability for each level 1 coefficient can be obtained by plugging estimated variances into the following equations:

$$reliability(\beta_{0j}) = \frac{\tau_{00}}{\tau_{00} + \left(\frac{\sigma^2}{n_j}\right)}$$

$$reliability(\beta_{1j}) = \frac{\tau_{11}}{\tau_{11} + \left(\frac{\sigma^2}{n_j}\right)} \quad (4.8)$$

$$reliability(\beta_{2j}) = \frac{\tau_{22}}{\tau_{22} + \left(\frac{\sigma^2}{n_j}\right)}$$

The estimated overall reliability of the level 1 coefficients can be obtained by plugging estimated variances into the following equation:

$$reliability = \frac{1}{pm} \times \sum_{j=1}^{m}\sum_{k=0}^{p-1} \left(\frac{\tau_{kk}}{\tau_{kk} + \left(\frac{\sigma^2}{n_j}\right)}\right) \quad (4.9)$$

where

j indexes the geographic units for $j = 1, 2, \ldots, m$ and m is the number of geographic units;

k indexes the explanatory variable, including the intercept ($k = 0$); and

p denotes the number of explanatory variables, including the intercept ($k = 0$).

The estimated reliability can then be used to reestimate level 1 coefficients by granting the reliable portion more weight. There is some theoretical justification for the estimates of level 1 coefficients provided by MLR to be more reliable than those provided by standard linear regression (Raudenbush & Bryk, 2002).

4.3.3 Cautions About MLR Models

MLR has several limitations (Raudenbush & Bryk, 2002):

- In an MLR model, each level has its specific assumptions, as does the standard linear regression model. A misspecification at one level can affect the results at other levels.

- Errors in level 2 models may correlate with each other; thus, the misspecification of one model can bias the estimates of others.

- The assumption of identical and independent error distribution in a standard linear regression model is likewise required for both levels in MLR. A departure from this assumption can affect the estimated standard errors at level 2 and the variance-covariance component estimates.

For contiguous geographic units, there likely is some spatial dependence in the process that departs from the assumption of independent errors at level 2. Spatial effects such as spatial lag could be included in level 2 models by a two-stage procedure (Sampson, Morenoff, & Earls, 1999).

4.3.4 Data Example

In this section, we continue to use Wisconsin as the study area, as in all the previous sections and chapters, but we use a different response variable—migration or not migration—as the response variable (a binary variable in this section). We structure a two-level linear regression model including both an individual/household level and an aggregated level; the response variable is an individual/household-level characteristic rather than an aggregated-level one. This data example is extracted from a study by Chi and Voss (2005). Here we focus on demonstrating the use of MLR models rather than a substantive discussion of migration. Please refer to the article for details.

The data used in this data example are extracted from the Wisconsin's 5 percent Public Use Microdata Sample (PUMS) file from Census 2000. The observations are householders who are twenty-five years old and older. The first level contains householders, and the second level contains the Public Use Microdata Areas (PUMAs) in Wisconsin (Figure 4.4).

At the first level, the response variable is whether a householder moved in the past five years or not. In total, there are 99,580 observations (i.e., householders). The explanatory variables include age (*AGE*), race (*NHWHITE*), education (*BACHLR*), marital status (*MARRIED*), married couple both working (*MCBW*), presence of children (*CHDR12*), female-headed household with children (*CHDR17*), female-headed household with children under eighteen years old (*HHFHHC*), rent or own

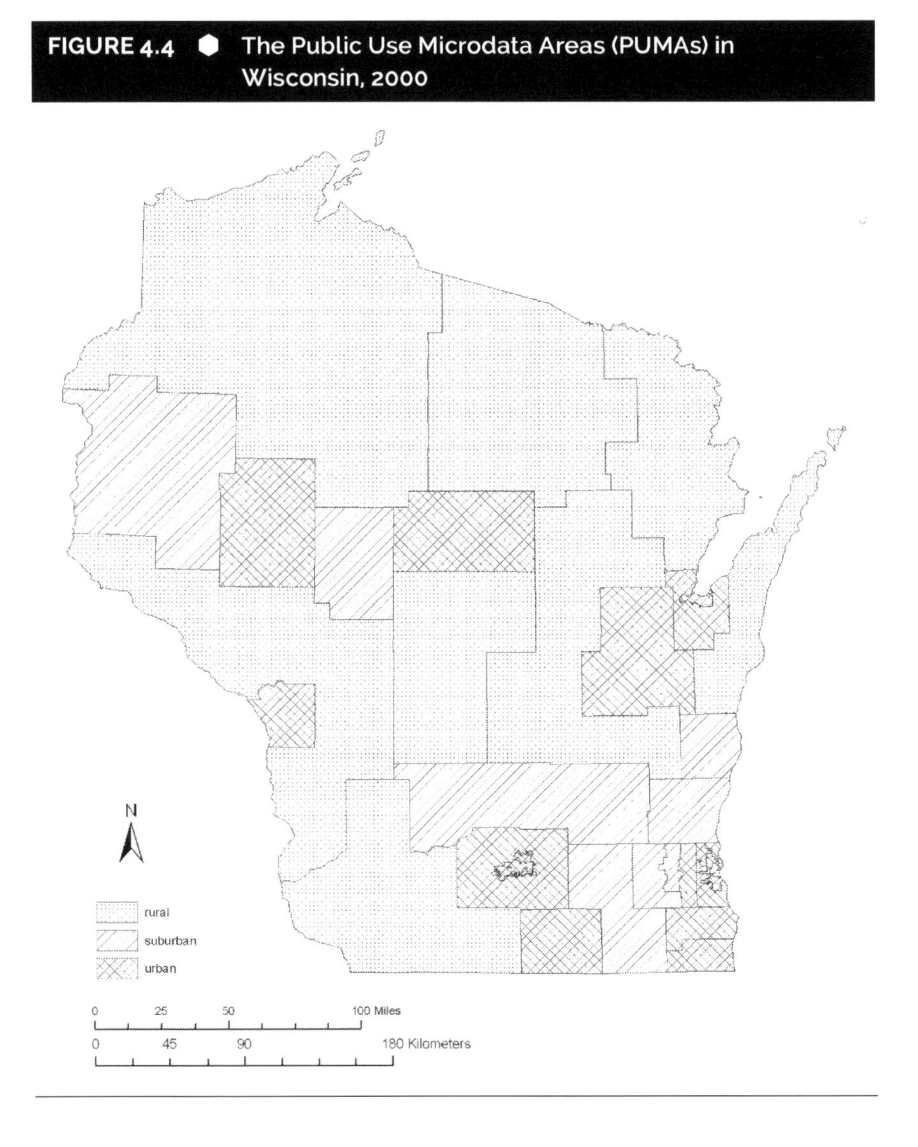

FIGURE 4.4 ● The Public Use Microdata Areas (PUMAs) in Wisconsin, 2000

(*OWNRENT*), and age of housing units (*HUYEAR*). We let *P* denote the probability of migration. The model for the log odds of migration, $P/(1 - P)$, is specified as

$$\ln[P/(1-P)]_{ij} = \beta_{0j} + \beta_{1j}(AGE)_{ij} + \beta_{2j}(OWNRENT)_{ij} + \beta_{3j}(MCBW)_{ij} + \\ \beta_{4j}(HHFHHC)_{ij} + \beta_{5j}(BACHLR)_{ij} + \beta_{6j}(NHWHITE)_{ij} + \beta_{7j}(MARRIED)_{ij} + \\ \beta_{8j}(HUYEAR)_{ij} + \beta_{9j}(CHDR12)_{ij} + \beta_{10j}(CHDR17)_{ij} + \varepsilon_{ij}, \; \varepsilon_{ij} \sim N(0, \sigma^2), \quad (4.10)$$

where *i* indexes an individual for $i = 1, \ldots, n$, *j* indexes PUMA for $j = 1, \ldots, m$

At level 1, we assume the error term (ε_{ij}) to be identically and independently distributed as normal distribution with mean 0 and variance σ^2. Notice, however, that the intercept and the coefficients are subscripted by *j*, which allows each PUMA to have its own intercept and coefficients. We express the expectations, variances, and covariances of the intercept and coefficients as follows:

$$E(\beta_{0j}) = \gamma_0, \text{Var}(\beta_{0j}) = \tau_{00} \\ E(\beta_{1j}) = \gamma_1, \text{Var}(\beta_{1j}) = \tau_{11} \\ \vdots \\ E(\beta_{9j}) = \gamma_9, \text{Var}(\beta_{9j}) = \tau_{99} \\ E(\beta_{10j}) = \gamma_{10}, \text{Var}(\beta_{10j}) = \tau_{1010} \\ \text{Cov}(\beta_{0j}, \beta_{1j}) = \tau_{01} \\ \text{Cov}(\beta_{0j}, \beta_{2j}) = \tau_{21} \\ \vdots \quad (4.11)$$

where

γ_0 is the expectation of the random intercept among PUMAs,

τ_{00} is the variance of the random intercept among PUMAs,

γ_1 is the expectation of the random coefficient for *AGE* among PUMAs,

τ_{11} is the variance of the random coefficient for *AGE* among PUMAs,

τ_{01} is the covariance between the random intercept and the random coefficient for *AGE*, and so on.

The intercept and the coefficients could vary greatly across the PUMAs (i.e., level 2), and they might be explained by some characteristics at the PUMA level. In theory, the response variables could include any coefficients from level 1. For the purpose of a simple demonstration, we choose to only model the intercept as a response variable at level 2. The explanatory variables are PUMA characteristics, including urban/suburban/rural status (*SUBURBAN*), highway expansion (*HWXP9095*), percent people moving (*MOVPERCT*), percent race (*PRTNHWHI*), percent house age (*PRTHU40Y*), and natural amenities (*AMENITY*). The level 2 equations are specified as

$$\beta_{0j} = \gamma_{00} + \gamma_{01}(HWXP9095)_j + \gamma_{02}(MOVPERCT)_j + \gamma_{03}(PRTNHWHI)_j + \\ \gamma_{04}(PRTHU40Y)_j + \gamma_{05}(SUBURBAN)_j + \gamma_{06}(AMENITY)_j + u_{0j}$$

$$u_{0j} \sim N(0, \tau_{00})$$
$$\beta_{1j} = \gamma_{10} + u_{1j} \quad u_{1j} \sim N(0, \tau_{11})$$
$$\beta_{2j} = \gamma_{20} + u_{2j} \quad u_{2j} \sim N(0, \tau_{22}) \quad (4.12)$$
$$\vdots$$
$$\beta_{9j} = \gamma_{90} + u_{9j} \quad u_{9j} \sim N(0, \tau_{99})$$
$$\beta_{10j} = \gamma_{100} + u_{10j} \quad u_{10j} \sim N(0, \tau_{1010})$$

The combined equation can be generated by replacing the coefficients in the level 1 equations with their corresponding coefficients in the level 2 equations:

$$\begin{aligned}\ln[P/(1-P)]_{ij} &= \gamma_{00} + \{\gamma_{01}(HWXP9095)_j + \gamma_{02}(MOVPERCT)_j + \\ &\quad \gamma_{03}(PRTNHWHI)_j + \gamma_{04}(PRTHU40Y)_j + \gamma_{05}(SUBURBAN)_j + \\ &\quad \gamma_{06}(AMENITY)_j + \gamma_{10}(AGE)_{ij} + \gamma_{20}(OWNRENT)_{ij} + \\ &\quad \gamma_{30}(MCBW)_{ij} + \gamma_{40}(HHFHHC)_{ij} + \gamma_{50}(BACHLR)_{ij} + \\ &\quad \gamma_{60}(NHWHITE)_{ij} + \gamma_{70}(MARRIED)_{ij} + \gamma_{80}(HUYEAR)_{ij} + \\ &\quad \gamma_{90}(CHDR12)_{ij} + \gamma_{100}(CHDR17)_{ij}\} + \{u_{0j} + u_{1j}(AGE)_{ij} + \\ &\quad u_{2j}(OWNRENT)_{ij} + u_{3j}(MCBW)_{ij} + u_{4j}(HHFHHC)_{ij} + \\ &\quad u_{5j}(BACHLR)_{ij} + u_{6j}(NHWHITE)_{ij} + u_{7j}(MARRIED)_{ij} + \\ &\quad u_{8j}(HUYEAR)_{ij} + u_{9j}(CHDR12)_{ij} + u_{10j}(CHDR17)_{ij}\} + \varepsilon_{ij}\end{aligned} \quad (4.13)$$

The error has unequal variances because it depends on the u_{xj} ($x = 0, 1, \ldots, 10$), which varies across PUMAs, and it depends on the values of the level 1 explanatory variables, which vary across individuals.

A logit multilevel model can be fitted for these data using the hierarchical linear model (HLM) software (Scientific Software International, Inc.). The output includes the coefficients and their significance test at level 1 (unit-specific and population-average models are used in this software), the coefficients and their significance test at level 2 (i.e., how level 2 variables affect their corresponding level 1 intercept and coefficients), and the variance and covariance components among levels (the variance can be divided into components within and between level 2 units).

Table 4.4 shows the coefficient estimates for both level 1 and level 2 variables. Note that the coefficients for level 2 variables are for explaining the intercept at level 1 (i.e., the variance of "initial" probability of migration among the PUMAs).

An advantage of hierarchical regression lies in the reliability estimates of level 1 coefficients (Table 4.5). If the within-group variance compared to the across-group variance is smaller, then the reliability will be larger and the multilevel regression coefficients will be more reliable. As we see from Table 4.5, some variables, such as age of householder (*AGE*), rent or own (*OWNRENT*), and age of housing unit

TABLE 4.4 ● Multilevel linear regression (MLR) model results

Variable	Coefficient	SE
Level 1		
AGE	−0.059	0.001***
NHWHITE	−0.290	0.048***
BACHLR	0.280	0.025***
MARRIED	−0.058	0.023*
MCBW	−0.253	0.024***
CHDR12	−0.165	0.027***
CHDR17	−0.427	0.021***
HHFHHC	0.123	0.033***
OWNRENT	−1.486	0.033***
HUYEAR	−0.021	0.001***
Level 2		
INTRCPT2	2.307	0.264***
HWXP9095	0.018	0.015
MOVPERCT	2.149	0.304***
PRTNHWHI	1.191	0.132***
PRTHU40Y	0.898	0.111***
SUBURBAN	0.063	0.016***
AMENITY	−0.025	0.007**

Note: SE = standard error.

*Significant at the α = .05 level. **Significant at the α = .01 level. ***Significant at the α = .001 level.

(*HUYEAR*), are quite reliable, while marital status (*MARRIED*), married couple both working (*MCBW*), female-headed household with children under eighteen years old (*HHFHHC*), and female-headed household with children (*CHDR17*) are less reliable. But the latter three variables are highly significant in the regression. How can we explain that? A small reliability value can be caused either by a smaller coefficient variance across PUMAs compared to within groups, a small sample size, or both (Raudenbush & Bryk, 2002). Since the sample size is not small here, the low reliabilities are likely the result of a smaller coefficient variance across groups. Table 4.6 reaffirms this conclusion: the coefficients of these three variables do not vary greatly across groups.

TABLE 4.5 ● Reliability estimates of level 1 coefficients in a multilevel linear regression (MLR) model

Random level 1 coefficient	Reliability estimate
INTRCPT1	0.682
AGE	0.714
OWNRENT	0.655
MCBW	0.339
HHFHHC	0.326
BACHLR	0.472
NHWHITE	0.436
MARRIED	0.310
HUYEAR	0.749
CHDR12	0.427
CHDR17	0.211

TABLE 4.6 ● Estimation of variance components in a multilevel linear regression (MLR) model

Random effect	SD	Variance component	p-value
INTRCPT1	0.511	0.261	.000
AGE slope	0.006	0.000	.000
OWNRENT slope	0.169	0.028	.000
MCBW slope	0.091	0.008	.034
HHFHHC slope	0.128	0.016	.236
BACHLR slope	0.108	0.012	.003
NHWHITE slope	0.200	0.040	.002
MARRIED slope	0.085	0.007	.042
HUYEAR slope	0.004	0.000	.000
CHDR12 slope	0.106	0.011	.002
CHDR17 slope	0.065	0.004	.301

Note: SD = standard deviation.

In this analysis, three advantages of MLR for studying migration are demonstrated:

- MLR can readily integrate heterogeneous variables at the aggregated level into the individual-level model, and their significance can be assessed.

- The coefficient reliability of level 1 variables can be estimated based on within- and across-group variance and can then be used to reestimate the coefficients of level 1 variables.

- The way that MLR combines both individual and aggregate characteristics helps to alleviate ecological fallacies. This is particularly important because individual behaviors tend to be influenced by, and their aggregation tends to influence, the characteristics of the residential area.

While the individual and areal linkage of migration studies is crucial for housing policy making, it has long been ignored (Li & Wu, 2004).

This section introduces a relatively simple MLR model and uses a data example of migration to illustrate its use. MLR models have also been used in studies of health (e.g., Bardenheier, Shefer, Barker, Winston, & Sionean, 2005; Suvak, Walling, Iverson, Taft, & Resick, 2009; Weinmayr, Dreyhaupt, Jaensch, Forastiere, & Strachan, 2017), education (e.g., Rocconi, 2013), crime (e.g., Rotarou, 2018), program evaluation (e.g., Lundgren & Rankin, 1998), social work (e.g., Kim, Solomon, & Zurlo, 2009), and energy consumption (e.g., Tso & Guan, 2014). MLR models could be further integrated with spatial regression models (Xu, 2014; Yamagata, Murakami, Yoshida, Seya, & Kuroda, 2016), qualitative comparative analysis (Meuer & Rupietta, 2017), and geographically weighted regression models (Chen & Truong, 2012). For more advanced MLR models, readers are referred to the corresponding MLR literature.

Study Questions

1. What is a spatial error model with spatially lagged responses (SEMSLR)? How is it different from a spatial lag model or a spatial error model?

2. How do we fit an SEMSLR? Which spatial weight matrices do we use in an SEMSLR? When is an SEMSLR needed?

3. What are the differences between an SEMSLR and a spatial autoregressive moving average (SARMA) model?

4. What is a spatial cross-regressive model? How is it different from a spatial lag model or a spatial error model? How is it related to a standard linear regression model?

5. How do we fit a spatial cross-regressive model? Which spatial weight matrices do we use in a spatial cross-regressive model? When is a spatial cross-regressive model needed?

6. Are the spatial parameters in a spatial cross-regressive model estimated endogenously or exogenously?

7. Which spatially lagged explanatory variables should be included in a spatial cross-regressive model?

8. What is a multilevel linear regression (MLR) model? When and why do we need an MLR model?

9. What issues is an MLR model best for dealing with?

10. How do we fit an MLR model? How do we interpret level 1 and level 2 effects from an MLR model? How are the reliability estimates related to within- and across-group variances?

11. How might an SEMSLR, spatial cross-regressive model, or MLR model be useful to your research?

12. What practical challenges could there be in fitting an SEMSLR, a spatial cross-regressive model, or an MLR model?

5

MODELS DEALING WITH SPATIAL HETEROGENEITY

LEARNING OBJECTIVES

- Become familiar with the traditional methods used in social science research to deal with spatial heterogeneity.

- Understand when and how to fit a spatial regime standard linear regression model, interpret the coefficients across different regimes, and use appropriate diagnostics to assess the model.

- Understand the strengths and weaknesses that spatial regime models have over the aspatial regression models dealing with spatial heterogeneity.

- Understand when and how to apply a geographically weighted regression method, describe its assumptions, interpret the estimates of the global and local coefficients, and use appropriate model diagnostics.

- Describe the differences in and cautions about using the three types of methods dealing with spatial heterogeneity.

As addressed in Section 2.3, **spatial heterogeneity,** or spatial variation, refers to differences in the mean, variance, and/or covariance structures, including spatial autocorrelation within a spatial region (Dutilleul, 2011; LeSage, 1999). In the context of spatial regression modeling, we categorize spatial heterogeneity into two types.

Spatial heterogeneity refers to differences in a spatial region in the mean, variance, or spatial covariance (or spatial correlation) structures.

The first type of spatial heterogeneity refers to spatial variations in individual variables, which could include both the response variable and explanatory variables. When we conduct an exploratory spatial data analysis (ESDA) for a variable of interest using local indicator of spatial association (LISA) techniques, we may find that some regions show positive spatial autocorrelation (places with high values are surrounded by neighbors with high values, or places with low values are surrounded by neighbors with low values) and other regions show negative spatial autocorrelation (places with high values are surrounded by neighbors with low values, or places with low values are surrounded by neighbors with high values). (Refer to Section 2.4 for details.) Examining this type of spatial heterogeneity is useful for identifying clusters, hotspots, corridors, and "pockets" as well as for detecting spatial outliers and regimes. However, the existence of spatial heterogeneity in individual variables does not necessarily require it to be incorporated into regression modeling; for example, spatial heterogeneity in the response variable may be explained by spatial heterogeneity in one or more of the explanatory variables of the model.

> One type of spatial heterogeneity refers to the spatial variations in an individual variable—either the response variable or an explanatory variable.

Most social science studies dealing with the first type of spatial heterogeneity focus on the response variable rather than the explanatory variables. These studies usually first investigate the possible spatial heterogeneity in the response variable and then fit regression models to explain that. For example, in one study, Wu and Gopinath (2008) first identified spatial variations in economic development in the United States and then sought and explained the factors driving the spatial variations in economic development using regression models. Investigating spatial heterogeneity (or variations) in the response variable and explanatory variables often results in insights into the phenomenon of study.

> Another type of spatial heterogeneity refers to the spatial variations of the relations between the explanatory variables and the response variable.

The second type of spatial heterogeneity, which refers to spatial variations of the relations between the explanatory variables and the response variable (i.e., the regression coefficients), has received much less attention than the first type of spatial heterogeneity in existing social science research, but attention to the second type has been increasing in recent years due to the development of methods and software packages for dealing with it. In this chapter, we exclusively focus on the second type of spatial heterogeneity and introduce models that deal with spatial heterogeneity of the regression coefficients rather than that of the individual variables. Because local patterns vary in ways traditional standard linear regression models with global regression coefficients cannot easily capture, spatial heterogeneity of the regression coefficients is possible (Partridge, Rickman, Ali, & Olfert, 2008a, 2008b). The estimates of regression coefficients in a standard linear regression reflect relations globally but generally do not reflect local variations of the relations between the response and the explanatory variables; therefore, it would not be adequate to apply the inferences about the global regression coefficients in the standard linear regression to explain local patterns. In this chapter, we introduce three methods that deal with spatial heterogeneity of the regression coefficients:

- aspatial regression methods,
- spatial regime models, and
- geographically weighted regression (GWR) methods.

5.1 ASPATIAL REGRESSION METHODS

5.1.1 The Methods

There are three often-used aspatial regression methods that deal with spatial heterogeneity in existing social science research. The first aspatial method is to use one or more dummy variables indicating the region into which each observation falls. For example, in many sociological studies that have been conducted at the state or county level in the United States, a dummy variable indicating the North versus the South or multiple dummy variables indicating finer classifications such as regions (Northeast, Midwest, South, and West) or divisions (there are nine divisions in the United States) are used (e.g., Iceland & Nelson, 2008; Logan, Oakley, & Stowell, 2008; Rugh & Massey, 2010; Zeng & Xie, 2004). Based on the coefficients of the dummy variables, we can draw an inference that, for example, everything else being equal, states or counties in the North are different from those in the South by $\hat{\beta}$ (the coefficient on the dummy variable) with higher (or lower) mean response if $\hat{\beta}$ is positive (or negative). Although this approach incorporates geographic information into the model, it only tells us the spatial heterogeneity in the mean of the response variable.

Three aspatial regression methods dealing with spatial heterogeneity are often used in existing social science research.

The second aspatial method is to add one or more interaction variables between the dummy variables and one or more explanatory variables. We could interpret that, for example, the regression coefficient estimates for the explanatory variable that interacts with the dummy variable (indicating the North versus the South) differ by $\hat{\beta}$ between the states or counties in the North and those in the South. Although this approach does provide the difference of regression coefficients among different regions, the addition of multiple interaction variables to examine the spatial variations of multiple explanatory variables' associations with the response variable makes the model complex and makes interpretation of the regression coefficients not always straightforward.

The third aspatial method[1] is to partition the data by the categories as indicated by dummy variables and fit regression models separately for each category (e.g., Blanchard, 2007). For example, suppose we have four regions in the data: Northeast, Midwest, West, and South. We can separate the data into the four categories. We can then fit standard linear regression models separately with observations from each of the four categories. Next, we present the results of the four regression models (or sometimes together with the model with pooled data) in one table, with regression coefficients for the same explanatory variables on the same row. With such a table, we can compare the magnitude and significance of each explanatory variable's association with the response variable across the four regions. We can further test the differences of the coefficients across the categories by using a *t*-test as addressed by Clogg, Petkova, and Haritou (1995).

5.1.2 Data Example

Here we illustrate the use of the three aspatial methods for addressing spatial heterogeneity by our example of population growth from 2000 to 2010 at the minor civil division (MCD) level in Wisconsin. Existing literature shows a history of recognizing spatial heterogeneity of population change and reveals that it is associated with economic geography, natural endowments, and accumulated human and physical capital (Wu & Gopinath, 2008). However, existing studies have tended to ignore the spatial heterogeneity of these factors' associations with population change. Traditional standard linear regression models with global regression coefficients cannot capture the variation in growth mechanisms of local areas (Partridge et al., 2008b). Although the global relations can be reflected by the estimates of the global regression coefficients, the local variations of the relations cannot be reflected; the information on local dynamics is inadequate.

We divide all MCDs ($n = 1,837$) into three groups: urban MCDs, suburban MCDs, and rural MCDs. Refer to Table 1.1 and Table 2.1 for the descriptive statistics of the variables across the three groups. MCDs are the smallest functioning governmental units in Wisconsin, which is composed of low-density rural areas; many small villages, towns, and cities; and a few large cities and surrounding neighboring suburbs. Thus, studying population growth across urban MCDs, suburban MCDs, and rural MCDs can provide insights into the possible local dynamics that may not be captured by analysis using the entire data set.

---

[1] It should be noted that the second and third methods could be argued to be *spatial*—both approaches can provide coefficients for each category of regions.

TABLE 5.1 ● Results for the standard linear regression model with urban-rural classifications

Variable	Coefficient	SE
Constant	0.058**	0.020
Previous growth	0.061**	0.021
Old	−0.277***	0.061
Unemployment	−0.233*	0.109
Airport	0.072	0.083
Forest	−0.073***	0.015
Land developability	0.044*	0.018
Urban-rural classification (rural = reference group)		
Urban	0.024	0.017
Suburban	0.040***	0.008
Measures of fit		
Log-likelihood	1,121.01	
AIC	−2,224.01	
BIC	−2,174.37	
n	1,837	

Note: AIC = Akaike's information criterion; BIC = Schwartz's Bayesian information criterion; SE = standard error.

*Significant at the α = .05 level. **Significant at the α = .01 level. ***Significant at the α = .001 level.

First, we add two dummy variables to refit the standard linear regression model as presented in Table 3.1. The two dummy variables indicate urban and suburban statuses, with rural status as the reference group. The results are presented in Table 5.1. This model is better fitted to data balanced with model parsimony than the standard linear regression model is, based on the fact that the Akaike's information criterion (AIC) and Schwartz's Bayesian information criterion (BIC) values are smaller for the former than for the latter. The negative residuals (Figure 5.1) appear to be smaller (in the absolute term) than those of the initial standard linear regression model (Figure 3.1) for some MCDs. The difference in population growth between the urban and rural MCDs is not statistically significant, but the difference between the suburban and rural MCDs is statistically significant. Everything else being equal, a suburban MCD has a 0.04 percent higher population growth rate in 2000 to 2010 than a rural MCD does. However, this only tells the spatial variation of population growth across the urban-rural continuum. It does not indicate spatial variation of the associations between the explanatory variables and population growth.

Second, we create two interaction variables between land developability and the urban-rural status and refit the standard linear regression model (Table 5.2). Note that we selected land developability from the six explanatory variables mainly for demonstration purposes; the other explanatory variables could also interact with the urban-rural status on population growth. This model with the interaction variables is slightly better fitted to data balanced with model parsimony than the standard linear regression model with dummy variables as presented in Table 5.1. There appear to be only a few MCDs in which the residuals of the model with interaction variables (Figure 5.2) are smaller (in the absolute term) than those of the model with dummy variables (Figure 5.1). The interaction between land developability and urban status is statistically significant (at the $\alpha = .05$ level) in

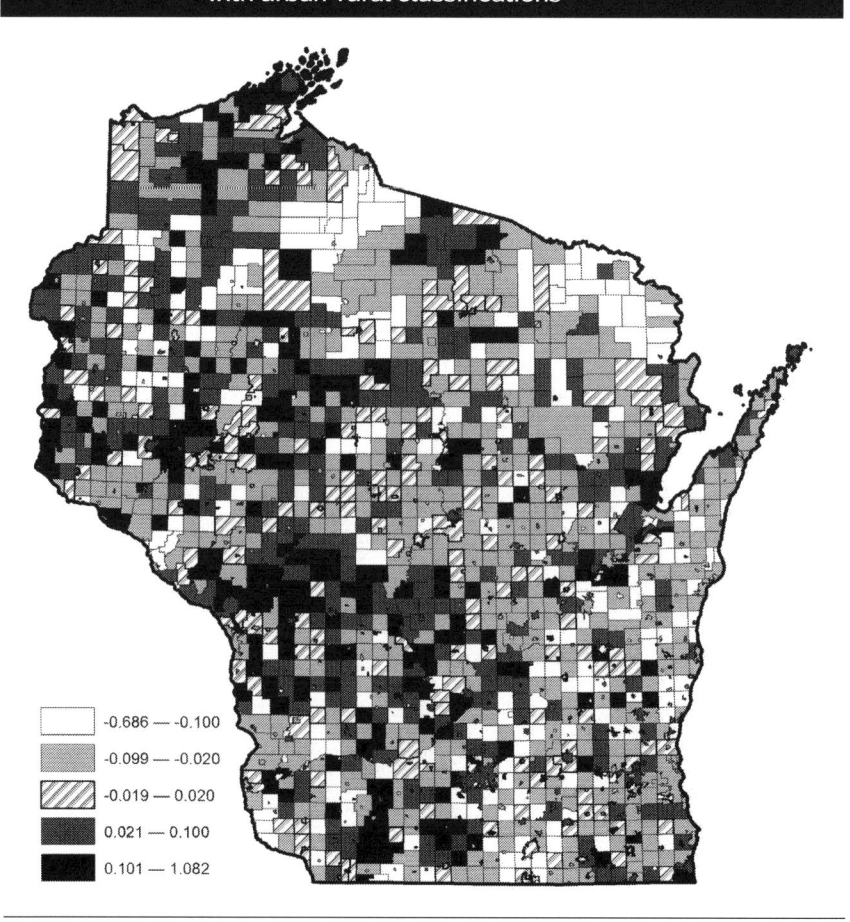

FIGURE 5.1 ● **Residuals of the standard linear regression model with urban-rural classifications**

-0.686 — -0.100
-0.099 — -0.020
-0.019 — 0.020
0.021 — 0.100
0.101 — 1.082

TABLE 5.2 ● Results for the standard linear regression model with urban-rural classifications and interaction variables

Variable	Coefficient	SE
Constant	0.054*	0.021
Previous growth	0.057**	0.021
Old	−0.276***	0.061
Unemployment	−0.219*	0.109
Airport	0.077	0.084
Forest	−0.075***	0.015
Land developability	0.049*	0.021
Urban/rural classification (rural = reference group)		
Urban	−0.053	0.041
Suburban	0.104**	0.036
Interaction variable (Developability × Urban)	0.153*	0.071
Interaction variable (Developability × Suburban)	−0.082	0.045
Measures of fit		
Log-likelihood	1,125.58	
AIC	−2,229.15	
BIC	−2,168.48	
n	1,837	

Note: AIC = Akaike's information criterion; BIC = Schwartz's Bayesian information criterion; SE = standard error.

*Significant at the α = .05 level. **Significant at the α = .01 level. ***Significant at the α = .001 level.

explaining population growth. Everything else being equal, a 1 percent increase in land developability in urban areas is associated with 0.15 percent more population growth than that in rural areas. The interaction between land developability and urban status is not statistically significant at the α = .05 level but is statistically significant at the α = .10 level in explaining population growth. Everything else being equal, a 1 percent increase in land developability in suburban areas is associated with 0.08 percent less population growth than that in rural areas. Although this provides the spatial variation of the association of one explanatory variable (land developability in this example) with population growth, it does not provide

FIGURE 5.2 ● Residuals of the standard linear regression model with urban-rural classifications and interaction variables

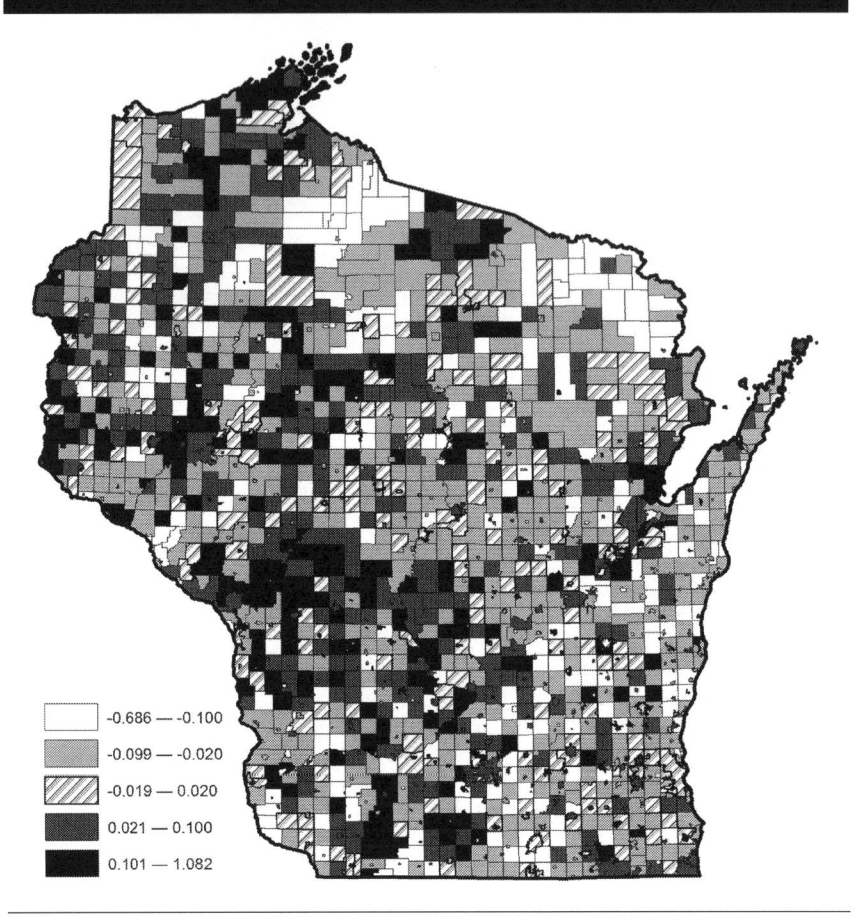

Legend
-0.686 — -0.100
-0.099 — -0.020
-0.019 — 0.020
0.021 — 0.100
0.101 — 1.082

interactions for other explanatory variables. While we could create more interaction variables, doing so would make the model complex.

Therefore, third, we partition the data by the urban-rural classification and fit a standard linear regression model separately for each classification. The results are presented in Table 5.3 and Figure 5.3, showing that the explanatory variables have varying associations with population growth across the urban-rural continuum in terms of the sign, magnitude, and significance of the coefficients. For example, previous growth has a negative association with population growth in rural areas but a positive association in urban and suburban areas. Proximity to airports has a much stronger association in rural areas than in suburban areas and a stronger association in suburban areas than in urban areas. Land developability has a statistically significant association with population growth in rural and urban areas but not in suburban areas.

TABLE 5.3 ● Results for standard linear regression models across the urban-rural continuum

	Rural		Suburban		Urban	
Variable	Coefficient	SE	Coefficient	SE	Coefficient	SE
Constant	0.052*	0.022	0.036	0.059	0.073	0.060
Previous growth	−0.044	0.023	0.288***	0.049	0.209**	0.071
Old	−0.282***	0.061	0.218	0.220	−0.792**	0.257
Unemployment	−0.182	0.108	−0.168	0.388	0.092	0.570
Airport	0.331	0.229	0.110	0.174	0.029	0.069
Forest	−0.065***	0.016	−0.069	0.046	0.104	0.087
Land developability	0.052**	0.019	0.008	0.052	0.110*	0.048
Measures of fit						
Log-likelihood	925.84		174.781		99.609	
AIC	−1,837.67		−335.561		−185.218	
BIC	−1,801.3		−307.329		−168.038	
n	1,334		417		86	

Note: AIC = Akaike's information criterion; BIC = Schwartz's Bayesian information criterion; SE = standard error.
*Significant at the α = .05 level. **Significant at the α = .01 level. ***Significant at the α = .001 level.

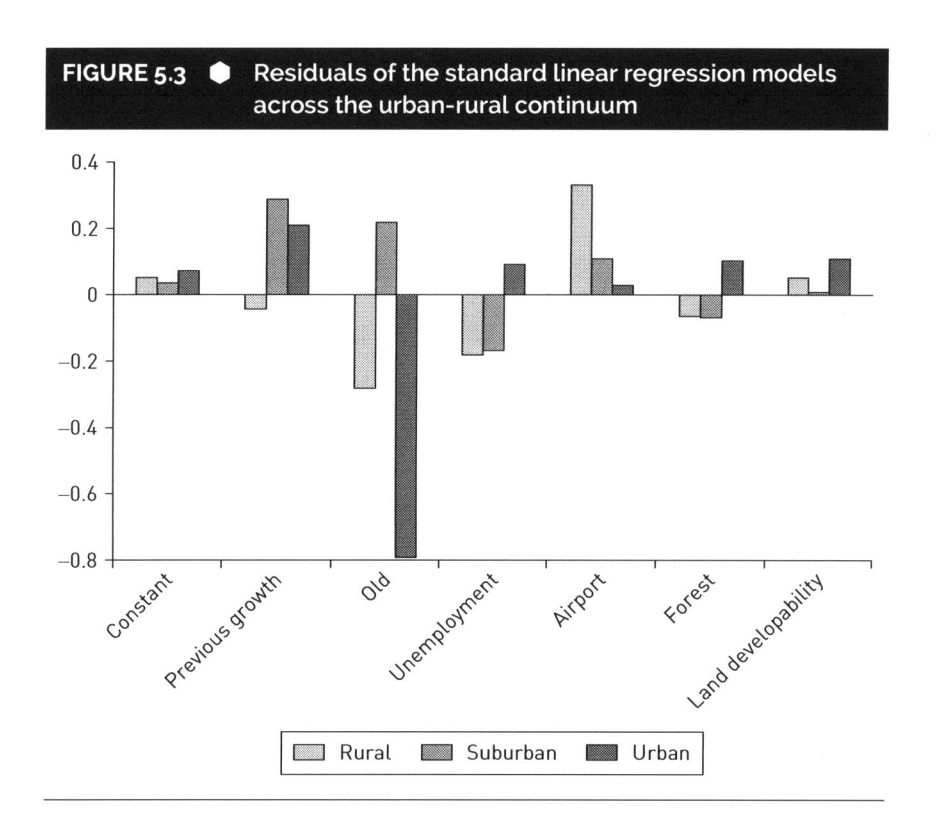

FIGURE 5.3 ● Residuals of the standard linear regression models across the urban-rural continuum

TABLE 5.4 ● Results of *t*-test of coefficient differences across the urban-rural continuum

Variable	Rural vs. Suburban	Suburban vs. Urban	Rural vs. Urban
Constant			
Previous growth	***		**
Old	*	**	
Unemployment			
Airport			
Forest			
Land developability			

*Significant at the $\alpha = .05$ level. **Significant at the $\alpha = .01$ level. ***Significant at the $\alpha = .001$ level.

In addition, the results according to Clogg et al.'s (1995) *t*-test on coefficient differences indicate that there are statistically significant differences across the three groups (Table 5.4). The relations between previous growth and population growth are statistically significantly different between rural and suburban areas and between rural and urban areas. The relations between the old population and population growth are statistically significantly different between rural and suburban areas and suburban and urban areas. The differences in the coefficients of other explanatory variables across the urban-rural continuum are not statistically significant.

5.2 SPATIAL REGIME MODELS

5.2.1 The Methods

Section 5.1 introduced three often-used aspatial regression methods for dealing with spatial heterogeneity in social science research. The second method, which is the use of interaction variables between the explanatory variables and the dummy variables indicating regions, can provide different coefficients for different regions; the differences of coefficients across the different regions can also be tested. However, the possibly large number of interaction variables makes the model complex and interpretation less straightforward.

The third method, which is a data partition approach, can also provide different coefficients for subsets of the data; the differences of coefficients across the different subsets of data can also be tested. However, it would be difficult or problematic to include spatial dependence in the data partition model; spatial regression models such as spatial lag models, spatial error models, and spatial error models with spatially lagged responses (SEMSLRs) require the study area to be contiguous—that is, the areal units (or locations) of the study area need to be connected and the potential existence of "island" areas would be difficult to include in the neighborhood structure. For example, although the entire study area of the lower forty-eight states of the United States is contiguous, subsets of the study area may not be contiguous, depending on the category from which subsets of the data are drawn. If we use two categories—say, metropolitan areas and nonmetropolitan areas—the geographic areas of the two subsets are not contiguous, as the subset data for metropolitan areas are composed of many "island" areas and the subset data for nonmetropolitan areas have many "holes." If we use the category of region—say, Northeast, Midwest, West, and South—each subset of the data is contiguous, but when we create a spatial weight matrix for each subset of the data, the neighbors in other subsets of the data will not be included (also known as the *edge effect*), which reduces the reliability of the spatial weight matrices.

> Including spatial dependence in a data partition model is problematic because spatial regression models such as spatial lag models, spatial error models, and SEMSLRs require the study area to be contiguous.

The spatial regime model, which was developed by Anselin (1988a), can deal with the limitations of the interaction variable method and the data partition method as discussed in Section 5.1. A spatial regime model fits to the entire data set and at the same time can estimate different sets of coefficients for subsets of the data. Because the model fits to the entire data set, spatial structure issues such as noncontiguity within each subset of the data (leading to island areas and hole areas) and edge effects can be dealt with, which allows for simultaneous estimates of spatial dependence and spatial heterogeneity (which are addressed in Chapter 6). In addition, the difference of each coefficient across subsets of the data (the structural stability for each variable) as well as the overall structural stability can be tested by the **spatial Chow test,** which was developed by Anselin (1990), who extended the classic Chow (1960) test to spatial regression models. The spatial Chow test is based on an asymptotic Wald statistic, distributed as a chi-square with $(m-1)p$ degrees of freedom (m = the number of regimes; p = the number of explanatory variables).

> Spatial regime models fit to the entire data set and estimate different sets of coefficients for data subsets.

> Spatial Chow test can be used to test the structural stability of each variable as well as the overall structural stability.

A spatial regime model in a standard linear regression form, which we call a **spatial regime standard linear regression (SRSLR) model,** is specified as

$$Y_r = X_r \beta_r + \varepsilon_r \qquad (5.1)$$

> Spatial regime standard linear regression (SRSLR) model considers a separate set of coefficients for each areal type, or regime.

where

r indexes the regime for $r = 1, 2, \ldots, m$ and m is the number of regimes;

Y_r is an n_r-by-1 vector of the n_r observations of the response variable in regime r;

X_r is an n_r-by-p design matrix of explanatory variables in regime r;

β_r is a p-by-1 vector of the regression coefficients in regime r; and

ε_r is an n_r-by-1 vector of error terms in regime r, and collectively, ε is an n-by-1 vector of $n = n_1 + n_2 + \cdots + n_m$ error terms that are independently and identically distributed as normal distribution with mean 0 and a constant variance.

> Spatial regime models convert a single explanatory variable into multiple new explanatory variables based on the categories chosen.

A spatial regime model transfers each explanatory variable into several new explanatory variables based on the category. If there are two categories, each explanatory variable will be transferred to two new explanatory variables. The values for the new variables correspond to the original variable when the observation falls into its regime (or category) but are zeros when the observation does not fall into its regime. For example, we have data for all counties in the continental United States, divided into North and South. Initially, we have a population growth variable, and each county has a value for that variable. A spatial regime model converts the population growth variable into two variables: a population growth North variable and a population growth South variable. Counties in the North would have their original population growth values in the population growth North variable but zeros in the population growth South variable; counties in the South would have their original population growth values in the population growth South variable but zeros in the population growth North variable.

The spatial regime model produces the exact same coefficients for subsets of data as the interaction variable method and the data partition method via a standard linear regression model using subsets of data. The standard errors of the coefficients are the same for the spatial regime method and the interaction variable method. The three model estimates have the same number of parameters (rp) and the same number of observations (n).

Despite the similarity between the three models, the spatial regime model has at least two advantages over the two aspatial models.

- The first advantage is that in practice it is easier to fit a spatial regime model than the interaction variable and data partition methods. We fit the spatial regime model only once to get the results, whereas for the interaction variable method, we need to create multiple interaction variables and calculate corresponding coefficients for each subset of data after fitting the model, and for the data partition method, we need to fit the standard linear regression model r times to get the results.

- The second and more important advantage is that the spatial regime model allows spatial lag and spatial error dependence (addressed in Chapter 6) more robustly than the data partition method does, as addressed earlier in this section.

Spatial regime models and their extensions have been used in many social science research areas, including regional development (e.g., Ertur, Le Gallo, & Baumont, 2006; Lim, 2016), population change and migration (e.g., Chi & Marcouiller, 2013), commodity and technology markets (e.g., Bille, Salvioni, & Benedetti, 2018; Myers & Jayne, 2012), taxes (e.g., Freret & Maguain, 2017), political science (e.g., Elhorst & Freret, 2009), health (e.g., Myers, Slack, Martin, Broyles, & Heymsfield, 2015), and others.

5.2.2 Model Fitting

Because an SRSLR model is estimated within the context of a standard linear regression model, it can be estimated via either ordinary least squares (OLS) or maximum likelihood estimation (MLE). Model fitting to data balanced with model parsimony can be measured by AIC or BIC values. Refer to Section 3.1 for estimation in detail.

Similar to diagnostics for other spatial regression models, there are usually two sets of model diagnostics to perform when fitting SRSLR models. The first sets of diagnostics are those performed after fitting a standard linear regression model, including diagnostics for possible multicollinearity, heteroscedasticity, and others. The second set of diagnostics is for detecting possible spatial dependence in model residuals. Refer to Section 3.2 for details. In addition, a third set of diagnostics is used to test the difference of each coefficient across subsets of the data (structural stability) and the overall structural stability by the spatial Chow test.

5.2.3 Data Example

Here we use our example of population growth from 2000 to 2010 at the MCD level in Wisconsin for demonstrating the use of SRSLR models. Spatial regime models with spatial lag and/or error dependence are addressed in Chapter 6.

In Section 5.1, we partitioned all MCDs ($n = 1,837$) in Wisconsin into three categories: rural MCDs ($n = 1,334$), suburban MCDs ($n = 417$), and urban MCDs ($n = 86$). These three areal types are seen as three *regimes*. The SRSLR model considers a separate set of coefficients for each of the three regimes. Then we use the spatial Chow test to diagnose the overall structural stability as well as the coefficient stability of each variable. The results are presented in Table 5.5.

The estimates of the regression coefficients for each regime are the same as those in the corresponding standard linear regression model with data partitions. The standard errors of the coefficients are slightly different. Different from the data partition method, in which the stability of each coefficient has to be calculated after fitting the models, the spatial regime model provides the stability test simultaneously. However, the stability test generated by the SRSLR model diagnoses structural instability across all three regimes rather than for two pairs of regimes at a time (although this could be calculated afterward). The results indicate statistically significant instabilities in the association of *previous growth* and *old* with population growth. In addition, a spatial Chow test for the overall coefficient stability is generated and suggests that, collectively, the relations between the explanatory variables and population growth differ across the three regimes.

A *spatial regime standard linear regression* (SRSLR) model generates a stability test that examines structural instability across all three regimes simultaneously.

The SRSLR model residuals are also diagnosed for possible spatial dependence based on the 4-nearest neighbor weight matrix (Table 5.5). The diagnostics based on forty spatial weight matrices are presented in online Appendix B.5 and illustrated in Figure 5.4 on page 128. The results show that there remains small but statistically significant dependence in the model residuals. The LM test and robust LM test for lag and error dependence indicate that both spatial lag and spatial error dependence remain in the spatial regime model residuals. Therefore, the spatial lag and spatial error dependence are further considered; these are addressed in Chapter 6, tying spatial dependence and spatial heterogeneity together.

TABLE 5.5 ● Results of the spatial regime standard linear regression model based on the 4-nearest neighbor weight matrix

Variable	Rural Coefficient	SE	Suburban Coefficient	SE	Urban Coefficient	SE	Instability
Constant	0.052*	0.023	0.036	0.048	0.073	0.099	
Previous growth	−0.044	0.025	0.288***	0.039	0.209	0.116	***
Old	−0.282***	0.065	0.218	0.178	−0.792	0.420	*
Unemployment	−0.182	0.116	−0.168	0.314	0.092	0.933	
Airport	0.331	0.246	0.110	0.140	0.029	0.114	
Forest	−0.065***	0.017	−0.069	0.037	0.104	0.143	
Land developability	0.052*	0.021	0.008	0.042	0.110	0.079	
Diagnostics for spatial dependence							
Moran's I	0.118***						
LM test (lag)	65.616***						
LM test (error)	55.598***						
Robust LM test (lag)	13.399***						
Robust LM test (error)	3.381						
LM test (lag and error)	68.997***						
Measures of fit							
Log-likelihood	1,156.16						
AIC	−2,270.32						
BIC	−2,154.48						
Spatial Chow test	6.84 with 14 degrees of freedom***						
n	1,837						

Note: AIC = Akaike's information criterion; BIC = Schwartz's Bayesian information criterion; LM = Lagrange multiplier; SE = standard error.

*Significant at the α = .05 level. ***Significant at the α = .001 level.

5.3 GEOGRAPHICALLY WEIGHTED REGRESSION

5.3.1 The Limitations of Spatial Regime Models

Section 5.2 introduces the spatial regime model for dealing with spatial heterogeneity. Specifically, the spatial regime model allows different sets of coefficients

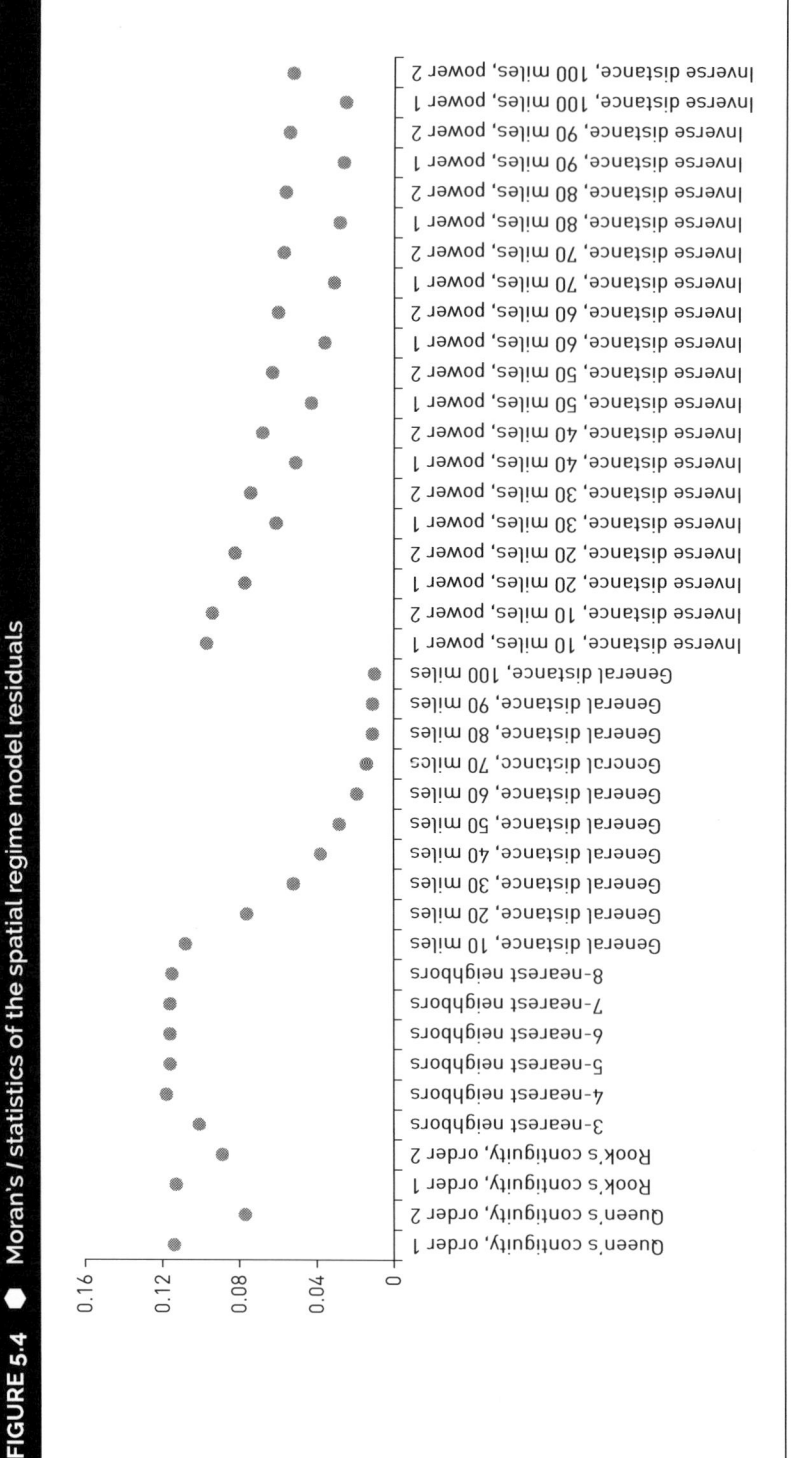

FIGURE 5.4 ● Moran's *I* statistics of the spatial regime model residuals

for the data in different regimes. The assumption is that the relations between the explanatory variables and the response variable are homogeneous within each regime but heterogeneous across regimes. However, this assumption could be easily violated—spatial heterogeneity could exhibit in subregimes of regimes of the data. One solution is to divide the data into more regimes by increasing the number of categories in a categorical variable or by using a more informative categorical variable. However, doing so increases the number of parameters relative to the sample size of the data rapidly, which in turn reduces the efficiency of model estimates.

Therefore, ideally, we would like an approach that enables different sets of coefficients and, to an extreme point, one set of coefficients for each areal unit. **Geographically weighted regression (GWR)** is capable of doing this under suitable conditions.

> **Geographically weighted regression (GWR)** is capable of estimating one set of coefficients for each areal unit under suitable conditions.

5.3.2 Model Specifications of GWR

GWR has received growing attention from social scientists to address the spatial heterogeneity of social science phenomena, such as rural development (e.g., Ali, Partridge, & Olfert, 2007), environmental justice (e.g., Mennis & Jordan, 2005), urban studies (e.g., Yu, Wei, & Wu, 2007), poverty (e.g., Longley & Tobón, 2004), public health and epidemiology (e.g., Fraser, Clarke, Cade, & Edwards, 2012; Yang & Matthews, 2012), homicide (e.g., Graif & Sampson, 2009), education (e.g., Ansong, Ansong, Ampomah, & Adjabeng, 2015), population forecasting (e.g., Chi & Wang, 2017), traffic safety (e.g., Liu, Khattak, & Wali, 2017), wildfire (e.g., Oliveira Pereira, San-Miguel-Ayanz, & Lourenço, 2014), environmental quality (e.g., Harris, Fotheringham, & Juggins, 2010), and others.

The principles of GWR are described in the book *Geographically Weighted Regression: The Analysis of Spatially Varying Relationships* (Fotheringham, Brunsdon, & Charlton, 2002). Here we provide a brief description of the basic idea behind GWR. For more advanced GWR-type approaches, we recommend that readers refer to the literature in their corresponding fields.

The key difference of GWR models compared to other regression models (spatial or aspatial) described in Chapters 3 to 4 and Sections 5.1 to 5.2 is that each of the regression coefficients can be a continuous function across space, meaning that the coefficients

- can vary across space and
- do so continuously (or smoothly).

A basic model in GWR is specified as

$$y_i = \sum_{k=1}^{p} \beta_k(u_i, v_i) x_{ik} + \varepsilon_i \tag{5.2}$$

where

i indexes the ith areal unit (or observation) in the study domain,

y_i denotes the response variable for the ith observation,

(u_i, v_i) denotes the coordinates of the centroid of the ith areal unit,

k indexes the kth explanatory variable,

p denotes the number of explanatory variables including the intercept ($k = 1$),

x_{ik} denotes the explanatory variable k for the ith observation,

$\beta_k(u_i, v_i)$ is the continuous function $\beta_k(u, v)$ for the ith areal unit, and

ε_i is the ith error term and the error terms are independently and identically distributed as normal distribution with mean 0 and a constant variance.

Equation (5.2) suggests that $\beta_k(u_i, v_i)$ could vary for each areal unit i. If we assume that the coefficients may vary freely, that leaves us with $np + 1$ parameters to estimate, which is more than what the n observations allow us to do. To solve this dilemma, GWR does not assume the coefficients to be unrestricted; rather, it assumes them to be deterministic functions of the spatial areal unit. The estimated regression coefficients depend on the response variables and explanatory variables, particularly those in areal unit i and its neighbors. This is similar to the spatial lag and spatial error models, where we have a neighborhood structure to define the neighbors and a spatial weight matrix to quantify the effects of each neighbor.

5.3.3 Spatial Weight Matrices for GWR Models

The spatial weight matrices used for GWR models are different from those used for spatial lag or spatial error models: the former are local matrices, but the latter are global matrices. In GWR, the local weight matrix is a kernel function that

- has a bandwidth (or threshold value) for selecting a subset of the observations and
- gives the nearer neighbors more weight than the farther ones.

Just as there are many spatial weight matrices for spatial lag and spatial error models, the GWR local weight matrices can be specified in different ways. For most GWR applications, the preferences are the continuous functions that produce smoothly decreasing weight as distance increases, such as the adaptive bi-square kernel function:

$$w_{ij} = \left(1 - \left(\frac{d_{ij}}{\theta_{i(l)}}\right)^2\right)^2 \text{ if } d_{ij} < \theta_{i(l)};\ w_{ij} = 0 \text{ otherwise} \quad (5.3)$$

where

w_{ij} is the weight value of observation at areal unit j for estimating the coefficient at areal unit i,

d_{ij} is the Euclidean (or flight) distance between areal unit i and areal unit j, and

$\theta_{i(l)}$ is an adaptive bandwidth defined as the distance between the lth nearest neighbor and the ith areal unit. It should be noted that the bandwidth controls the smoothness of the GWR results. The bandwidth can either vary by location (adaptive bandwidth) or be fixed (fixed bandwidth), in which case $\theta_{i(l)}$ is θ for all areal units i.

A distinct difference between a GWR and a spatial lag or spatial error model is that in the former, often only a subset of observations is used to estimate each coefficient, while in the latter, all observations are used to estimate the coefficients. For example, when we estimate $\beta(u_i, v_i)$, we are using the explanatory variables and response variable at areal unit i as well as its neighbors selected based on a weight function w_{ij}. There are multiple ways to define w_{ij}. We do not discuss them here; rather, we recommend readers refer to the corresponding literature (e.g., Fotheringham et al., 2002).

> In GWR, effectively only a subset of observations is used to estimate each coefficient, while in a spatial lag or spatial error model, all observations are used to estimate the coefficients.

5.3.4 Model Fitting

The GWR is carried out based on a local log-likelihood function, which essentially minimizes the sum of squares of the difference between the observed value and the fitted value of the response variable. We suggest readers refer to Fotheringham et al. (2002, pp. 87–92) for details. The performance of models can be measured by AIC_c (a GWR version of AIC) and BIC that balance model fitting to data and model parsimony. A smaller AIC_c or BIC value indicates a better fitted model.

5.3.5 Model Diagnostics

A major model diagnostic for GWR is a test for spatial heterogeneity. An essential feature of GWR is that the relations between the explanatory variables and the

> In GWR models, the relations between the response variable and the explanatory variables vary spatially.

response variable can vary spatially. After we fit a GWR model, we can test whether the spatial effects are statistically significant. In the standard GWR software package, there is a statistic called **diff-criterion** that is based on a set of model-fitting measures, including AIC_c, AIC, BIC, and cross-validation (CV). A rule of thumb is that when the diff-criterion value for a given explanatory variable is smaller than -2, there is indication that spatial heterogeneity exists for this explanatory variable. If the diff-criterion value is -2 or larger, the corresponding explanatory variable is to be treated as having a spatially homogeneous relation with the response variable and the GWR model is to be refitted with a global regression coefficient for the explanatory variable.

5.3.6 Strength and Limitation of GWR

The strength of GWR is that it can estimate one set of coefficients for each areal unit; that is, the coefficients vary from one areal unit to another, and smoothly (Yu, 2006). This strength can be better illustrated in the data example at the end of this section.

However, the same capability of GWR that leads to its strength has its limitation. The capability of smoothly estimating varying coefficients requires an assumption: if there exists local variation of the associations of explanatory variables with the response variable, the associations need to vary smoothly across space. Such an assumption may not hold in practice. Some researchers favor GWR methods because the smoothly varying coefficients as presented in a map have visual appeal and intuitive explanations; other researchers are skeptical of GWR methods because the map is too "beautiful" to be trusted. In addition, GWR has computational drawbacks, especially for large data sets: model fitting is computationally demanding; optimizing the spatial weight function and the selection of kernel bandwidth would further challenge the computational power (Matthews & Parker, 2013). Furthermore, GWR methods require a normality assumption (Yu, Peterson, & Reid, 2009), are sensitive to the bandwidth selection (Cho, Lambert, & Chen, 2010), and can suffer from multicollinearity among local estimates and multiple comparisons when conducting significance tests (Griffith, 2008; Wheeler & Tiefelsdorf, 2005).

Now a practical question becomes, should one use GWR or not? There is not really a straightforward answer, as GWR has been used a lot but also has been criticized a lot. Our suggestion is to base the decision on your research question and your data. If the goal is to study the spatial pattern of the coefficients and it is expected that the coefficients vary smoothly in space, GWR could be a reasonable choice. GWR is a tool more for exploratory analysis than explanatory analysis (Yang &

Matthews, 2012). If it is of interest to study the spatial variation of the coefficients but the coefficients are expected to vary across a limited number of subsets of the data, spatial regime models might be a more reasonable choice.

5.3.7 Data Example

To illustrate the use of GWR methods, we consider our example of population growth from 2000 to 2010 at the MCD level in Wisconsin. We use the same set of explanatory variables as was used in previous chapters: *previous growth* (population growth rate from 1990 to 2000), *old* (the percentage of old population in 2000), *unemployment* (unemployment rate in 2000), *airport* (proximity to the nearest major commercial airport), *forest* (the percentage of forest coverage), and *land developability* (the percentage of land available for development).

We first apply GWR to the data by assuming that all the explanatory variables have spatially heterogeneous associations with population growth from 2000 to 2010 (i.e., for any explanatory variable, its coefficients vary across each MCD). The descriptive statistics of the coefficients of each explanatory variable (including the intercept) are presented in Table 5.6, which highlights the minimum,

TABLE 5.6 ● Local coefficient estimates of the initial geographically weighted regression (GWR)

Variable	Minimum	Lower quartile	Median	Upper quartile	Maximum	Diff-criterion
Constant	−0.219	−0.021	0.061	0.140	0.605	25.574
Previous growth	−0.626	−0.158	0.037	0.252	0.594	−160.569
Old	−1.601	−0.499	−0.230	0.034	1.237	3.298
Unemployment	−2.836	−0.818	−0.398	0.059	1.922	10.393
Airport	−11.763	0.051	0.514	1.894	17.486	0.014
Forest	−0.928	−0.234	−0.049	0.046	0.425	−35.901
Land developability	−0.382	−0.058	0.006	0.072	0.241	23.971
Measures of fit						
Adjusted R^2	0.298					
AIC	−2,574.385					
Bandwidth size	140					
n	1,837					

Note: Positive value of the diff-criterion suggests no spatial variability in terms of model selection criteria. Bandwidth size refers to the number of nearest neighbors. AIC = Akaike's information criterion.

lower quartile, median, upper quartile, and maximum of the coefficients of each explanatory variable.

The estimated coefficients are further illustrated in Figure 5.5. The estimated coefficients for each explanatory variable vary smoothly across space. The darker shading (red*) highlights larger coefficient values and the lighter shading (blue*) highlights smaller coefficient values. For example, previous growth has strong and positive effects in southeast Wisconsin but strong and negative effects in central Wisconsin. Southeast Wisconsin MCDs that experienced population growth in the 1990s continued the trend into the 2000s, but central Wisconsin MCDs that experienced population growth in the 1990s reversed the trend in the 2000s. One possible reason is the sudden economic recession that occurred in the late 2000s—southeast Wisconsin, which has been dominated by service and manufacturing industries, fared better than central Wisconsin, which relied on agriculture in the economic recession. The reason for the spatial heterogeneity of the effects needs further investigation, but the focus in this section is to illustrate how coefficients could vary spatially.

A legitimate question that always arises when fitting regression models is related to statistical significance—in the GWR case, is the spatial heterogeneity statistically significant? That leads us to calculate the *t*-value of each coefficient by comparing the estimate of the coefficient to its standard error in each areal unit. Figure 5.6 presents the *t*-statistics for the coefficients of each explanatory variable in each MCD. It appears that each explanatory variable is statistically significant in explaining population growth in some MCDs but not all MCDs. For example, *previous growth* has more statistically significant associations in many MCDs than *land developability*. The question now becomes: should one still use the local coefficients if many or a majority of them are not statistically significant?

> Whether to use global or local coefficients in a GWR model can be determined by the diff-criterion value.

To answer this question, we use the diff-criterion to determine whether an explanatory variable has spatially heterogeneous associations with the response variable (i.e., whether to use the global or local coefficients). A diff-criterion value smaller than −2 suggests that local coefficients are more appropriate, whereas a value larger than −2 suggests that a global coefficient is more appropriate. Table 5.7 indicates that only *previous growth* and *forest* have negative diff-criterion values smaller than −2, meaning that each of the two explanatory variables has spatially heterogeneous associations with population growth while the other explanatory variables do not.

In the next step, we treat *previous growth* and *forest* as having spatially heterogeneous associations and the rest of the explanatory variables as having spatially homogeneous associations with population growth and refit the GWR model.

---

*Full-color shading of Figure 5.5 uses red and blue, as can be seen at **study.sagepub.com/researchmethods/quantitative-statistical-research/chi**

FIGURE 5.5 • Local coefficient estimates of initial geographically weighted regression (GWR)

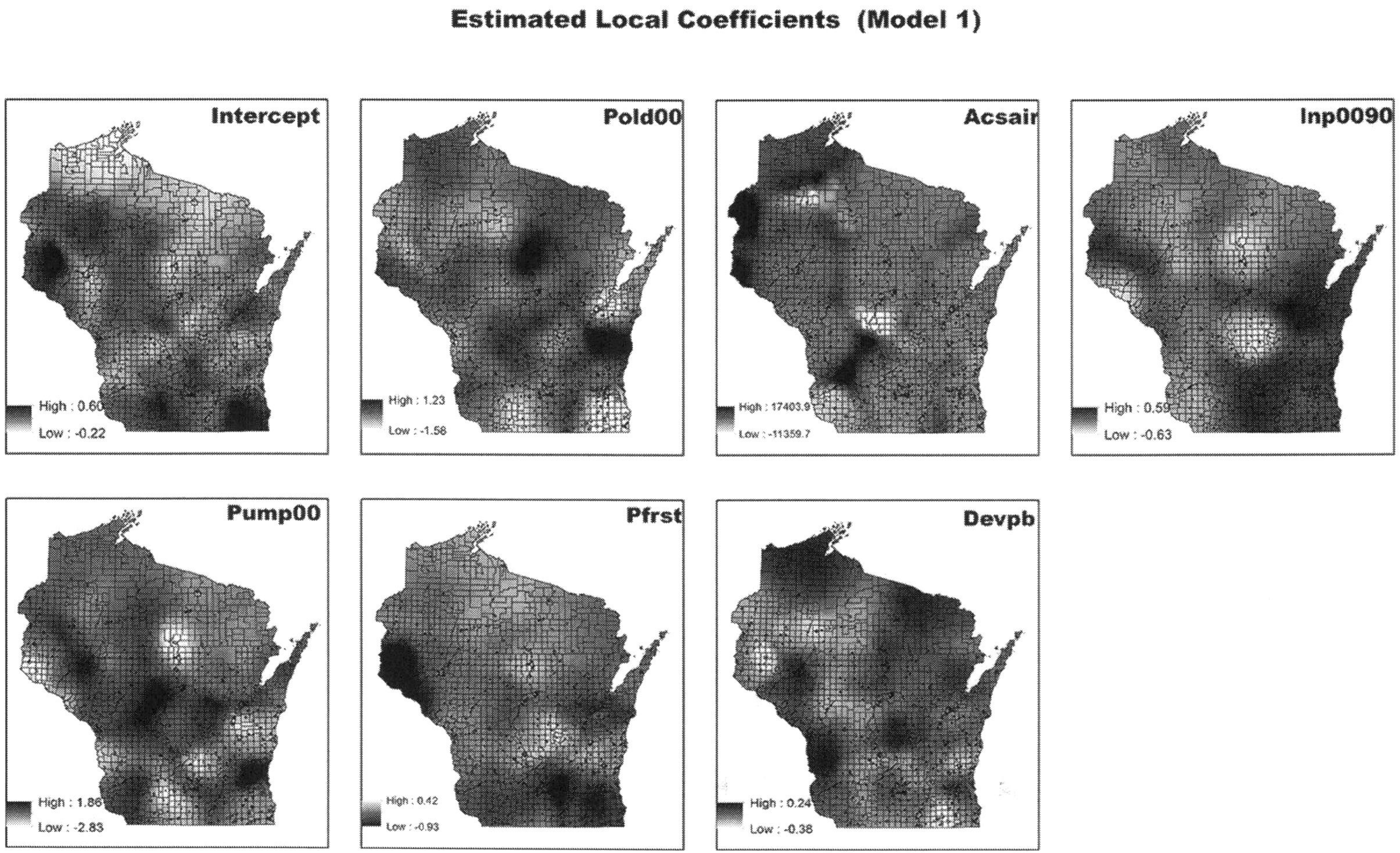

Estimated Local Coefficients (Model 1)

FIGURE 5.6 ● The *t*-values of initial geographically weighted regression (GWR) coefficients

T-statistics (model 1)

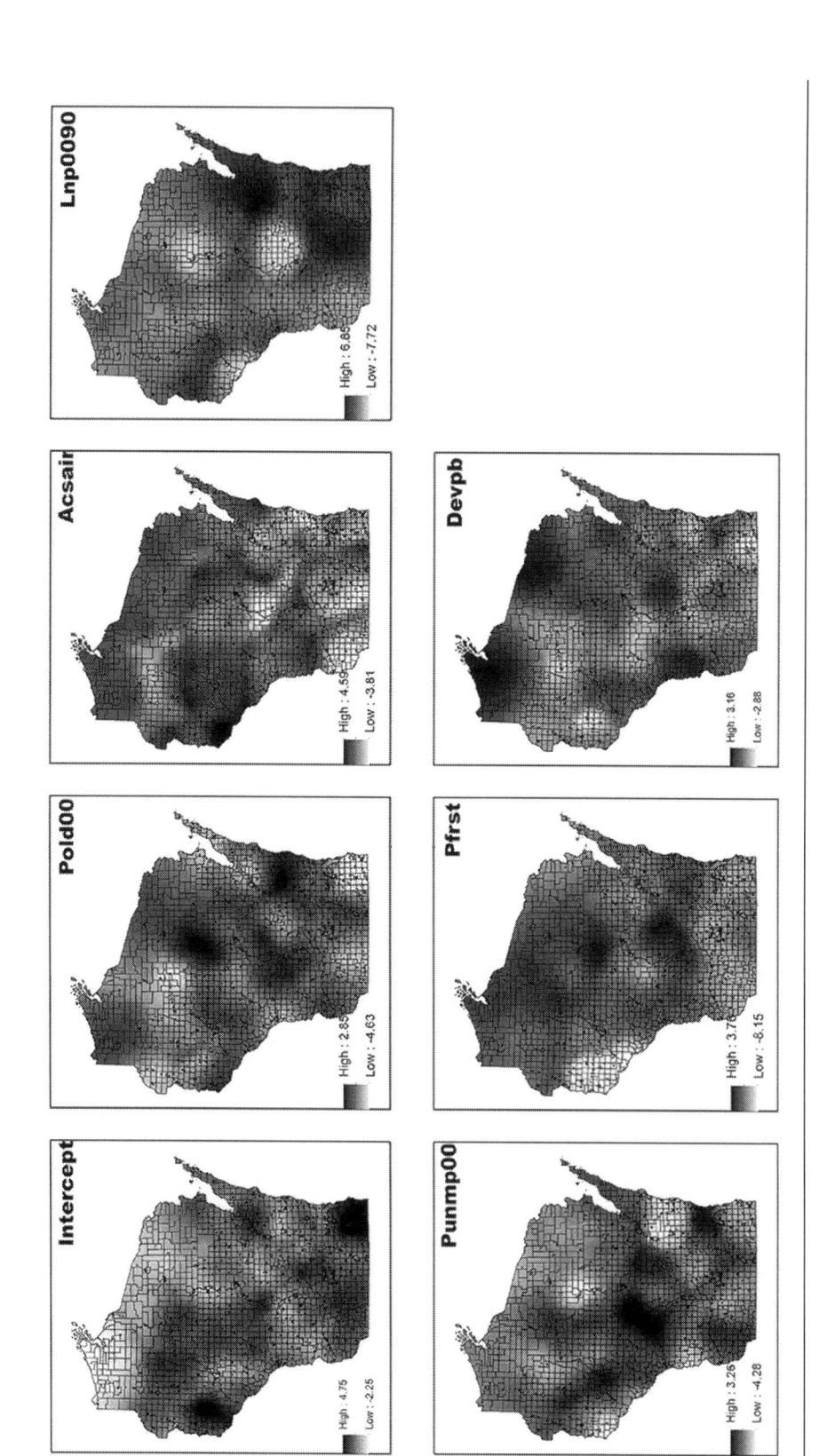

TABLE 5.7 ● Global and local coefficients of the final geographically weighted regression (GWR) model

Local variable	Minimum	Lower quartile	Median	Upper quartile	Maximum
Previous growth	−0.917	−0.166	0.044	0.300	1.090
Forest	−1.272	−0.175	−0.070	0.021	0.792
Global variables	Estimate	SE			
Constant	0.044	0.020			
Old	−0.199	0.058			
Unemployment	−0.194	0.105			
Airport	0.067	0.074			
Land developability	0.037	0.017			
Measures of fit					
Adjusted R^2	0.324				
AIC	−2,666.614				
Bandwidth size	57				
n	1,837				

Note: Bandwidth size refers to the number of nearest neighbors. AIC = Akaike's information criterion; SE = standard error.

FIGURE 5.7 ● Local coefficients and *t*-values of final geographically weighted regression (GWR)

Local Estimates (model2)

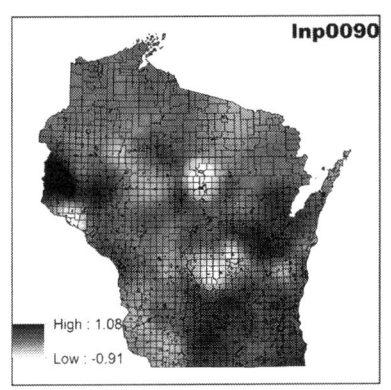

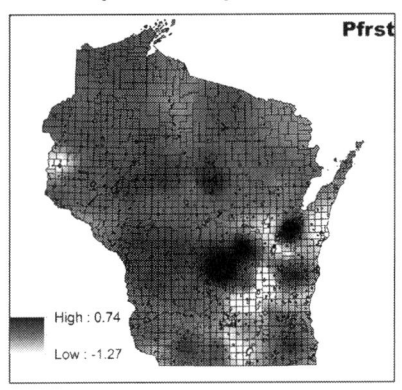

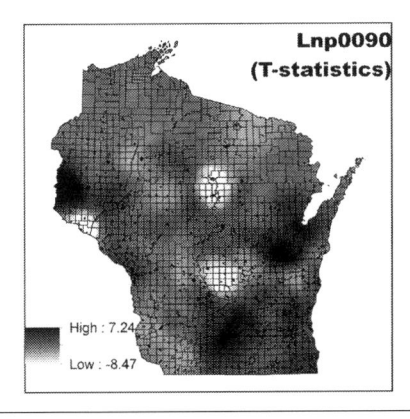

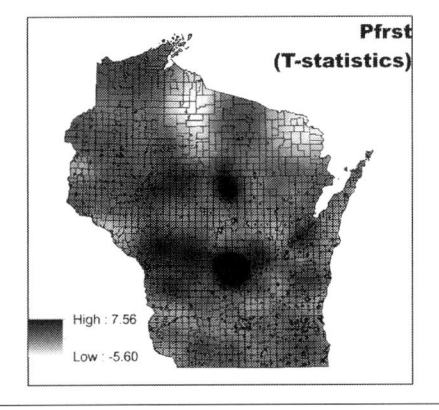

lnp0090 — High: 1.08, Low: −0.91

Pfrst — High: 0.74, Low: −1.27

Lnp0090 (T-statistics) — High: 7.24, Low: −8.47

Pfrst (T-statistics) — High: 7.56, Low: −5.60

The results are presented in Table 5.7. The explanatory variables that have spatially heterogeneous associations are presented with descriptive statistics of their estimated coefficients, and the explanatory variables that have spatially homogeneous associations are presented with their estimated coefficients and standard errors. The local coefficients and t-values of the final model are presented in Figure 5.7.

As this example demonstrates, the GWR is different from standard linear regression models that do not consider spatial heterogeneity and where only one global coefficient applies to all the MCDs. The GWR is also different from spatial regime models that do consider spatial heterogeneity but in a different way: the former presents the variation smoothly across space, but the latter presents the variation of the associations by a few sets of regression coefficients.

Study Questions

1. What is spatial heterogeneity? How is it different from spatial dependence?

2. What methods can be used to deal with spatial heterogeneity of the regression coefficients?

3. How do you use dummy variables and/or interaction variables (in traditional, aspatial regression models) to deal with spatial heterogeneity?

4. How does the data partition approach deal with spatial heterogeneity?

5. What is a spatial Chow test? How are the structural stability for each variable and the overall structural stability diagnosed?

6. When fitting the same data set using a spatial regime model, the interaction variable method, and the data partition method, how do the estimated coefficients and their standard errors compare among the methods?

7. What are the strengths and weaknesses that spatial regime models have over the aspatial regression models dealing with spatial heterogeneity?

8. What is a geographically weighted regression (GWR)? What is the key difference between GWR models and other regression (spatial or aspatial) models?

9. How are spatial weight matrices for GWR different from those for spatial lag or spatial error models?

10. What are the strengths and weaknesses of GWR?

11. How do you choose between GWR and spatial regime models in dealing with spatial heterogeneity?

12. By using spatial regime models or GWR models, how might the interpretation of the results help you make a (spatial) theoretical contribution to your area of research?

6

MODELS DEALING WITH BOTH SPATIAL DEPENDENCE AND SPATIAL HETEROGENEITY

LEARNING OBJECTIVES

- Understand how to incorporate spatial dependence and spatial heterogeneity simultaneously within the spatial regime context.
- Understand how to fit a spatial regime lag model, a spatial regime error model, and a spatial regime error and lag model.
- Understand how to interpret the spatial effects and different sets of coefficients across regimes in spatial regime models.
- Interpret the spatial Chow test.

So far, we have introduced models dealing with spatial dependence (Chapters 3 and 4) and spatial heterogeneity (Chapter 5) separately. Can we relatively easily model both spatial dependence and spatial heterogeneity? The answer is yes. Our approach is to incorporate spatial dependence into spatial regime models.[1] This approach incorporates spatial dependence and spatial heterogeneity simultaneously within the spatial regime context. We discuss this approach in this chapter because it builds upon the models covered in Chapters 3 to 5 and is relatively straightforward to understand and apply.

We consider models with both spatial dependence and spatial heterogeneity by incorporating spatial dependence into spatial regime models.

---

[1]Another approach is to build extensions of geographically weighted regression (GWR) by considering spatial dependence within a GWR framework. This has been addressed by Páez, Uchida, and Miyamoto (2002) and Shoff, Chen, and Yang (2014). However, these extensions of GWR are not easy to estimate. Readers who are interested in this approach are referred to the relevant literature.

An approach for simultaneously considering spatial dependence and spatial heterogeneity is to place spatial regression models dealing with spatial dependence within a spatial regime context (Anselin, 1988a, 1990; Chi, 2010a; Patton & McErlean, 2003). In this chapter, we introduce spatial regime models in combination with spatial lag models, spatial error models, and spatial error models with spatially lagged responses.

6.1 SPATIAL REGIME LAG MODELS

We refer to the combination of a spatial regime model and a spatial lag model as a **spatial regime lag model (SRLM)**. An SRLM is specified as

$$Y_r = X_r \beta_r + \rho W_r Y_r + \varepsilon_r \qquad (6.1)$$

where

The **spatial regime lag model (SRLM)** combines the spatial regime model and the spatial lag model.

r denotes the regime for $r = 1, 2, \ldots, m$ and m is the number of regimes;

Y_r is an n_r-by-1 vector of the n_r observations of the response variable in regime r;

X_r is an n_r-by-p design matrix of the explanatory variables in regime r;

β_r is a p-by-1 vector of the regression coefficients in regime r;

W_r is an n_r-by-n_r spatial weight matrix;

$W_r Y_r$ denotes a spatially lagged response variable in regime r in the sense that it is a weighted average of the response variables in the neighborhood;

ρ is a scalar spatial lag parameter; and

ε_r is an n_r-by-1 vector of error terms in regime r, and collectively, ε is an n-by-1 vector of $n = n_1 + n_2 + \ldots + n_m$ error terms that are normally and independently but not necessarily identically distributed.

The terms Y_r, X_r, and β_r are denoted as in a standard linear regression model, but the remainder terms of the model W_r, ρ, and ε_r are not.

Three things should be noted here:

- Because the regression coefficients β vary by r, which indicates the number of regimes, there are r sets of coefficients—one set for each regime.
- The possible neighbors of an areal unit include not only those falling into the same regime but also those falling into other regimes. Because of that,

there will be only one spatial parameter ρ instead of a unique ρ for each regime. The assumption here is that the heterogeneity is in the regression mean but not in the covariance. We make this assumption for the SRLM because the primary interest is in the regression and the lag parameter is to account for the additional, global spatial lag dependence.

- The selection of an appropriate spatial weight matrix can follow the same procedure as for a spatial lag model, for which a more appropriate spatial weight matrix can be the one that captures the maximum spatial dependence of the response variable in combination with a high level of statistical significance, or the one that leads to the best model fitting to data.

6.2 SPATIAL REGIME ERROR MODELS

Let us call the combination of a spatial regime model and a spatial error model a **spatial regime error model (SREM)**. An SREM is specified as

$$Y_r = X_r \beta_r + u_r, \quad u_r = \rho W_r Y_r + \varepsilon_r \tag{6.2}$$

*The **spatial regime error model (SREM)** combines the spatial regime model and the spatial error model.*

where

r denotes the regime for $r = 1, 2, \ldots, m$ and m is the number of regimes;

Y_r is an n_r-by-1 vector of the n_r observations of the response variable in regime r;

X_r is an n_r-by-p design matrix of the explanatory variables in regime r;

β_r is a p-by-1 vector of the regression coefficients in regime r;

u_r is an n_r-by-1 vector of error terms in regime r;

W_r is an n_r-by-n_r spatial weight matrix;

$W_r u_r$ denotes a spatially lagged error term in regime r in the sense that it is a weighted average of the error terms in the neighborhood;

ρ is a scalar spatial error parameter; and

ε_r is an n_r-by-1 vector of error terms in regime r, and collectively, ε is an n-by-1 vector of $n = n_1 + n_2 + \cdots + n_m$ error terms that are normally and independently but not necessarily identically distributed.

The terms Y_r, X_r, and β_r are denoted as in a standard linear regression model, but the remainder terms of the model W_r, ρ, u_r, and ε_r are not.

Three things should also be noted here:

- Because the regression coefficients β vary by *r*, which indicates the number of regimes, there are *r* sets of coefficients—one set for each regime.

- The possible neighbors of an observation include not only those falling into the same regime but also those falling into other regimes. Because of that, there will be only one spatial parameter ρ instead of a unique ρ for each regime. The assumption here is that the heterogeneity is in the regression mean but not in the covariance. We make this assumption for the SREM because the primary interest is in the regression and the spatial parameter ρ is to account for the additional, global spatial error dependence.

- The selection of an appropriate spatial weight matrix can follow the same procedure as for a spatial error model, for which a more appropriate spatial weight matrix can be the one that captures the maximum spatial dependence of the spatial regime model residuals in combination with a high level of statistical significance, or the one that leads to the best model fitting to data.

6.3 SPATIAL REGIME ERROR AND LAG MODELS

We now consider the combination of a spatial regime model and a spatial error model with spatially lagged responses, which will be referred to as a **spatial regime error and lag model (SRELM)**. An SRELM is specified as

$$Y_r = X_r \beta_r + \theta_r W_{1r} Y_r + u_r, u_r = \rho W_{2r} u_r + \varepsilon_r \tag{6.3}$$

where

r denotes the regime for $r = 1, 2, \ldots, m$ and *m* is the number of regimes;

Y_r is an n_r-by-1 vector of the n_r observations of the response variable in regime *r*;

X_r is an n_r-by-*p* design matrix of the explanatory variables in regime *r*;

β_r is a *p*-by-1 vector of the regression coefficients in regime *r*;

W_{1r} is an n_r-by-n_r spatial weight matrix for the response variables;

$W_{1r} Y_r$ is a spatially lagged response variable in regime *r* in the sense that it is a weighted average of the response variables in the neighborhood;

Spatial regime error and lag model is a relatively more flexible model that deals with spatial dependence and spatial heterogeneity simultaneously by considering spatial lag dependence, spatial error dependence, and spatial heterogeneity.

θ_r is a scalar coefficient for the spatially lagged response variables in regime r;

u_r is an n_r-by-1 vector of error terms in regime r;

W_{2r} is an n_r-by-n_r spatial weight matrix for the error terms;

$W_{2r}u_r$ denotes a spatially lagged error term in regime r in the sense that it is a weighted average of the error terms in the neighborhood;

ρ is a scalar coefficient for the spatially lagged error terms; and

ε_r is an n_r-by-1 vector of error terms in regime r, and collectively, ε is an n-by-1 vector of $n = n_1 + n_2 + \cdots + n_m$ error terms that are normally and independently but not necessarily identically distributed.

The terms Y_r, X_r, and β_r are denoted as in a standard linear regression model, but the remaining terms of the model W_{1r}, W_{2r}, θ_r, ρ, u_r, and ε_r are not.

Four things should be noted here:

- Because β and θ vary by r, which indicates the number of regimes, there are r sets of coefficients—one set for each regime.

- Because the spatially lagged response variable ($W_{1r}Y_r$) is treated exogenously as an explanatory variable, there are r sets of coefficients—one set for each regime. This is different from the SRLM in which the spatially lagged response variable is treated endogenously and thus there is only one spatial parameter.

- The possible neighbors of an observation include not only those falling into the same regime but also those falling into other regimes. Because of that, there will be only one spatial parameter ρ instead of a unique ρ for each regime. The assumption here is that the heterogeneity is in the regression mean and spatially lagged response variable but not in the covariance of the spatial errors. We make this assumption for the SRELM because the primary interest is in the regression while the spatial parameter ρ is to account for the additional, global spatial error dependence.

- The selection of an appropriate spatial weight matrix can follow the same procedure as for a spatial error model with spatially lagged responses (SEMSLR): a more appropriate spatial weight matrix for the spatial lag dependence can be the one that captures the maximum spatial dependence of the response variable or the one that leads to the best model fitting to data, and a more appropriate matrix for the spatial error dependence can be the one that captures the maximum spatial dependence of the SRLM residuals or the one that leads to the best model fitting to data.

The SRELM simultaneously considers spatial lag dependence, spatial error dependence, and spatial heterogeneity. Therefore, the SRELM is a relatively more flexible model dealing with both spatial dependence and spatial heterogeneity.

6.4 MODEL FITTING

The SRLM, SREM, and SRELM can be estimated and inferred via maximum likelihood, like their corresponding spatial lag models, spatial error models, and SEMSLRs. Model fitting to data balanced with model parsimony can be measured by Akaike's information criterion (AIC) or Schwartz's Bayesian information criterion (BIC). Refer to Chapter 3 for details.

Similar to diagnostics for spatial regime standard linear regression (SRSLR) models, there are usually three sets of model diagnostics to perform when fitting the SRLM, SREM, or SRELM. The first set includes diagnostics performed after fitting a standard linear regression model, including those for possible multicollinearity, heteroscedasticity, and others. The second set is to detect possibly remaining spatial dependence after accounting for it. The third set of diagnostics tests the differences of each coefficient across subsets of the data (structural stability) and the overall structural stability by the spatial Chow test. Refer to Section 5.2 for details.

6.5 DATA EXAMPLE

Here we continue to use the example of population growth from 2000 to 2010 at the minor civil division (MCD) level in Wisconsin for demonstrating the application of the SRLM, SREM, and SRELM. Essentially, we account for both spatial dependence and spatial heterogeneity in data modeling. The possible spatial dependence includes both spatial lag dependence and spatial error dependence. The possible spatial heterogeneity of the coefficients that explanatory variables have on population growth is dealt with across the urban-rural continuum.

The results of the SRSLR model (Table 5.5) suggest that the explanatory variables have varying associations with population growth and that the spatial variation of the associations is sometimes statistically significant. The diagnostics for the SRSLR residuals (online Appendix B.5 and Figure 5.4) further indicate that there remains statistically significant spatial lag and error dependence after accounting for the spatial heterogeneity. Therefore, we consider a model that accounts for spatial lag and spatial error dependence as well as spatial heterogeneity in the coefficients, which can be achieved by an SRELM. For demonstration purposes, we first apply an SRLM and an SREM.

The results of the SRLM are presented in Table 6.1 and Figure 6.1. Similar to the results of the SRSLR model, the coefficients vary across rural, suburban, and urban areas in terms of the sign, magnitude, and significance. For example, *previous growth* has a negative association with population growth in rural areas but a positive association in suburban and urban areas, the associations are statistically

TABLE 6.1 ● **Results of the spatial regime lag model (SRLM)**

	Rural		Suburban		Urban		Instability
Variable	Coefficient	SE	Coefficient	SE	Coefficient	SE	
Constant	0.041	0.023	0.022	0.046	0.057	0.096	
Previous growth	−0.057*	0.024	0.270***	0.038	0.179	0.113	***
Old	−0.237***	0.063	0.316	0.173	−0.743	0.409	**
Unemployment	−0.156	0.113	−0.211	0.305	0.036	0.907	
Airport	0.246	0.239	0.065	0.137	0.029	0.110	
Forest	−0.047**	0.017	−0.057	0.036	0.102	0.139	
Land developability	0.046*	0.020	−0.011	0.041	0.113	0.076	
Spatial lag	0.234***	0.030					
Measures of fit							
Log-likelihood	1,185.200						
AIC	−2,326.390						
BIC	−2,205.040						
Spatial Chow test	87.75 with 14 degrees of freedom***						
n	1,837						

Note: The 4-nearest neighbor weight matrix is used here. AIC = Akaike's information criterion; BIC = Schwartz's Bayesian information criterion; SE = standard error.

*Significant at the $\alpha = .05$ level. **Significant at the $\alpha = .01$ level. ***Significant at the $\alpha = .001$ level.

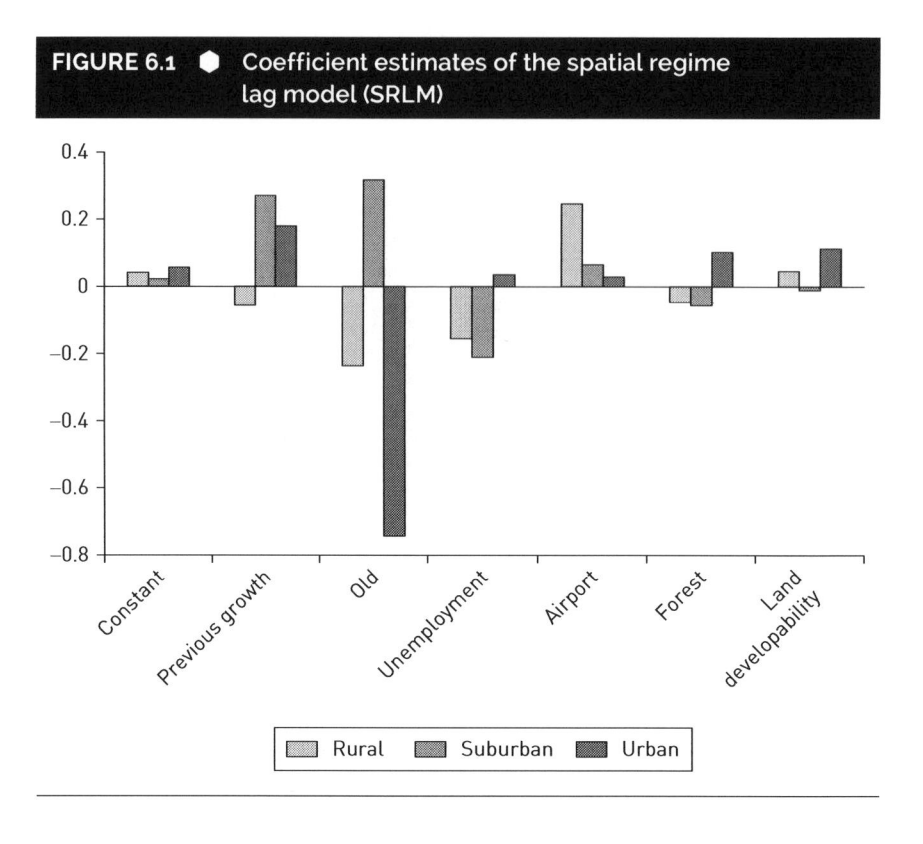

FIGURE 6.1 ● Coefficient estimates of the spatial regime lag model (SRLM)

[Bar chart showing coefficient estimates across Constant, Previous growth, Old, Unemployment, Airport, Forest, and Land developability for Rural, Suburban, and Urban categories. Y-axis ranges from −0.8 to 0.4.]

significant in rural and suburban areas but insignificant in urban areas, and the associations are much larger in suburban areas than in rural areas. The instability of coefficients is statistically significant for previous growth and the old population. Overall, the coefficients across the urban-rural continuum are unstable. The spatial lag dependence has a statistically significant association with population growth. One percent of the weighted neighbor average of population growth is associated with a 0.23 percent population growth, with all the other explanatory variables held constant. Compared to the SRSLM, the incorporation of spatial lag dependence also improves model fitting to data balanced to model parsimony, based on AIC and BIC. Figure 6.2 shows the distribution of the SRSLM residuals. There is no apparent difference of residual distributions between the SRSLM and the standard linear regression models with urban-rural classifications (Figures 5.1 and 5.2).

The results of the SREM are presented in Table 6.2 and Figure 6.3. The results are similar to those generated from the SRLM and the SRSLR model. The explanatory variables have varying associations with population growth across the urban-rural continuum; the spatial variation of the associations is statistically significant for previous growth and the old population. The considered spatial error dependence is

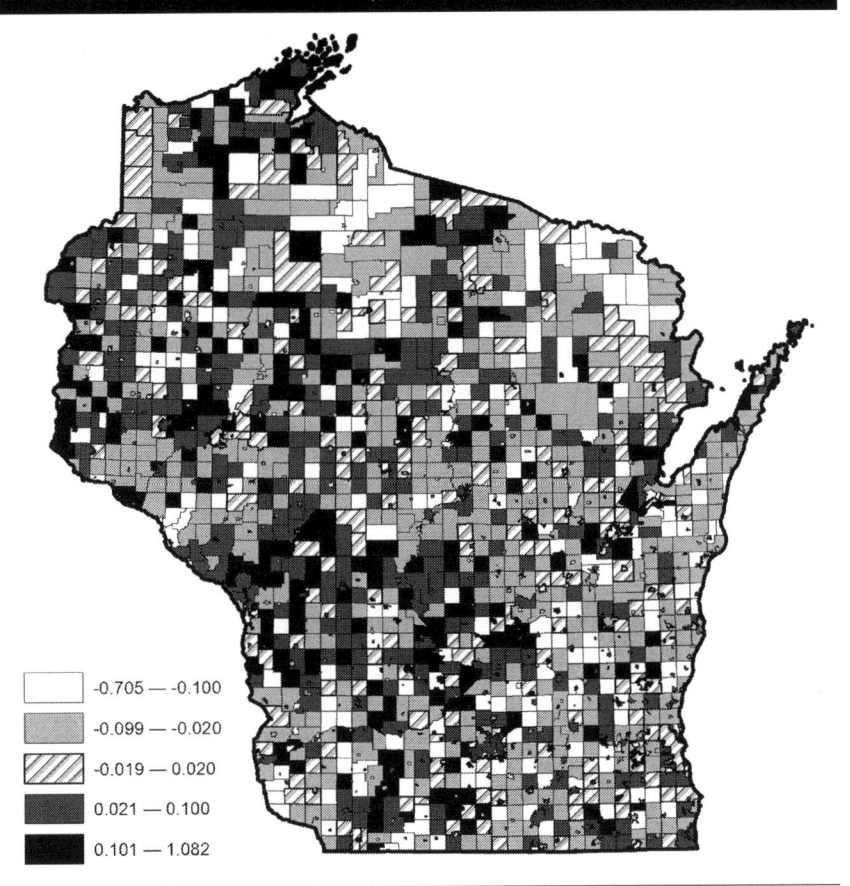

Chapter 6 ■ Models Dealing With Both Spatial Dependence and Spatial Heterogeneity **147**

FIGURE 6.2 ● Residuals of the spatial regime lag model (SRLM)

- ☐ -0.705 — -0.100
- ▨ -0.099 — -0.020
- ▧ -0.019 — 0.020
- ▪ 0.021 — 0.100
- ■ 0.101 — 1.082

TABLE 6.2 ● Results of the spatial regime error model (SREM)

	Rural		Suburban		Urban		Instability
Variable	Coefficient	SE	Coefficient	SE	Coefficient	SE	
Constant	0.050*	0.025	0.070	0.050	0.082	0.104	
Previous growth	−0.077**	0.025	0.262***	0.039	0.195	0.114	***
Old	−0.239***	0.065	0.308	0.175	−0.788	0.436	**
Unemployment	−0.158	0.114	−0.342	0.320	−0.052	0.970	
Airport	0.303	0.278	0.019	0.159	0.020	0.117	
Forest	−0.064***	0.019	−0.071	0.042	0.065	0.174	
Land developability	0.049*	0.022	−0.031	0.044	0.125	0.084	
Spatial error	0.242***	0.031					

(Continued)

TABLE 6.2 ● (Continued)

	Rural	Suburban	Urban	Instability
Measures of fit				
Log-likelihood	1,196.03			
AIC	−2,350.07			
BIC	−2,234.23			
Spatial Chow test	99.50 with 14 degrees of freedom***			
n	1,837			

Note: The 4-nearest neighbor weight matrix is used here. AIC = Akaike's information criterion; BIC = Schwartz's Bayesian information criterion; SE = standard error.

*Significant at the α = .05 level. **Significant at the α = .01 level. ***Significant at the α = .001 level.

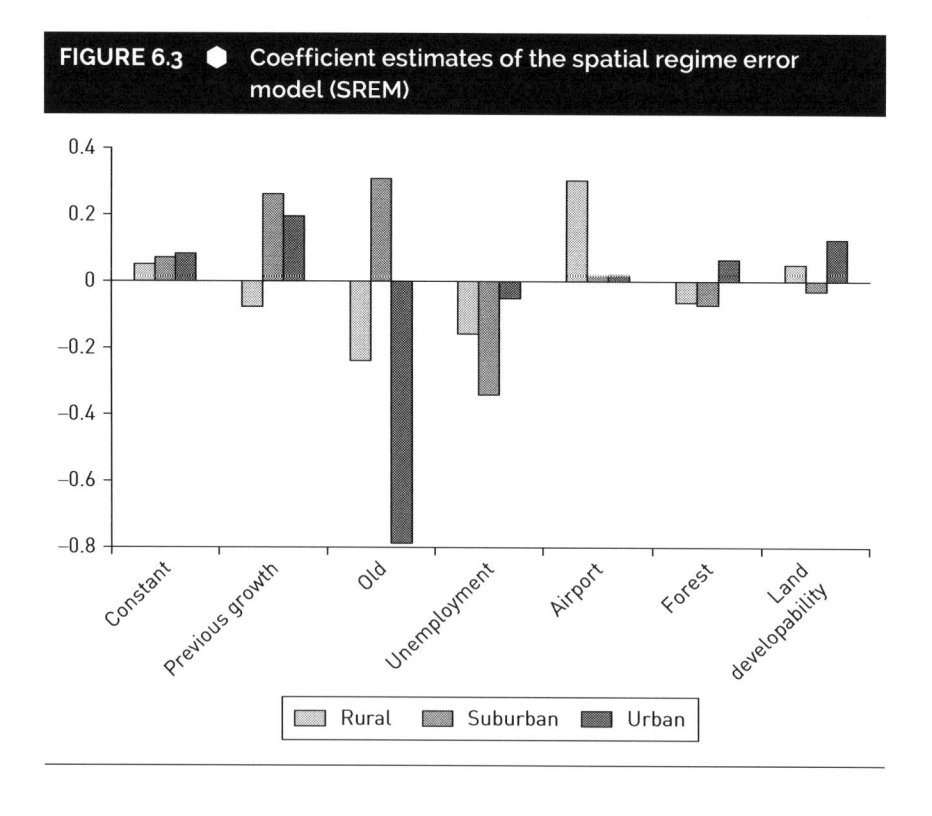

FIGURE 6.3 ● Coefficient estimates of the spatial regime error model (SREM)

statistically significant in associating with population growth. The SREM is better fitted to data than the SRLM and the SRSLR model based on the measures of fit, but it appears that more MCDs have larger residuals (in the absolute term) in the SREM (Figure 6.4) than in the SRLM (Figure 6.2).

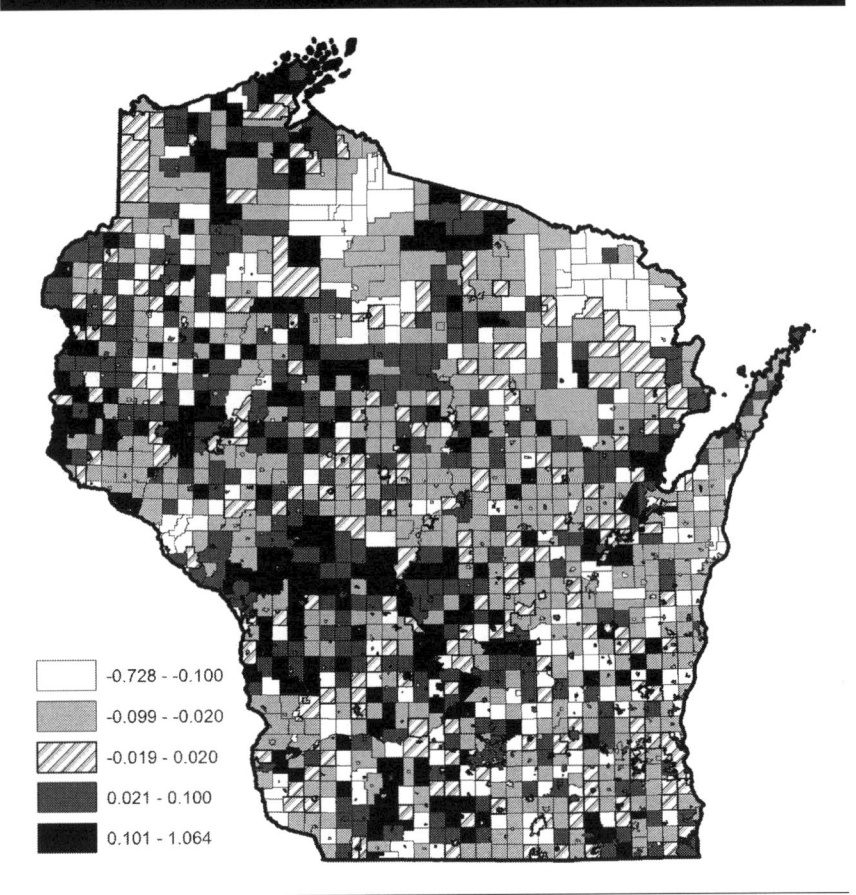

FIGURE 6.4 ● Residuals of the spatial regime error model (SREM)

-0.728 - -0.100
-0.099 - -0.020
-0.019 - 0.020
0.021 - 0.100
0.101 - 1.064

Finally, we fit an SRELM since both spatial lag and error dependence as well as spatial heterogeneity exist in the associations of explanatory variables with the response variable. We need two spatial weight matrices, one for the spatial lag dependence and the other for the spatial error dependence. The 4-nearest neighbor weight matrix (W_1) is selected for the spatial lag dependence as it captures the maximum spatial dependence of population growth. To find a more appropriate spatial weight matrix for the spatial error dependence, we diagnose the potential spatial dependence in the SRLM residuals (online Appendix B.6). The 30-mile general distance weight matrix captures the maximum spatial dependence in the SRLM residuals and thus is used as W_2 (Figure 6.5).

The results of the SRELM are presented in Table 6.3 and Figure 6.6. The SRELM is better fitted to data than any of the previous models based on the

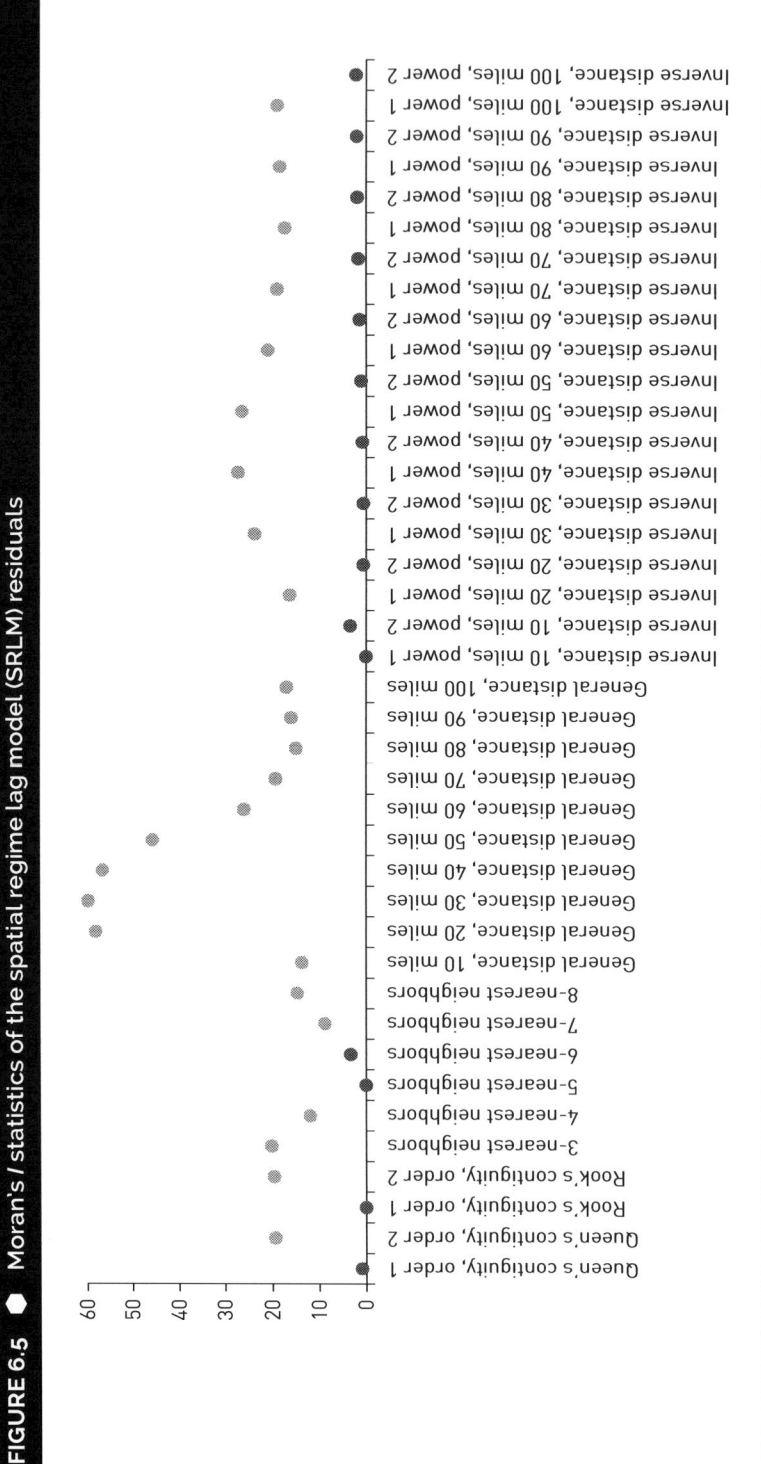

FIGURE 6.5 Moran's *I* statistics of the spatial regime lag model (SRLM) residuals

TABLE 6.3 ● **Results of the spatial regime error and lag model (SRELM)**

	Rural		Suburban		Urban		Instability
Variable	Coefficient	SE	Coefficient	SE	Coefficient	SE	
Constant	0.025	0.025	0.062	0.052	0.162	0.102	
Previous growth	−0.083***	0.025	0.266***	0.038	0.197	0.116***	***
Old	−0.184**	0.066	0.375*	0.176	−0.832*	0.412**	**
Unemployment	−0.169	0.114	−0.309	0.314	−0.556	0.990	
Airport	0.235	0.275	0.053	0.142	0.020	0.110	
Forest	−0.023	0.021	−0.076	0.050	−0.098	0.212	
Land developability	0.040	0.021	−0.034	0.043	0.121	0.079	
Spatial lag	0.268***	0.054	0.264***	0.071	0.024	0.206	
Spatial error	0.578***	0.083					
Measures of fit							
Log-likelihood	1,216.03						
AIC	−2,384.06						
BIC	−2,251.68						
Spatial Chow test	95.41 with 16 degrees of freedom***						
n	1,837						

Note: The 4-nearest neighbor weight matrix is used for W_1 and the 30-mile general distance weight matrix is used for W_2. AIC = Akaike's information criterion; BIC = Schwartz's Bayesian information criterion; SE = standard error.

*Significant at the $\alpha = .05$ level. **Significant at the $\alpha = .01$ level. ***Significant at the $\alpha = .001$ level.

fact that the AIC and BIC values are the smallest among all models covered in the book. The explanatory variables have varying associations with population growth across the urban-rural continuum in terms of sign, magnitude, and significance; the overall variation is statistically significant. The variation of the association of previous growth and the old population is also statistically significant. The spatial lag dependence has a statistically significant association with population growth in rural and suburban areas but not in urban areas. The included spatial error dependence is also statistically significant. The SRELM residuals (Figure 6.7) seem to be smaller than the SRLM and SREM residuals.

FIGURE 6.6 ● Coefficient estimates of the spatial regime error and lag model (SRELM)

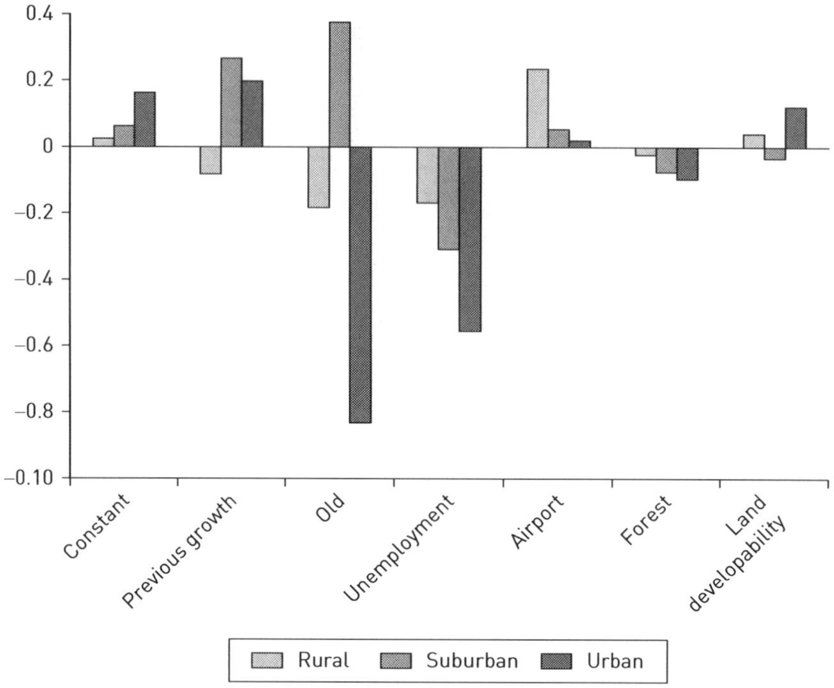
0.4
0.2
0
−0.2
−0.4
−0.6
−0.8
−0.10
Constant
Previous growth
Old
Unemployment
Airport
Forest
Land developability
Rural
Suburban
Urban

Note: The 4-nearest neighbor weight matrix is used for calculating the spatially lagged responses; the 30-mile general distance weight matrix is used for controlling for the spatial error dependence.

FIGURE 6.7 ● Residuals of the spatial regime error and lag model (SRELM)

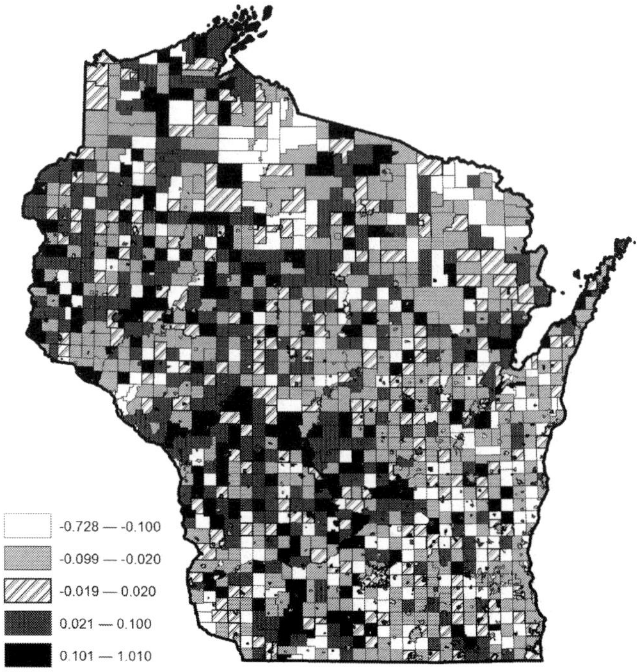
-0.728 — -0.100
-0.099 — -0.020
-0.019 — 0.020
0.021 — 0.100
0.101 — 1.010

Study Questions

1. How could spatial dependence and spatial heterogeneity be modeled simultaneously?

2. How are regimes specified?

3. How is a spatial regime lag model (SRLM) fitted? How is the spatial lag effect interpreted? How are different sets of coefficients across regimes interpreted?

4. How is a spatial regime error model (SREM) fitted? How is the spatial error effect interpreted? How are different sets of coefficients across regimes interpreted?

5. How is a spatial regime error and lag model (SRELM) fitted? How are the spatial lag and spatial error effects interpreted? How are different sets of coefficients across regimes interpreted?

6. What spatial weight matrix or matrices are used in an SRLM, an SREM, or an SRELM?

7. Could an SRLM, an SREM, or an SRELM be used in your research? If so, how might the interpretation of the results help you make a (spatial) theoretical contribution to your area of research?

7

ADVANCED SPATIAL REGRESSION MODELS

> ### LEARNING OBJECTIVES
>
> - Understand how to fit a spatio-temporal regression model, interpret the spatial and/or temporal lag effects, and use appropriate diagnostics to assess the model.
> - Understand how to use spatio-temporal regression models for forecasting purposes.
> - Understand how to use geographically weighted regression models for forecasting purposes.

Previous chapters focus on the spatial aspects of a research problem and deal with data that have spatial information. What if the data are both geographically referenced and longitudinal? Such rich information could be considered in more advanced models. Could we use the spatial and longitudinal nature of the data for forecasting?

In this chapter we first introduce spatio-temporal regression models that consider both spatial and temporal dependence exhibited in the data (Section 7.1). Second, we transform spatial regression models for forecasting purposes (Section 7.2). Third, we introduce a version of the geographically weighted regression (GWR) model that can be used for forecasting purposes (Section 7.3).

7.1 SPATIO-TEMPORAL REGRESSION MODELS

Spatio-temporal regression models refer to regression models that consider both spatial and temporal dependence exhibited in the data. Spatio-temporal regression models can be used to analyze spatial panel data, which are geographically referenced and have observations at each areal unit over multiple time points. Spatio-temporal regression is related to spatial panel data analysis methods, which deal with various aspects of spatial panel data.

Spatio-temporal regression models refer to regression models that consider both spatial and temporal dependence exhibited in the data.

7.1.1 Why Use Spatio-temporal Regression Models?

So far, we have introduced spatial regression models dealing with spatial dependence. These models consider spatial lag dependence and error dependence, either separately or simultaneously. Regarding dependence, the temporal dependence was addressed long before the spatial dependence in the social sciences. Time-series analysis has been used widely to account for the temporal dependence in studies falling into many social science disciplines. Although spatial regression models have received increasing attention among social scientists, time-series analysis is still more familiar to social scientists.

The question of interest here is, what should we do with the temporal dimension when we consider the spatial dimension? Could we simply ignore the temporal dimension in dealing with the spatial dimension? Or should we consider both of the dimensions, but separately? If the data are geographically referenced and have information over multiple time points—data often referred to as **spatial panel data**—it may not be appropriate for us to ignore the temporal dimension. Spatial panel data might exhibit both spatial dependence among observations of areal units at each time point and temporal dependence among observations of each areal unit over time. Such spatial panel data present researchers with various modeling possibilities. Ignoring the temporal or spatial dependence from the data might result in less reliable statistical inference.

Spatial panel data are geographically referenced and have observations at each areal unit over multiple time points.

The question now becomes, is it possible to consider both the spatial and temporal dependence when we conduct analysis? The short answer is yes. There are many approaches for spatial panel data analysis and many versions of spatio-temporal regression models. Here we introduce two approaches that build upon the models dealing with spatial dependence addressed in the previous chapters.

7.1.2 Two General Approaches for Spatio-temporal Regression Modeling

The first approach for spatio-temporal regression modeling is to fit spatial regression models separately for each time point (or period) and then compare the results, especially model parameters (including regression coefficients, variance components, and spatial parameters), across the multiple time points (or periods). However, the temporal dimension is considered only by comparing the temporal difference of model parameters rather than through temporal dependence. Therefore, this approach does not consider both spatial dependence and temporal dependence simultaneously, although it allows us to conduct spatial panel data analysis without knowledge beyond the spatial regression models that we have learned so far—spatial lag models, spatial error models, and spatial error models with spatially lagged responses—while at the same time providing insights into the spatial dependence in the data and the temporal variation of the model parameters.

The second approach for spatio-temporal regression modeling is to formally consider spatial and temporal dependence simultaneously in linear regression models. There are a number of spatio-temporal regression models, and each has different strengths and limitations. For a review of these models, please refer to Elhorst (2001). Based on these models, Elhorst (2001, 2010a) proposed a first-order serial and spatial autoregressive distributed lag model, which is a simple but relatively comprehensive and robust spatio-temporal regression method. In this section, we focus on Elhorst's model.

7.1.3 From Standard Linear Regression to Spatio-temporal Regression

Before we introduce Elhorst's (2001) spatio-temporal linear regression model, let us start with the standard linear regression model and discuss how we can go from a standard linear regression model to a spatio-temporal linear regression model step by step.

A standard linear regression model has two components for the response variable—a linear regression mean involving explanatory variables and a random error term:

$$Y = X\beta + \varepsilon \qquad (7.1)$$

where

Y is an n-by-1 vector of n observations on the response variable,

X is an n-by-p design matrix with a vector of n 1s in the first column for the intercept and $p - 1$ vectors (n-by-1) of explanatory variables in the remaining columns,

β is a p-by-1 vector of regression coefficients, and

ε is an n-by-1 vector of n error terms that are independently and identically distributed as normal distribution with mean 0 and a constant variance.

A spatial lag model has three components for the response variable—a linear regression mean involving explanatory variables, a spatially lagged response variable, and a random error term:

$$Y = X\beta + \rho WY + \varepsilon \qquad (7.2)$$

where

Y is an n-by-1 vector of response variables,

X is an n-by-p design matrix of explanatory variables,

β is a p-by-1 vector of regression coefficients,

W is an n-by-n spatial weight matrix,

ρ is a scalar spatial lag parameter, and

ε is an n-by-1 vector of error terms that are normally and independently but not necessarily identically distributed.

A spatial error model is specified as

$$Y = X\beta + u, u = \rho Wu + \varepsilon \qquad (7.3)$$

where

Y is an n-by-1 vector of response variables,

X is an n-by-p design matrix of explanatory variables,

β is a p-by-1 vector of regression coefficients,

u is an n-by-1 vector of error terms,

W is an n-by-n spatial weight matrix,

ρ is a scalar spatial error parameter, and

ε is an n-by-1 vector of error terms that are normally and independently but not necessarily identically distributed.

With some algebraic manipulation, we can rearrange equation (7.3) to be

$$Y = X\beta + \rho WY - \rho WX\beta + \varepsilon \qquad (7.4)$$

Therefore, a spatial error model has four components for the response variable—a linear regression mean involving explanatory variables, a spatially lagged response variable, spatially lagged explanatory variables, and a random error term.

All the terms in a spatial error model are at the same time point. Let's denote the time point as t. The spatial error model now becomes

$$Y_t = X_t\beta + \rho WY_t - \rho WX_t\beta + \varepsilon_t \qquad (7.5)$$

For each of the four components in the spatial error model specified in equation (7.5), if we add their corresponding temporally lagged components (at time $t-1$) to the right side of the model, it becomes

$$Y_t = X_t\beta + \rho WY_t - \rho WX_t\beta + \tau_1 Y_{t-1} + \\ X_{t-1}\tau_2 + \tau_3 WY_{t-1} + WX_{t-1}\tau_4 + \varepsilon_t \qquad (7.6)$$

where

Y_t is an n-by-1 vector of response variables at time t,

Y_{t-1} is an n-by-1 vector of response variables at time $t-1$,

X_t is an n-by-p design matrix of explanatory variables at time t

β is a p-by-1 vector of regression coefficients for X_t at time t,

X_{t-1} is an n-by-p design matrix of explanatory variables at time $t-1$,

W is an n-by-n spatial weight matrix,

ρ is a scalar spatial parameter,

τ_1 is a scalar coefficient for Y_{t-1} at time $t-1$,

τ_2 is a p-by-1 vector of coefficients for the explanatory variables X_{t-1} at time $t-1$,

τ_3 is a scalar coefficient for WY_{t-1} at time $t-1$,

τ_4 is a p-by-1 vector of coefficients for the explanatory variables WX_{t-1} at time $t-1$, and

ε_t is an n-by-1 vector of error terms.

This model consists of eight components for the response variable—a linear regression mean involving

- explanatory variables,
- a spatially lagged response variable,
- spatially lagged explanatory variables,
- a temporally lagged response variable,
- temporally lagged explanatory variables,
- a spatially and temporally lagged response variable,
- spatially and temporally lagged explanatory variables, and
- a random error term.

Equation (7.6) is the general first-order serial and spatial autoregressive distributed lag model first introduced by Elhorst (2001). It should be noted that our spatio-temporal regression model is specified in different notations from Elhorst's model for the purpose of illustrating how we can go from a standard linear regression model to a spatio-temporal regression model. Elhorst's original model is specified as

$$Y_t = \tau Y_{t-1} + \rho W Y_t + \eta W Y_{t-1} + X_t \beta_1 + X_{t-1} \beta_2 + W X_t \beta_3 + W X_{t-1} \beta_4 + \varepsilon_t \tag{7.7}$$

where

Y_t is an n-by-1 vector of response variables at time t,

Y_{t-1} is an n-by-1 vector of response variables at time $t-1$,

τ is a scalar coefficient for Y_{t-1} at time $t-1$,

ρ is a scalar spatial parameter,

W is an n-by-n spatial weight matrix,

η is a scalar spatial parameter,

X_t is an n-by-p design matrix of explanatory variables at time t,

β_1 is a p-by-1 vector of coefficients for X_t at time t,

X_{t-1} is an n-by-p design matrix of explanatory variables at time $t-1$,

β_2 is a p-by-1 vector of coefficients for X_{t-1} at time $t-1$,

β_3 is a p-by-1 vector of coefficients for the explanatory variables WX_t at time t,

β_4 is a p-by-1 vector of coefficients for the explanatory variables WX_{t-1} at time $t-1$, and

ε_t is an n-by-1 vector of error terms at time t.

Elhorst's (2001) model has three strengths. First, it is a formal spatio-temporal regression model that considers spatial and temporal dependence simultaneously. Second, this model can be modified to a variety of simpler models by assuming one or more of the parameters to be zero; Elhorst derived ten restricted models from the general first-order serial and spatial autoregressive distributed lag model. Third, because this model is companioned with multiple restricted models, they can be compared to determine which one provides the better model fitting to data balanced with model parsimony based on the likelihood ratio test (LRT), Akaike's information criterion (AIC), and Schwartz's Bayesian information criterion (BIC).

It should be noted that there are several other approaches and several more advanced methods for spatio-temporal regression modeling and spatial panel data analysis. For example, Elhorst (2003, 2010a) proposed four spatial panel data models: a fixed-effects spatial lag model, a fixed-effects spatial error model, a random-effects spatial lag model, and a random-effects spatial error model. Readers are referred to these and other methods for a comprehensive review of spatio-temporal regression models (e.g., Anselin, 1988b; Anselin & Bera, 1998; Baltagi & Li, 2004; Cressie, 1993; Elhorst, 2010b; Huang, Wu, & Barry, 2010; Lee & Yu, 2010; LeSage & Pace, 2009). We choose to introduce the Elhorst (2001) model because it falls into the line of spatial regression models as addressed in this book and is relatively straightforward to understand and apply.

7.1.4 How to Fit the Spatio-temporal Regression Model

In addition to building the spatio-temporal regression models (Elhorst, 2001, 2003, 2010a), Elhorst provided code to fit the models using MATLAB.[1] The code, however, might be difficult to understand for those who have little background in coding and MATLAB. Here we propose a relatively easy approach to fit the spatio-temporal regression model (however, it should be noted that Elhorst's code will result in more robust results than our approach).

Essentially, our approach is to fit a spatial error model but at the same time to incorporate a temporally lagged response variable, temporally lagged explanatory variables, and temporally and spatially lagged explanatory variables.

---

[1] www.regroningen.nl/elhorst/software.shtml

A spatial error model at time t is defined as

$$Y_t = X_t\beta + u_t, u_t = \rho W u_t + \varepsilon_t \tag{7.8}$$

If we add the temporally lagged response variable and temporally lagged explanatory variables to the right side of the first part of the model, it becomes

$$Y_t = X_t\beta_1 + \beta_2 Y_{t-1} + X_{t-1}\beta_3 + u_t, u_t = \rho W u_t + \varepsilon_t \tag{7.9}$$

With some algebra, it becomes

$$\begin{aligned}Y_t = {} & Y_{t-1}\beta_2 + \rho W Y_t - \rho\beta_2 W Y_{t-1} + X_t\beta_1 + \\ & X_{t-1}\beta_3 - W X_t \rho\beta_1 - W X_{t-1}\rho\beta_3 + \varepsilon_t\end{aligned} \tag{7.10}$$

This formula corresponds to the terms presented in our spatio-temporal regression model (equation [7.6]) and Elhorst's (2001) general first-order serial and spatial autoregressive distributed lag model (equation [7.7]). It should be noted that our equation (7.10) is more constrained than equation (7.7), but in practice we can fit a spatial error model by adding a temporally lagged response variable and temporally lagged explanatory variables to generate the parameters for a spatio-temporal regression model (Chi & Voss, 2011). The temporally lagged response variable and temporally lagged explanatory variables can be treated on the right side of the model in the same way as other explanatory variables.

Fitting such an "enriched" spatial error model can provide us with estimates of coefficients (β) and the spatial parameter (ρ). With corresponding coefficients and/or the spatial parameter, we can calculate the effect that each term has on the response variable by following Table 7.1.

Which spatial weight matrix is to be used for fitting a spatio-temporal regression model? Because we fit it as an "enriched" spatial error model, which basically is a spatial error model, we can follow the procedure for selecting an appropriate spatial weight matrix for a spatial error model as discussed in Section 3.3. We can first fit a standard linear regression model with the temporally lagged response variable and the temporally lagged explanatory variables included. We can then examine the spatial dependence of the residuals, which can be measured by Moran's I statistic based on a variety of spatial weight matrices. The spatial weight matrix that we deem most appropriate is the one that captures the maximum spatial dependence of the standard linear regression residuals companioned with a high level of statistical significance. Refer to Section 3.3 for more details and cautions in using this approach.

TABLE 7.1 ● The seven effects in a spatio-temporal regression model

Variable	Variable symbol	Effect symbol as in an "enriched" spatial error model (equation [7.10])	Effect symbol in the Elhorst (2001) model (equation [7.7])	Effect symbol as in our spatio-temporal regression model (equation [7.6])
Explanatory variable	X_t	β_1	β_1	β
Spatially lagged response variable	WY_t	ρ	ρ	ρ
Spatially lagged explanatory variable	WX_t	$-\rho\beta_1$	β_3	$-\rho\beta$
Temporally lagged response variable	Y_{t-1}	β_2	τ	τ_1
Temporally lagged explanatory variable	X_{t-1}	β_3	β_2	τ_2
Spatially and temporally lagged response variable	WY_{t-1}	$-\rho\beta_2$	η	τ_3
Spatially and temporally lagged explanatory variable	WX_{t-1}	$-\rho\beta_3$	β_4	τ_4

7.1.5 Data Example

To illustrate the application of the spatio-temporal regression model, we continue using our example that examines population growth from 2000 to 2010 and its relation to its explanatory variables at the minor civil division (MCD) level in Wisconsin. For purposes of simplicity, we use only one explanatory variable, *old* (the percentage of the old population [age sixty-five and older]), in the model. This variable is often found to be associated with population growth in the existing literature (e.g., Humphrey, 1980). In addition, the percentage of the old population in 2000 is a statistically significant variable in all the models that we have fit so far. It has a negative relation to population change; places with a higher percentage of the old population are associated with population decline.

As discussed in this section as well as in previous chapters, the use of different spatial weight matrices could result in different model parameter estimates. One approach to choose an appropriate spatial weight matrix is to choose the matrix that captures the maximum spatial dependence of the standard linear regression residuals companioned with a high level of statistical significance. We first fit a standard linear regression model with population growth from 2000 to 2010 as the response variable and population growth from 1990 to 2000, the old population in 2000, and the old population in 1990 as the explanatory variables. The model residuals are examined for spatial dependence based on Moran's I statistics. Based on Table 7.2, the standard linear regression model residuals having the highest Moran's I value are based on the 4-nearest neighbor weight matrix among forty spatial weight matrices. Thus, the 4-nearest neighbor weight matrix is selected for fitting the "enriched" spatial error model; the results are presented in online Appendix B.7 and Figure 7.1.

The results of Table 7.2 include the estimates of the coefficients of the population growth rate from 1990 to 2000, the old population in 2000, and the old population in 1990, as well as the estimate of a spatial parameter. The distribution of model residuals is shown in Figure 7.2. While we could interpret the estimated coefficients and the spatial parameter companioned with their statistical significance, decomposing them into the seven components as presented in Table 7.1 could provide more meaningful interpretations of the spatial and temporal effects. Therefore, we use the estimates of the coefficients and the spatial parameter in Table 7.2 to evaluate the effect that each term has on the response variable. The results are presented in Table 7.3.

> A spatio-temporal regression model can be decomposed into seven components.

TABLE 7.2 ⬢ Spatio-temporal regression model fitting results based on the 4-nearest neighbor weight matrix

Variable	Coefficient	Standard error
Constant	0.087***	0.010
Previous growth	0.033	0.021
Old 2000	−0.209*	0.087
Old 1990	−0.167*	0.079
Spatial lag (ρ)	0.276***	0.030
Measures of fit		
Log-likelihood	1,127.97	
AIC	−2,247.93	
BIC	−2,225.87	
n	1,837	

Note: AIC = Akaike's information criterion; BIC = Schwartz's Bayesian information criterion.
*Significant at the α = .05 level. ***Significant at the α = .001 level.

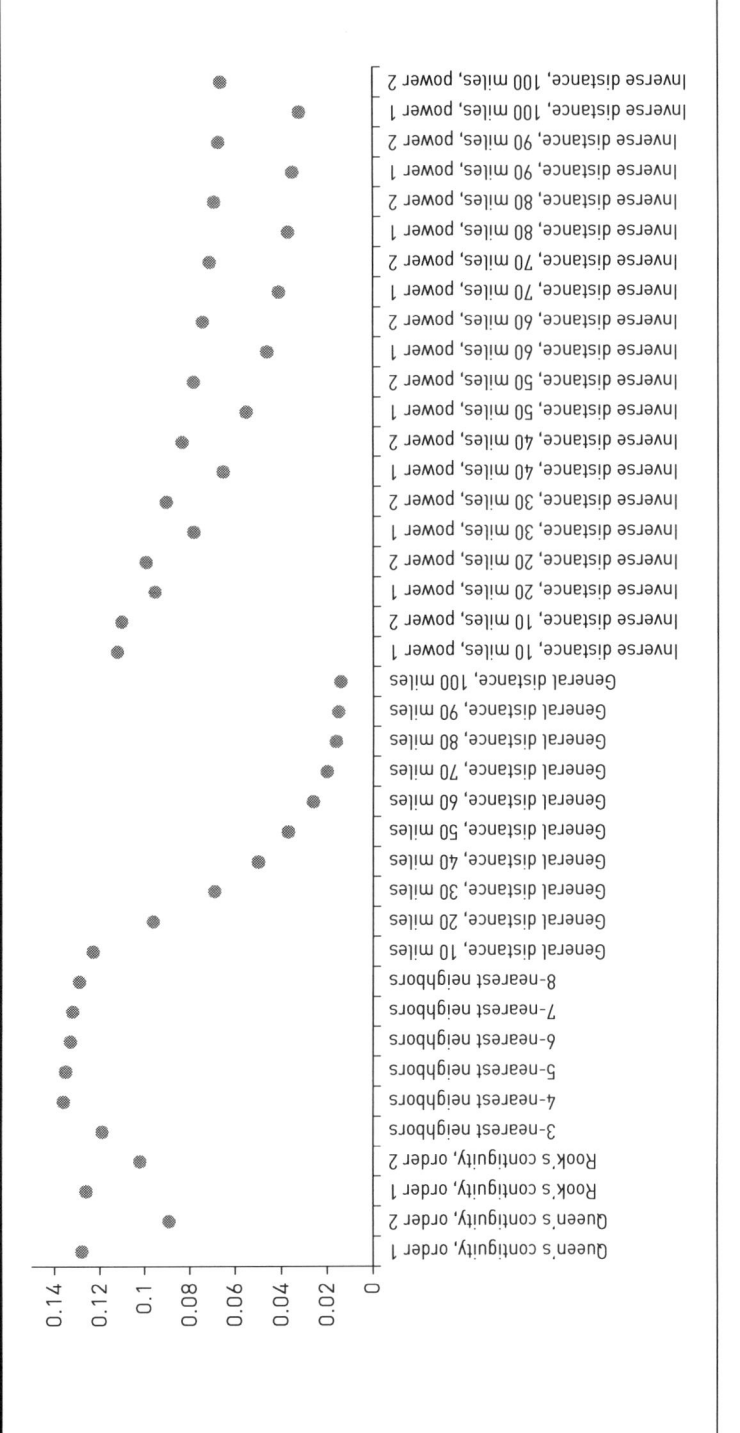

FIGURE 7.1 ● Moran's *I* statistics for residuals of a standard linear regression model

FIGURE 7.2 ● Residuals of the spatio-temporal regression model based on the 4-nearest neighbor weight matrix

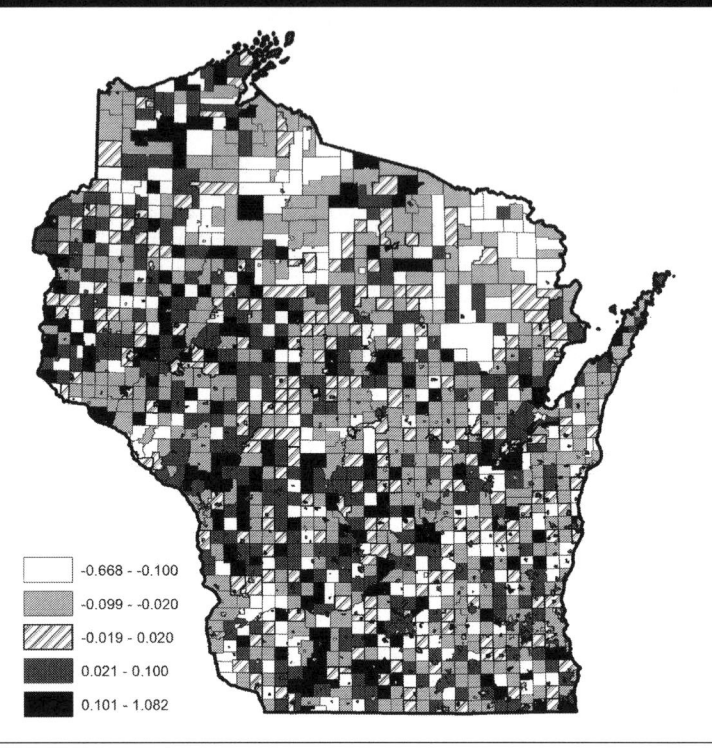

- −0.668 - −0.100
- −0.099 - −0.020
- −0.019 - 0.020
- 0.021 - 0.100
- 0.101 - 1.082

TABLE 7.3 ● The seven effects on population growth in the spatio-temporal regression model

Variable	Variable symbol	Effect symbol as in an "enriched" spatial error model (equation [7.10])	Effect
Old population in 2000	X_t	β_1	−0.209
Neighborhood average of population growth rate 2000–2010	WY_t	ρ	0.276
Neighborhood average of the old population in 2000	WX_t	$-\rho\beta_1$	0.058
Population growth rate 1990–2000	Y_{t-1}	β_2	0.033
Old population in 1990	X_{t-1}	β_3	−0.167
Neighborhood average of population growth rate 1990–2000	WY_{t-1}	$-\rho\beta_2$	−0.009
Neighborhood average of the old population in 1990	WX_{t-1}	$-\rho\beta_3$	0.046

The seven components that are associated with population growth are the old population in 2000 (explanatory variable); neighborhood average of population growth rate from 2000 to 2010 (the spatially lagged response variable); neighborhood average of the old population in 2000 (the spatially lagged explanatory variable); population growth rate from 1990 to 2000 (the previous growth rate, i.e., the temporally lagged response variable); the old population in 1990 (the temporally lagged explanatory variable); neighborhood average of population growth rate from 1990 to 2000 (the spatially and temporally lagged response variable); and neighborhood average of the old population in 1990 (the spatially and temporally lagged explanatory variable). Four components have positive relations with population growth and three components have negative relations with population growth.

By comparing the magnitudes of the associations (based on the absolute values of the estimated coefficients), we observe two notable phenomena. First, variables that are measured at the current time (or period) have stronger associations than those measured with temporal lags. For example, the old population in 2000 has a stronger association with population growth than does the old population in 1990. Neighborhood average of the old population in 2000 has a stronger association with population growth than does that in 1990. Neighborhood average of population growth rate from 2000 to 2010 has a stronger association with population growth than does that from 1990 to 2000. Second, the variables themselves have stronger associations than their corresponding neighborhood averages. For instance, the old population in 2000 has a stronger association with population growth than its neighborhood average does. The old population in 1990 has a stronger association with population growth than its neighborhood average does. Population growth rate from 1990 to 2000 has a stronger association with population growth than its neighborhood average does. Although the spatial and temporal effects are smaller than their corresponding components, the spatial and temporal effects do play strong roles in explaining the response variable and therefore deserve to be considered in the analysis.

7.2 SPATIAL REGRESSION FORECASTING MODELS

Forecasting products for population, school enrollment, transportation demand, energy demand, and many others have been playing important roles in planning, managing, and allocating resources for promoting growth and development and addressing their associated issues (Armstrong, 2001). The methods for forecasting are vast, ranging from extrapolation to expert-based to rule-based to econometric models. However, the potential use of spatial regression methods for forecasting purposes has not received as much attention in social science research. There is value in incorporating spatial effects into the forecasting process of social science phenomena—the spatial effects related to social science phenomena become stronger as the interactions among areal units, near ones or far ones, become more intensive largely due to the innovation and development in transportation and communication tools and international trades (Chi & Wang, 2018).

That said, forecasting models that could be considered "spatial" have been used in social science research, including a spatial regression forecasting approach (Chi & Voss, 2011), a Bayesian statistical approach (e.g., Assunção, Schmertmann, Potter, & Cavenaghi, 2005), an agent-based approach (e.g., Liu et al., 2007), integrated land use models (e.g., Tayman, 1996), spatial microsimulation methods (e.g., Ballas, Clarke, & Wiemers, 2005), and grid cell-based forecasting (e.g., Riahi & Nakicenovic, 2007). Refer to Chi (2009) and Wilson and Rees (2005) for a review of the literature. In the context of spatial regression models, this section focuses on spatial regression forecasting models.

7.2.1 What Is a Standard Regression Forecasting Model?

To begin, let us start with a standard regression forecasting model, which is using a regression approach for forecasting. A standard regression forecasting method proceeds in two steps. In step 1, it establishes a relation between the response variable and its explanatory variables measured at an earlier time point, because forecasting is to project the future with current and past information. The first part of a regression forecasting model is specified as

$$Y_t = \alpha Y_{t-1} + X_{t-1} \beta + \varepsilon_t \tag{7.11}$$

where

Y_t is an n-by-1 vector of response variables at time t,

Y_{t-1} is an n-by-1 vector of response variables at time $t - 1$,

α is a scalar coefficient for Y_{t-1} at time $t - 1$,

X_{t-1} is an n-by-p design matrix of explanatory variables at time $t - 1$,

β is a p-by-1 vector of regression coefficients for X_{t-1} at time $t - 1$, and

ε_t is an n-by-1 vector of error terms.

The reason for including Y_{t-1} is that the target to be forecasted, the response variable, is often affected by its previous existence and thus is often used in regression forecasting models.

In step 2, we use the estimated coefficients, the explanatory variables at time t, and the response variable at time t to forecast the response variable at time $t + 1$.

$$\hat{Y}_{t+1} = \hat{\alpha} Y_t + X_t \hat{\beta} \qquad (7.12)$$

where

$\hat{Y}_{t+1}$ is an n-by-1 vector of forecasted response variables at time $t + 1$,

Y_t is an n-by-1 vector of observed response variables at time t,

X_t is an n-by-p design matrix of observed explanatory variables at time t, and

$\hat{\alpha}$ and $\hat{\beta}$ are the estimates of the coefficients from fitting the model specified in equation (7.11).

The critical assumption is that the relations between the explanatory variables and the response variable, established in the base period (step 1), hold over time and can thus be used to forecast the response variable beyond the base period where the relations (the estimated coefficients) are established.

7.2.2 What Is a Spatial Regression Forecasting Model?

A **spatial regression forecasting** model can be built by adding the spatially lagged terms to the standard regression forecasting model. Let us start with the spatial error model as addressed in Section 3.3. The first part of the spatial error model equation (equation [3.3]) can be written as

To build a **spatial regression forecasting model**, we can add the spatially lagged terms to a standard regression forecasting model.

$$u = Y - X\beta \qquad (7.13)$$

Putting equation (7.13) into the second part of equation (3.3) generates

$$Y = X\beta + \rho WY - \rho WX\beta + \varepsilon \qquad (7.14)$$

On the right side of the model, there are explanatory variables (X), weighted averages of the response variables in the neighborhood (WY), and weighted averages of the explanatory variables in the neighborhood (WX). These variables are in the same time point as the response variable (Y):

$$Y_t = X_t \beta + \rho WY_t - \rho WX_t \beta + \varepsilon \qquad (7.15)$$

If we add temporally lagged terms of each of the four terms to the right side of the model, it becomes

$$Y_t = X_t\beta + \rho WY_t - \rho WX_t\beta + \tau_1 Y_{t-1} + X_{t-1}\tau_2 + \tau_3 WY_{t-1} - WX_{t-1}\tau_4 + \varepsilon_t \quad (7.16)$$

This is a general first-order serial and spatial autoregressive distributed lag model developed by Elhorst (2001, 2010a) and discussed in Section 7.1. However, for forecasting purposes, we cannot have the explanatory variables in the same time point as the response variable because we are forecasting the future that is unknown. By dropping the explanatory variables measured in time t from the right side of equation (7.16), we get a spatial regression forecasting model:

$$Y_t = \rho WY_t + \tau_1 Y_{t-1} + X_{t-1}\tau_2 + \tau_3 WY_{t-1} - WX_{t-1}\tau_4 + \varepsilon_t \quad (7.17)$$

This model can also be written as

$$Y_t = (I - \rho W)^{-1}(\tau_1 Y_{t-1} + X_{t-1}\tau_2 + \tau_3 WY_{t-1} - WX_{t-1}\tau_4 + \varepsilon_t) \quad (7.18)$$

where I is an identity matrix.

Now, all the terms on the right side of equation (7.18) are temporally lagged and include

- the temporally lagged response variable (Y_{t-1}),
- temporally lagged explanatory variables (X_{t-1}),
- the temporally lagged weighted average of the response variable in the neighborhood (WY_{t-1}), and
- the temporally lagged weighted average of the explanatory variables in the neighborhood (WX_{t-1}).

This model can be used for forecasting purposes by following the two steps for the standard regression forecasting model.

Furthermore, the term ρWY_t can be dropped from equation (7.17), resulting in a simpler spatial regression forecasting model (Chi & Voss, 2011):

$$Y_t = \tau_1 Y_{t-1} + X_{t-1}\tau_2 + \tau_3 WY_{t-1} - WX_{t-1}\tau_4 + \varepsilon_t \quad (7.19)$$

This model is used for illustrating the data example in this section by following the two steps for the standard regression forecasting model.

7.2.3 What Spatial Weight Matrices Should We Use in a Spatial Regression Forecasting Model?

There are no strict rules about the selection of spatial weight matrices because the spatial regression forecasting model is estimated exogenously and is less like a formal spatial regression model and more like a spatial cross-regressive model (addressed in Section 4.2). We could identify an appropriate spatial weight matrix for each temporally lagged variable based on their corresponding spatial dependence as measured by Moran's I.

7.2.4 Practical Considerations in Forecasting

In practice, regression forecasting is often followed by forecast adjustments and evaluations. Forecast adjustments modify the forecasting results by using existing information to improve the performance of forecasting. Forecast evaluations are often conducted to assess the performance of the forecasting (with statistical measures such as the mean algebraic percent error, the mean absolute percent error, and the root mean squared percent error), which informs users of the accuracy of the forecasting. These practical perspectives should be considered in spatial regression forecasting as well. In this section, we focus on the model rather than practical perspectives. The practical perspectives can be found in a large body of literature (e.g., Alho & Spencer, 2005; Armstrong, 2001; Chi, 2009; Pittenger, 1976; Smith et al., 2013).

7.2.5 Data Example

To illustrate the use of spatial regression forecasting models, we continue to use our example of population growth from 2000 to 2010 at the MCD level in Wisconsin. We also continue to use the explanatory variables that were used in the previous chapters, which are *previous growth, old, unemployment, airport, forest,* and *land developability*. We use population growth rate rather than population size as the response variable because the explanatory variables mentioned are more closely related to population growth rate than population size (Chi, 2009). Based on the forecasted population growth rate, we can calculate the forecasted population size.

First, we select an appropriate spatial weight matrix for each of the explanatory variables based on their corresponding spatial dependence (online Appendix B.8). Appropriate spatial weight matrices are the 5-nearest neighbor weight matrix for *previous growth* (Figure 7.3), the 10-mile general distance weight matrix for *old*, the first-order rook's contiguity weight matrix for *unemployment*, the 3-nearest neighbor weight matrix for *airport*, the first-order rook's contiguity weight matrix for *forest*, and the first-order queen's contiguity weight matrix for *land developability*.

The selection of spatial weight matrices does not have strict restrictions because spatial regression forecasting models are estimated exogenously and are similar to spatial cross-regressive models.

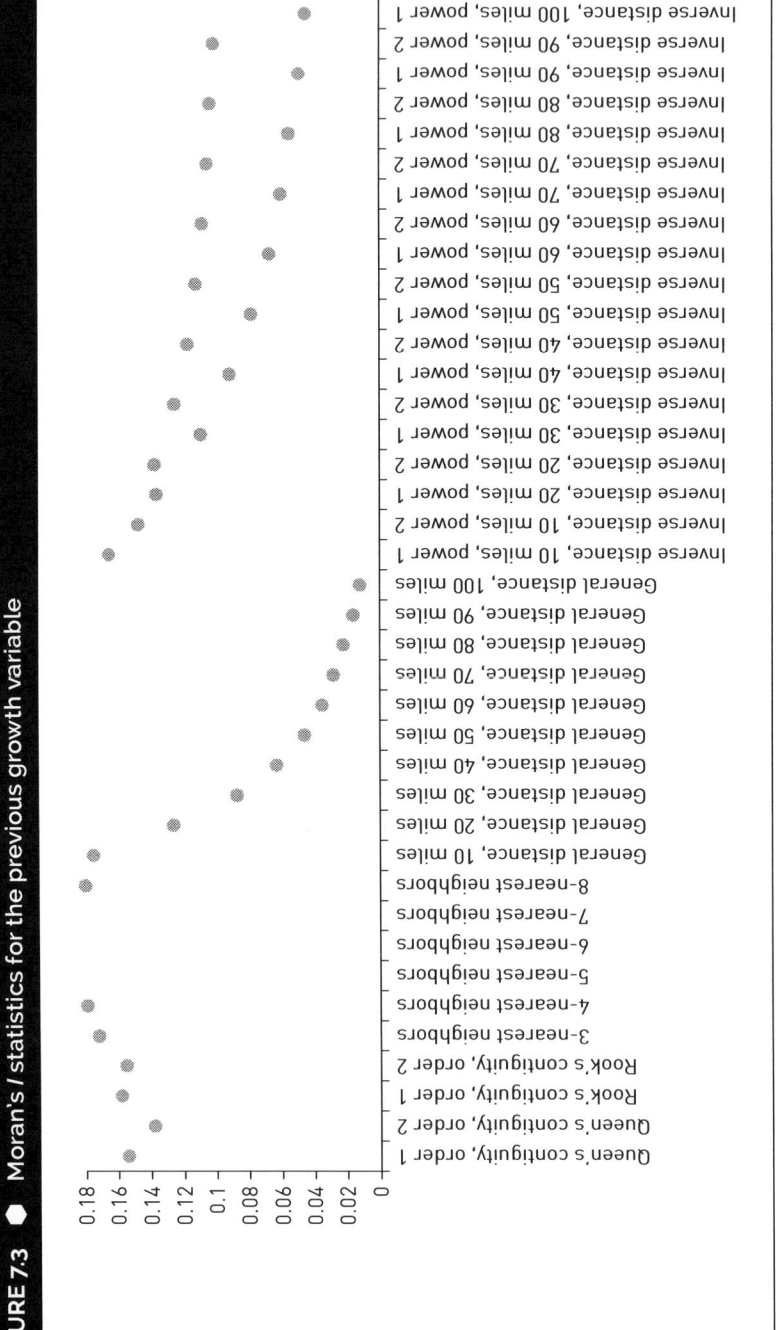

FIGURE 7.3 Moran's *I* statistics for the previous growth variable

These weight matrices are used to calculate their corresponding spatially lagged explanatory variables.

Second, we estimate the relation of population growth from 1990 to 2000 to population growth from 1980 to 1990, spatially lagged population growth from 1980 to 1990, explanatory variables in 1990, and spatially lagged explanatory variables in 1990 (equation [7.20]). To eliminate any background change in processes of population redistribution, the intercept, a constant term that is identical for all MCDs and indicates the overall growth rate, is excluded from the regression model. This exclusion forces the overall growth rate into the coefficients of explanatory variables (Chi, 2009). The regression results are presented in Table 7.4, and the model residuals are shown in Figure 7.4.

$$Y_{1990-2000} = \alpha Y_{1980-1990} + X_{1990}\beta + \lambda W Y_{1980-1990} + W X_{1990}\rho + \varepsilon \quad (7.20)$$

TABLE 7.4 ● **Model-fitting results of initial spatial regression**

Variable	Coefficient	SE
Previous growth	0.230***	0.029
Old	0.105	0.065
Unemployment	0.057	0.101
Airport	−0.089	0.116
Forest	0.152***	0.031
Land developability	0.030	0.023
Spatially lagged previous change	0.627***	0.050
Spatially lagged old	0.207	0.112
Spatially lagged unemployment	−0.171	0.168
Spatially lagged airport	0.179	0.144
Spatially lagged forest	−0.134***	0.038
Spatially lagged land developability	0.033	0.026
Measures of fit		
Log-likelihood	1,005.240	
AIC	−1,986.480	
BIC	−1,920.290	
n	1,837	

Note: AIC = Akaike's information criterion; BIC = Schwartz's Bayesian information criterion; SE = standard error.

***Significant at the α = .001 level.

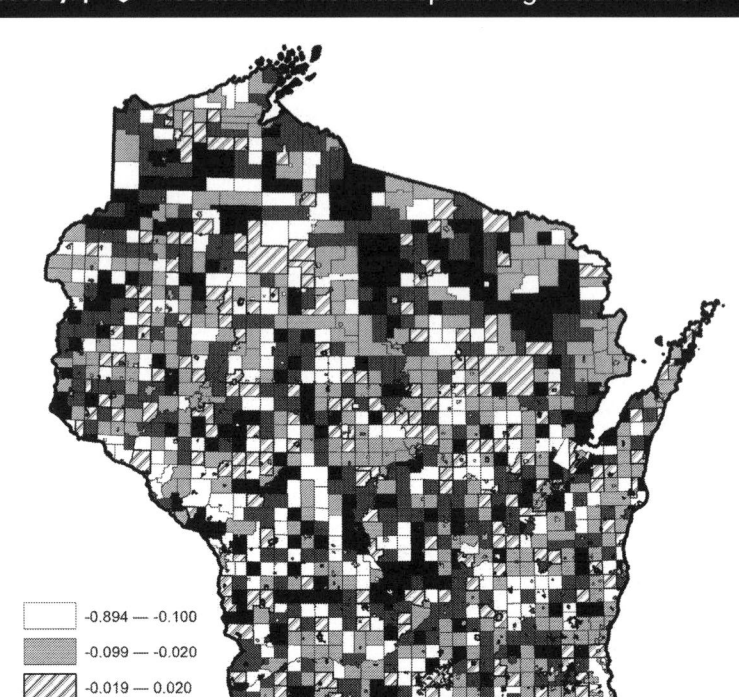

FIGURE 7.4 ● Residuals of the initial spatial regression model

Legend:
- -0.894 — -0.100
- -0.099 — -0.020
- -0.019 — 0.020
- 0.021 — 0.100
- 0.101 — 1.082

Third, explanatory variables showing lower levels of significance are discarded from the regression model until all variables become statistically significant at the α = .10 level. The results for the final spatial regression are presented in Table 7.5, and the model residuals are shown in Figure 7.5. It should be noted that the selection of an α-value as the threshold for including or excluding variables follows the backward elimination approach (Agresti & Finlay, 2009) but is arbitrary. A practical idea is to select a set of explanatory variables that includes neither too many nor too few—too many would not be easily handled in a forecasting process, and too few would lose the explanatory power and reduce the forecasting accuracy (Chi, 2009). Selecting a balanced number of explanatory variables maintains a reasonable accuracy and workload for interpretation and estimation.

TABLE 7.5 ● Model-fitting results of final spatial regression

Variable	Coefficient	SE
Previous growth	0.237***	0.029
Old	0.111	0.062
Forest	0.142***	0.031

Variable	Coefficient	SE
Spatially lagged previous change	0.665***	0.050
Spatially lagged old	0.562***	0.075
Spatially lagged forest	−0.166***	0.036
Measures of fit		
Log-likelihood	993.254	
AIC	−1,974.510	
BIC	−1,941.410	
n	1,837	

Note: AIC = Akaike's information criterion; BIC = Schwartz's Bayesian information criterion; SE = standard error.

***Significant at the $\alpha = .001$ level.

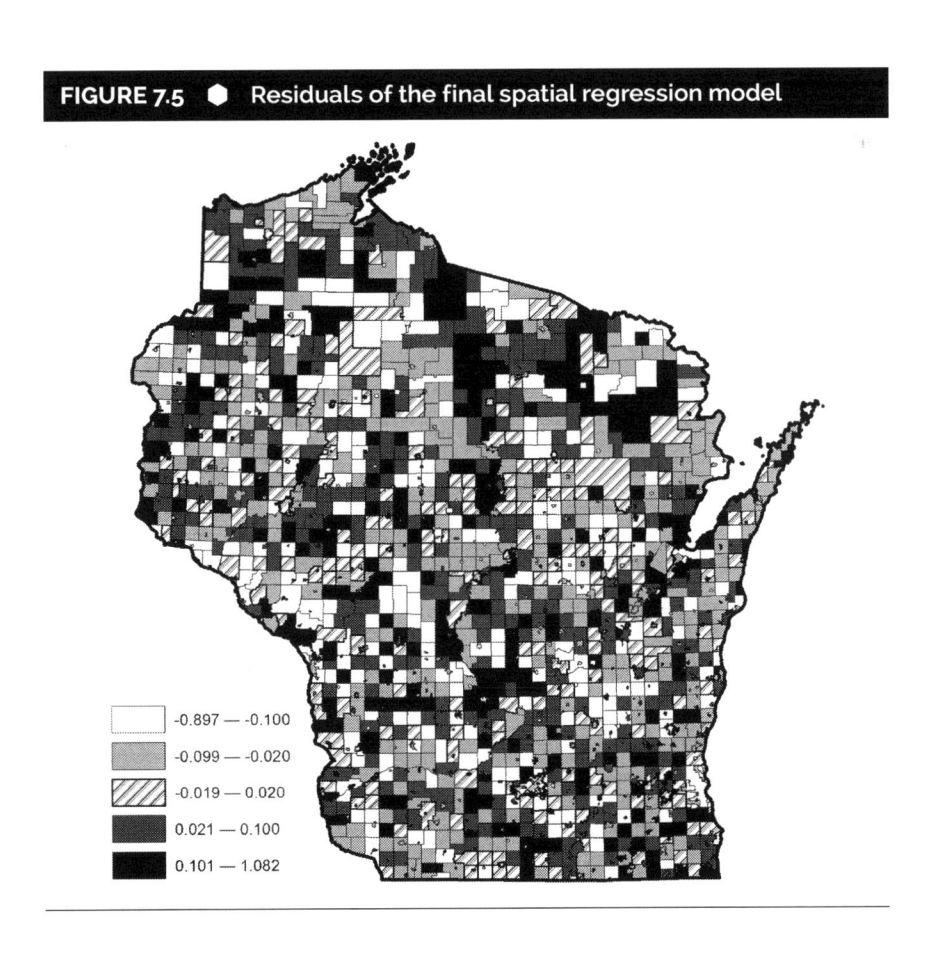

FIGURE 7.5 ● Residuals of the final spatial regression model

Fourth, we calculate the population growth rate from 2000 to 2010 based on equation (7.21) by using the estimated coefficients, population growth from

1990 to 2000, spatially lagged population growth from 1990 to 2000, explanatory variables in 2000, and spatially lagged explanatory variables in 2000.

$$\hat{Y}_{2000-2010} = \hat{\alpha} Y_{1990-2000} + X_{2000}\hat{\beta} + \hat{\lambda} WY_{1990-2000} + WX_{2000}\hat{\rho} \qquad (7.21)$$

Finally, based on the predicted population growth rate from 2000 to 2010 and the population size in 2000, we can calculate the predicted 2010 population size. As a "golden" standard in the field of applied demography, the accuracy of population projections should be evaluated (Chi, 2009; Smith et al., 2013). We can compare the predicted 2010 population to the 2010 census-based population estimate by applying quantitative measures such as mean percentage error, mean absolute percentage error, and root mean squared percentage errors. Here we focus on introducing spatial regression models and thus do not provide the evaluation results. Interested readers can refer to the population projection literature (e.g., Chi, 2009; Chi & Voss, 2011; Chi & Wang, 2018).

7.3 GEOGRAPHICALLY WEIGHTED REGRESSION FOR FORECASTING

7.3.1 The Methods

Just as spatial lag and spatial error models can be used for forecasting purposes (Section 7.2), geographically weighted regression (GWR) can be used for forecasting as well. The basic idea is to apply the parameters estimated from the observation period to the model in the forecasting period. This is typically done in two steps.

In step 1, we establish a relation between the response variable and its explanatory variables measured at an earlier time point, because forecasting is projecting the future with current and past information. The first part of a GWR forecasting model is specified as

$$y_{it} = \sum_{k=1}^{p} \beta_{k(t-1)}(u_i, v_i) \cdot x_{ik(t-1)} + \theta_{t-1}(u_i, v_i) \cdot y_{i(t-1)} + \varepsilon_{it} \qquad (7.22)$$

where

i indexes the ith areal unit in space;

t indexes the time point t;

$t-1$ indexes the previous time point $t-1$;

y_{it} denotes the response variable for the ith areal unit at time t;

k indexes the explanatory variable, including the intercept ($k = 1$);

p denotes the number of explanatory variables, including the intercept ($k = 1$),

(u_i, v_i) denotes the coordinates of the centroid of the ith areal unit in space;

$x_{ik \cdot (t-1)}$ denotes the kth explanatory variable for the ith areal unit at time $t - 1$;

$y_{i \cdot (t-1)}$ denotes the response variable for the ith areal unit at time $t - 1$;

$\beta_{k \cdot (t-1)}(u_i, v_i)$ denotes a continuous function $\beta_k(u,v)$ at areal unit i at time $t - 1$;

$\theta_{t-1}(u_i, v_i)$ denotes a continuous function $\theta(u,v)$ at areal unit i at time $t - 1$; and

ε_{it} denotes the ith error at time t, and the error terms are independently and identically distributed as normal distribution with mean 0 and a constant variance.

We include $y_{(t-1)}$ because the target to be forecasted, the response variable, is often affected by its previous existence, which is often used in regression forecasting models.

If any variable on the right-hand side of the model does not exhibit spatial heterogeneity, we refit the model by treating that variable's effects as spatially homogeneous, which would result in a global coefficient (that is, a single coefficient value) for that particular variable.

In step 2, we use the estimated coefficients, the explanatory variables at time t, and the response variable at time t to forecast the response variable at time $t + 1$:

$$\hat{y}_{i(t+1)} = \sum_{k=1}^{p} \hat{\beta}_{k \cdot t}(u_i, v_i) \cdot x_{i \cdot k \cdot t} + \hat{\theta}_t(u_i, v_i) \cdot y_{i \cdot t} \qquad (7.23)$$

where

$\hat{y}_{i(t+1)}$ is the response variable for the ith areal unit at time $t + 1$,

$y_{i \cdot t}$ is the response variable for the ith areal unit at time t,

$x_{i \cdot k \cdot t}$ is the kth explanatory variable for the ith areal unit at time t,

$\hat{\beta}_{k \cdot t}(u_i, v_i)$ are coefficients estimated from step 1, and

$\hat{\theta}_t(u_i, v_i)$ is the coefficient estimated from step 1.

7.3.2 Data Example

To illustrate the use of GWR for population forecasting, we continue to use our example of population growth from 2000 to 2010 at the MCD level in Wisconsin. The procedure for using the GWR method for population forecasting is similar to those for using standard regression and spatio-temporal regression methods (Section 7.2). In general, a regression forecasting approach is composed of four steps:

1. estimating the parameters in the observation period (typically by moving the time point backward),
2. applying the estimated parameters to the projection period for population projection,
3. adjusting the projection based on established practical procedures (Chi, 2009), and
4. evaluating the performance of the projection by comparing the projected population to the actual population.

As our purpose here is to demonstrate the use of the GWR method for population projection rather than to develop a better-performing population projection method, we focus on only the first two steps.

In step 1, we fit a GWR forecasting model to the data in the observation period. The response variable is population growth from 1990 to 2000, and the explanatory variables are measured in 1990, including *previous growth* (population growth rate from 1980 to 1990), *old* (the percentage of the old population [sixty-five and older] in 1990), *unemployment* (unemployment rate in 1990), *airport* (proximity to the nearest major commercial airport), *forest* (the percentage of forest coverage), and *land developability* (the percentage of land available for development), in the function of

$$y_{i.(1990-2000)} = \sum_{k=1}^{p} \beta_k(u_i, v_i) . x_{ik.1990} + \theta(u_i, v_i) . y_{i.(1980-1990)} + \varepsilon_i \qquad (7.24)$$

Table 7.6 presents the descriptive statistics of the coefficients for each explanatory variable. As indicated by the diff-criterion, two variables (*airport* and *land developability*) do not exhibit spatially heterogeneous associations with population growth. Thus, we treat their associations as spatially homogeneous and reapply a GWR to the data. Table 7.7 presents the results for the refined GWR model. The local coefficients and their t-values for each explanatory variable are shown in Figure 7.6 and Figure 7.7, respectively. The local R^2 is illustrated in Figure 7.8.

In step 2, we use the estimated parameters (including the local coefficients and global coefficients) to project population growth in 2000 to 2010. The explanatory variables are measured in 2000. The function for the projection is

$$\hat{y}_{i.(2000,2010)} = \sum_{k=1}^{p} \hat{\beta}_k(u_i, v_i) . x_{i.k.2000} + \hat{\theta}(u_i, v_i) . y_{i.(1990-2000)} \qquad (7.25)$$

Based on the predicted population growth rate from 2000 to 2010 and the population size in 2000, we can forecast the 2010 population size.

TABLE 7.6 ● GWR forecasting initial model

Variable	Minimum	Lower quartile	Median	Upper quartile	Maximum	Diff-criterion
Constant	−0.552	−0.081	0.030	0.148	0.327	−17.596
Previous growth	−1.033	−0.307	−0.054	0.221	1.095	−12.597
Old	−5,036.870	−289.074	70.777	677.984	22,353.330	5.296
Unemployment	−0.250	0.059	0.238	0.421	0.779	−29.670
Airport	−3.760	−0.386	0.008	0.477	2.008	−14.172
Forest	−0.379	−0.006	0.118	0.257	0.685	−26.634
Land developability	−0.185	−0.039	0.037	0.112	0.308	7.719
Measures of fit						
Adjusted R^2	0.225					
AIC	−2,060.377					
Bandwidth size	165					
n	1,837					

Note: Positive value of the diff-criterion suggests no spatial variability in terms of model selection criteria. Bandwidth size refers to the number of nearest neighbors. AIC = Akaike's information criterion.

TABLE 7.7 ● GWR forecasting final model

Variable	Minimum	Lower quartile	Median	Upper quartile	Maximum
Local variables					
Constant	−0.036	0.085	0.117	0.162	0.239
Previous growth	0.034	0.171	0.276	0.432	0.569
Old	−0.565	−0.278	−0.136	−0.002	0.406
Unemployment	−1.979	−0.263	0.031	0.284	0.711
Forest	−0.113	0.025	0.113	0.159	0.409
Global variables	Estimate	SE			
Airport	−62.635	94.965			
Land developability	−0.035	0.031			
Measures of fit					
Adjusted R^2	0.142				
AIC	−1,942.71				
Bandwidth size	454				
n	1,837				

Note: Bandwidth size refers to the number of nearest neighbors. AIC = Akaike's information criterion; SE = standard error.

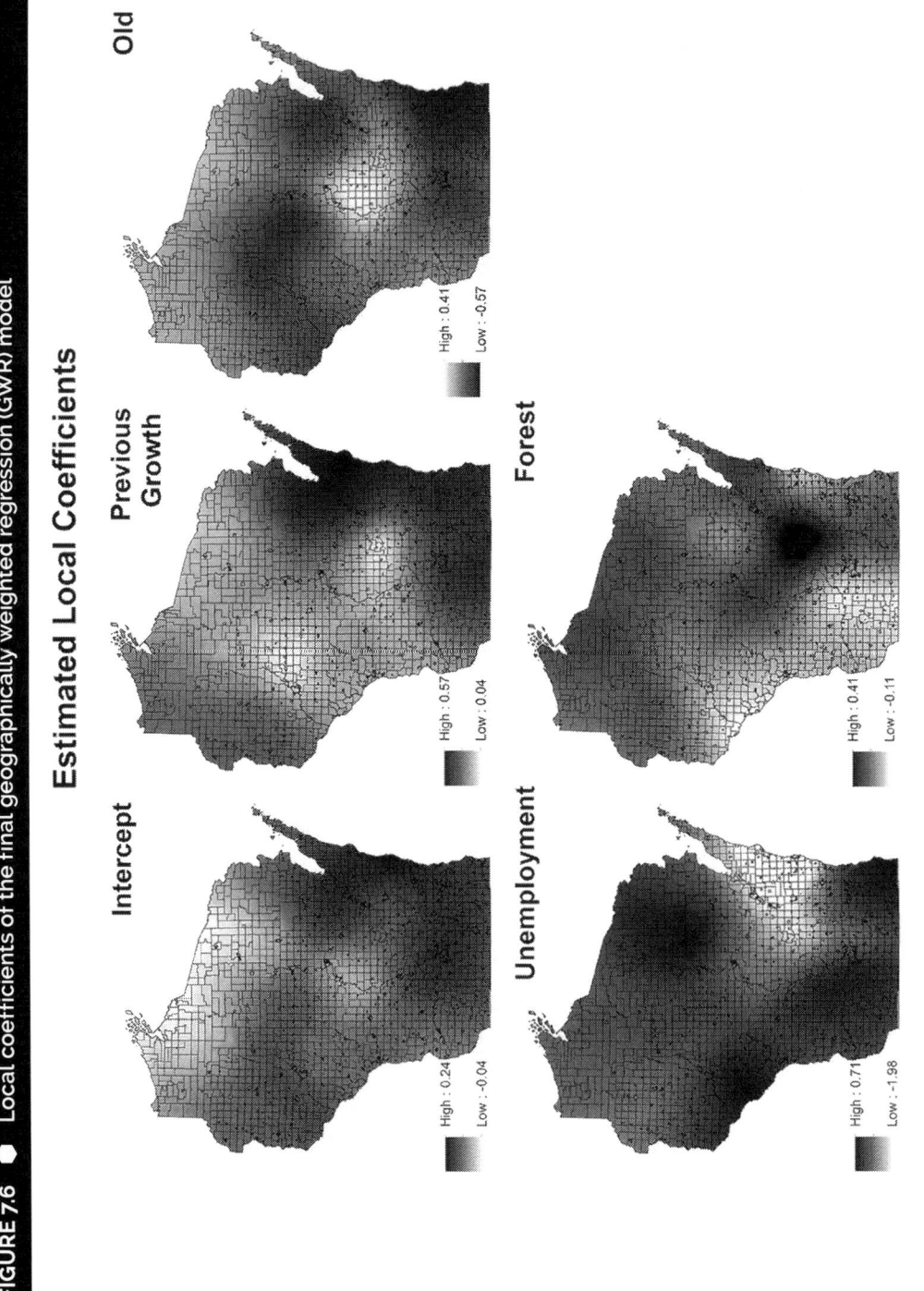

FIGURE 7.6 Local coefficients of the final geographically weighted regression (GWR) model

Estimated Local Coefficients

Intercept
High: 0.24
Low: -0.04

Previous Growth
High: 0.57
Low: 0.04

Old
High: 0.41
Low: -0.57

Unemployment
High: 0.71
Low: -1.98

Forest
High: 0.41
Low: -0.11

FIGURE 7.7 The *t*-values of the final geographically weighted regression (GWR) coefficients

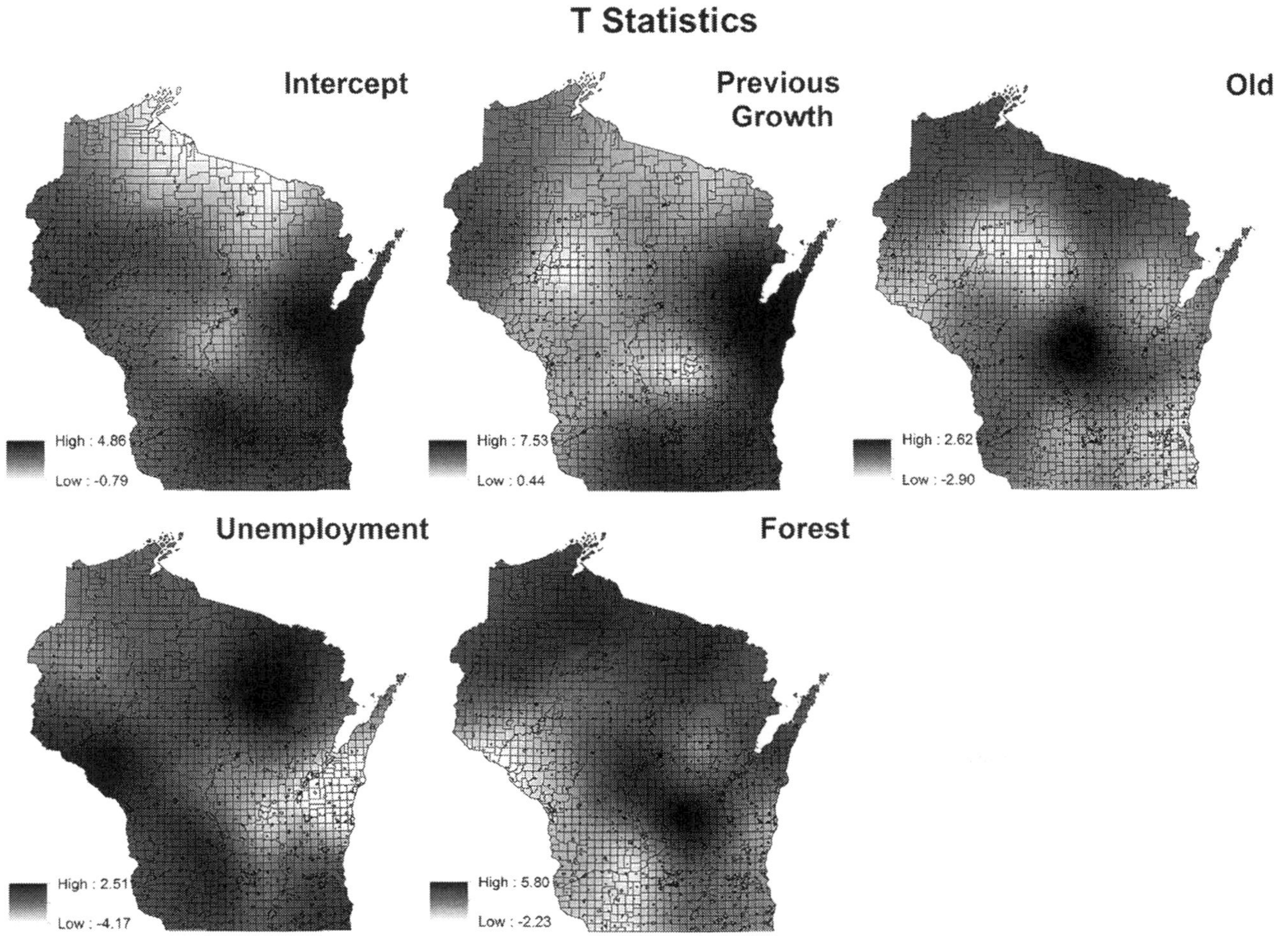

FIGURE 7.8 ● Local R^2 of the geographically weighted regression (GWR) model

Local R-square

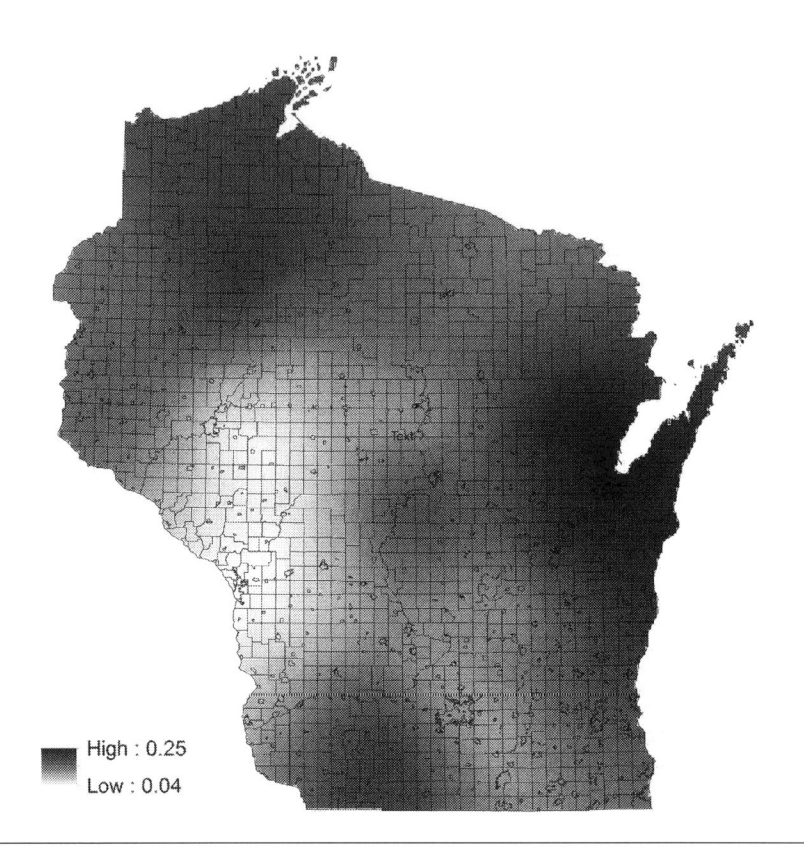

High : 0.25
Low : 0.04

Study Questions

1. What are spatial panel data?

2. How is spatial panel data analysis different from spatial regression analysis and time-series analysis?

3. How is a spatio-temporal regression model fitted?

4. What are the seven effects in a spatio-temporal regression model?

5. How are spatial forecasting regression models fitted? How are appropriate spatial weight matrices selected?

6. How is geographically weight regression (GWR) used for forecasting purposes?

7. Could any of the three advanced spatial regression models be useful for your research? If so, how?

8. Is there any spatial aspect of your research that cannot be addressed by the methods covered in this book?

8

PRACTICAL CONSIDERATIONS FOR SPATIAL DATA ANALYSIS

LEARNING OBJECTIVES

- Gain a basic understanding of spatial regression analysis of areal data in the R environment.
- Become familiar with a practical procedure of spatial data analysis.
- Choose between a theory-based approach and a data-driven approach for spatial regression modeling.
- Summarize the methods involved in spatial data analysis and understand their advantages and disadvantages.
- Develop a practical procedure of spatial data analysis for your own research.

In this chapter, we illustrate the procedure of spatial regression analysis by

- using a new data example of U.S. poverty and
- demonstrating the data analyses in R.

Throughout this book, we have primarily used the population change example for illustration purposes; a different data example provides a fresh view of spatial data analysis. We chose R for running the data analysis for the U.S. poverty example because R is an open-source statistical software environment that is gaining increasing popularity among social scientists (R Development Core Team, 2008). In this chapter, we provide code for data analysis in the R environment, and readers can modify the code for their own data analyses. We also present results in their raw format to help readers become familiar with the R environment.

This chapter also covers other practical considerations for spatial data analysis and proposes a general modeling procedure for studying social science phenomena with the spatial dimension in mind. This procedure, which is based off some of the methods covered in this book, deals with spatial dependence and spatial heterogeneity while simultaneously addressing other common issues associated with regression models.

8.1 DATA EXAMPLE OF U.S. POVERTY IN R

Throughout human history, poverty has been associated with many social problems and historic events, including inequality, wars, and revolutions. Even in developed countries, poverty persists. Thus, it is not a surprise that poverty is a topic that has been studied in many social science disciplines, generating a large body of literature. Poverty, like many other social phenomena, can be spatial. Scholars of poverty research have long recognized that the poor are not uniformly distributed across space (Nord, Luloff, & Jensen, 1995; Thiede, Kim, & Valasik, 2018; Voss, Long, Hammer, & Friedman, 2006; Weber, Jensen, Miller, Mosley, & Fisher, 2005). Understanding the spatial distribution of poverty is important because it helps us understand place-based structural inequalities (Lobao, Hooks, & Tickamyer, 2008; Tickamyer & Duncan, 1990). This school of research is also referred to as the study of "place poverty," in contrast with "people poverty," as the former emphasizes structural and contextual forces while the latter emphasizes individual or family forces (Voss et al., 2006).

Among the existing place poverty studies, county is often used as the unit of analysis; counties are salient units in policy making and planning perspectives such that many policy decisions potentially relevant to poverty rates are made at the county level (Greenlee & Howe, 2009; Lichter & Johnson, 2007; Thiede et al., 2018; Voss et al., 2006). Moreover, compared with the boundaries of other administrative units, county boundaries are subject to little boundary change, therefore facilitating scholarly study of poverty trends over time. Studies have found that county-level poverty is associated with many other structural disadvantages, especially when it comes to some major health indicators, such as stage cancer (Greenlee & Howe, 2009), obesity (Bennett, Probst, & Pumkam, 2011), and HIV prevalence (Vaughan, Rosenberg, Shouse, & Sullivan, 2014). Commonly identified factors associated with the spatial concentration of county-level poverty rates include economic structure (Goetz & Swaminathan, 2006; Lobao et al., 2008), racial composition (Thiede et al., 2018; Wimberley & Morris, 2002), and human capital stock (Levernier, Partridge, & Rickman, 2000).

This chapter provides an example of quantifying the spatial pattern of county-level poverty rates in the United States and assessing the relationship between county-level poverty rates and several socioeconomic factors. The response variable of interest is *povty,* measured as the percentage of individuals ages 18 to 64 living in poverty in a county in the year 2000. We include a set of economic, social, and demographic factors that may relate with county-level poverty rates. Specifically, three variables, *ag, manu,* and *retail,* are the percentages of workers in the agricultural sector, the manufacturing sector, and the retail sector, respectively. For socially related factors, *foreign* is the percentage of the foreign-born population in a county and *feemp* is the percentage of female employment to total population. Human capital stock is captured by *hsch,* which indicates the percentage of the population that completed a high school education. Finally, we use *black* (percentage Blacks) and *hisp* (percentage Hispanics) to capture racial and ethnic compositions.

We focus on data for the census year 2000 in the forty-eight states of the contiguous United States. The original data at the individual level are aggregated to the county level. The counties are identified by the five-digit federal information processing (FIP) standards code, with the first two digits corresponding to a state code and the last three digits corresponding to a county code.

8.1.1 Standard Exploratory Data Analysis

After the census data are downloaded and the variables of interest are extracted, we further streamline the data and save them to a proper data file to be read into R as a data frame before performing statistical data analysis:

```
povdf = read.table("poverty2000.csv", header = TRUE, sep=",")
nrow(povdf)
```

```
## [1] 3070
```

The data frame *povdf* features the poverty rate and the socioeconomic variables from the census year 2000 and in the 3,070 counties of the forty-eight contiguous states.

In exploratory data analysis, the summary statistics and graphical methods most commonly used are either applied to one variable at a time (univariate) or applied to two variables at a time (bivariate).

Using the R function *head()*, we view the first six counties in the data frame *povdf*:

head(povdf)

```
##   FIPS_N povty    ag  manu retail foreign feemp  hsch black hisp
## 1  56001 23.64  3.13  4.15   9.94    3.80 62.74 21.90  1.11 7.49
## 2  56015 13.23 12.03  4.42  10.94    1.89 52.08 33.43  0.20 8.83
## 3  56045  7.89  5.70  7.10  10.19    0.77 50.06 40.21  0.12 2.06
## 4  56017 10.77  8.03  3.13   6.63    1.31 59.48 36.13  0.35 2.38
## 5  56039  5.88  2.87  1.97  10.95    5.88 71.88 18.91  0.15 6.49
## 6  56003 12.11 10.79  5.77  10.83    2.21 48.56 34.13  0.11 6.17
```

To perform exploratory data analysis, we use summary statistics and graphical methods. Most commonly used summary statistics and graphical methods for exploratory data analysis are applied to either one variable at a time (i.e., univariate) or two variables at a time (i.e., bivariate).

Using the R function *summary()*, we obtain several univariate summary statistics for each of the variables in the data frame *povdf*:

summary(povdf)

```
##      FIPS_n          povty              ag              manu       
##  Min.   : 1001   Min.   : 2.04   Min.   : 0.030   Min.   : 0.000  
##  1st Qu.:19032   1st Qu.: 8.51   1st Qu.: 1.680   1st Qu.: 8.945  
##  Median :29178   Median :11.61   Median : 3.790   Median :14.965  
##  Mean   :30457   Mean   :12.69   Mean   : 6.129   Mean   :15.938  
##  3rd Qu.:45047   3rd Qu.:15.70   3rd Qu.: 7.810   3rd Qu.:21.997  
##  Max.   :56045   Max.   :53.83   Max.   :55.600   Max.   :48.550  
##      retail         foreign           feemp            hsch      
##  Min.   : 1.72   Min.   : 0.000   Min.   :23.21   Min.   :10.93  
##  1st Qu.:10.30   1st Qu.: 0.890   1st Qu.:46.94   1st Qu.:30.86  
##  Median :11.56   Median : 1.710   Median :51.88   Median :34.91  
##  Mean   :11.48   Mean   : 3.419   Mean   :51.64   Mean   :34.80  
##  3rd Qu.:12.72   3rd Qu.: 3.900   3rd Qu.:56.30   3rd Qu.:38.99  
##  Max.   :26.90   Max.   :50.940   Max.   :78.47   Max.   :53.25  
##      black             hisp       
##  Min.   : 0.000   Min.   : 0.080  
##  1st Qu.: 0.290   1st Qu.: 0.910  
##  Median : 1.675   Median : 1.780  
##  Mean   : 8.710   Mean   : 6.230  
##  3rd Qu.: 9.865   3rd Qu.: 5.107  
##  Max.   :86.490   Max.   :97.540  
```

For a continuous variable, the summary statistics are its minimum, first quartile, median, mean, third quartile, and maximum. The summary statistics of the response variable of poverty rate show that the lowest county-level poverty rate was 2.04 percent and the highest county-level poverty rate was 53.83 percent among the 3,070 counties in the contiguous United States in 2000. The center of the county-level poverty rates is 11.61 percent measured by median and 12.69 percent measured by mean (i.e., average). In addition, the interquartile range is between the first quartile of 8.51 percent and the third quartile of 15.70 percent. That is, half of the counties had poverty rates below 11.61 percent and the other half had poverty rates above 11.61 percent, while the middle half of the counties had poverty rates between 8.51 percent and 15.70 percent. Among the explanatory variables, here let's use the female employment rate as an example. The summary statistics of the female employment rate tell us that county-level female employment rates ranged between the lowest at 23.21 percent and the highest at 78.47 percent among the 3,070 counties in the contiguous United States in 2000. Half of the counties had female employment rates below the median of 51.88 percent and the other half had female employment rates above 51.88 percent, while the middle half of the counties had female employment rates between 46.94 percent and 56.30 percent.

Using the R function *cor()*, we obtain the sample correlation, a bivariate summary statistic, between poverty rate and any given socioeconomic factor. For example, the correlation between poverty rate and female employment rate is

```
cor(povdf$povty, povdf$feemp)
## [1] -0.6900635
```

The sign of this sample correlation is negative, indicating a negative correlation between the poverty and female employment rates. That is, higher female employment rates are associated with lower poverty rates, whereas lower female employment rates are associated with higher poverty rates. The magnitude of this correlation is 0.69 (rounded from 0.6900635) and reflects a moderate amount of association between the poverty and female employment rates for such an observational study in the social sciences.

Among the many graphical methods used for exploratory data analysis, in this chapter, we demonstrate two often-used graphs, one univariate and the other bivariate. In particular, we draw a histogram and a scatterplot by the R functions *hist()* and *plot()*, respectively:

```
par(mfrow=c(1,2))
hist(povdf$povty, freq=FALSE, main="(a)", xlab="Poverty Rate")
plot(povdf$feemp, povdf$povty, main="(b)", cex=0.1, xlab="Female
Employment Rate", ylab="Poverty Rate")
```

Figure 8.1 shows the histogram of *povty* and the scatterplot for *povty* by *feemp*. The histogram shows that the range of poverty rates is between 0 and 55 percent with a center around 10 percent (Figure 8.1a). The histogram is also right skewed, revealing counties with high poverty rates in the right tail. The histogram is based on density such that the areas of the vertical bars at 5 percent increments add up

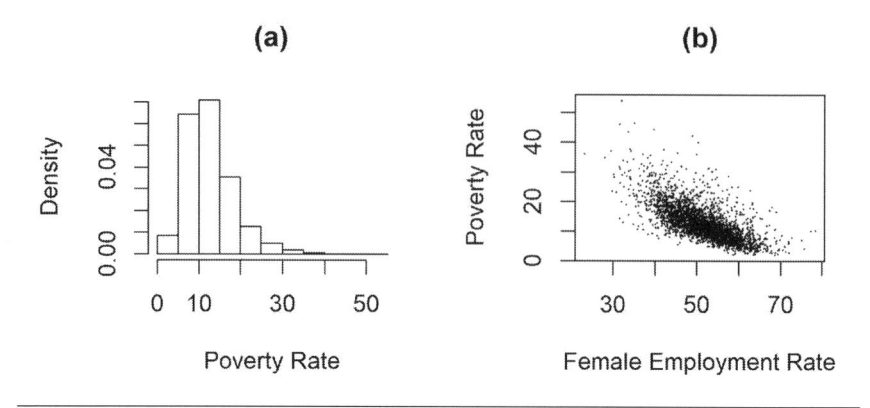

FIGURE 8.1 ● Histogram of poverty (a) and scatterplot between the poverty rate and the female employment rate (b)

to a total probability of 1. Alternatively, we could plot the histogram by the number of counties at 5 percent increments and the shape of the histogram would be the same.

The scatterplot shows a negative trend (Figure 8.1b). As the female employment rate increases from 20 percent to nearly 80 percent, the poverty rate declines. This finding is consistent with the negative sample correlation, indicating a negative association between female employment rate and poverty rate.

8.1.2 Standard Linear Regression
8.1.2.1 Model Fitting

To quantify the relationships between the poverty rate and the socioeconomic variables, we perform standard linear regression such that the response variable is poverty rate and the eight explanatory variables are percentage of agricultural workers (*ag*), percentage of manufacturing workers (*manu*), percentage of retail workers (*retail*), percentage of foreign-born residents (*foreign*), percentage of female employment (*feemp*), percentage of high school graduates (*hsch*), percentage of Blacks (*black*), and percentage of Hispanics (*hisp*).

The R function *lm()* is applied to the data frame *povty* and the output *m1* is an *lm* object. We then apply the R function *summary()* to the *m1* object and obtain the results of the standard linear regression:

```
m1 = lm(povty ~ ag + manu + retail + foreign + feemp + hsch + black +
hisp, data=povdf)
summary (m1)
```

```
## 
## Call:
## lm(formula = povty ~ ag + manu + retail + foreign + feemp + hsch +
##     black + hisp, data = povdf)
## 
## Residuals:
##      Min       1Q   Median       3Q      Max
## -12.9991  -2.2388  -0.3421   1.7029  29.0205
## 
## Coefficients:
##              Estimate Std. Error t value Pr(>|t|)
## (Intercept) 46.462367   1.019860  45.558  < 2e-16 ***
## ag           0.104110   0.012701   8.197 3.58e-16 ***
## manu        -0.028851   0.009740  -2.962  0.00308 **
## retail      -0.064335   0.039627  -1.624  0.10458
## foreign     -0.171651   0.021274  -8.069 1.01e-15 ***
## feemp       -0.526357   0.011166 -47.141  < 2e-16 ***
## hsch        -0.188037   0.014749 -12.749  < 2e-16 ***
## black        0.081289   0.005466  14.872  < 2e-16 ***
## hisp         0.061865   0.008176   7.567 5.03e-14 ***
## ---
## Signif. codes:  0 '***' 0.001 '**' 0.01 '*' 0.05 '.' 0.1 ' ' 1
## 
## Residual standard error: 3.809 on 3061 degrees of freedom
## Multiple R-squared:  0.5861, Adjusted R-squared:  0.585
## F-statistic: 541.7 on 8 and 3061 DF,  p-value: < 2.2e-16
```

There are four parts to the summary of this standard linear regression. The initial function call is echoed in the first part. The second part reports the summary statistics of residuals (minimum, first quartile, median, third quartile, and maximum). Here the residual is defined as the difference between an observed response (poverty rate) and its fitted value by the linear regression. We use residuals for model diagnostics near the end of this subsection. The third part reports, for each explanatory variable, a fitted regression coefficient (under *Estimate*), its standard errors (under *Std. Error*), the ratio of the two values as a *T*-test statistic (under *t value*), and a *p*-value for testing whether the true regression coefficient is zero or not (under *Pr(>|t|)*). For example, the estimated regression coefficient for *feemp* is −0.526 (rounded from *-0.52635676*) with standard error *0.011166*. The *T*-test statistic is −47.141 and the *p*-value is <2E−16. This tells us that a 1 percent increase in the female employment rate is associated with a 0.526 percent decrease in the poverty rate when all other explanatory variables are held constant. How significant is this result? Relative to the standard error of about 1.12 percent, the *T*-statistic is very large and the *p*-value is extremely small. There is very strong evidence that the true regression coefficient for female employment rate is not zero. The last part of the output provides a residual standard 3.809 on 3,061 degrees of freedom, which estimates the standard deviate of the error term in the standard linear regression model. In addition, a multiple and an adjusted *R*-squared are reported, indicating that about 58 percent of the variation in the response variable of poverty rate is explained by the relationship with the socioeconomic variables considered herein. Finally, an *F*-test is carried out for testing whether all of the regression coefficients are zero. The *p*-value is <2.2E–16, and there is very strong evidence that not all of the regression coefficients are zero.

In addition, we may extract the estimated regression coefficients and the corresponding 95 percent confidence intervals by applying the R functions *coef()* and *confint()* to the *m1* object. By the R function *cbind()* below, we combine these results into a table of three columns, one for the estimated regression coefficients (named *coefest*) and the other two for the lower and upper limits of the 95 percent confidence intervals.

```
cbind(coefest = coef(m1), confint(m1))
```

```
##                  coefest        2.5 %       97.5 %
## (Intercept) 46.46236736  44.46268723  48.462047496
## ag           0.10410987   0.07920740   0.129012335
## manu        -0.02885059  -0.04794830  -0.009752886
## retail      -0.06433542  -0.14203379   0.013362963
## foreign     -0.17165122  -0.21336404  -0.129938403
## feemp       -0.52635676  -0.54824943  -0.504464081
## hsch        -0.18803678  -0.21695614  -0.159117430
## black        0.08128912   0.07057202   0.092006219
## hisp         0.06186454   0.04583405   0.077895030
```

For example, the estimated regression coefficient for *feemp* is −0.526 with a 95 percent confidence interval of [−0.548, −0.504]. That is, there is a 95 percent confidence of between a 0.504 percent and 0.548 percent decrease in the poverty rate associated with a 1 percent increase in the female employment rate when all other explanatory variables are held constant.

8.1.2.2 Model Selection

Among the socioeconomic explanatory variables, one of them, *retail*, is not significant ($p = 0.10458$). It is common practice to perform model selection in search of a more parsimonious model that has possibly fewer explanatory variables. We use the R function *step()* to perform a backward elimination based on Akaike's information criterion (AIC) and save the result to an *Lm* object *m2*. That is, we start with the full model *m1*, which has all the socioeconomic explanatory variables, and we drop the explanatory variable that results in the largest decrease in AIC iteratively until there is no further decrease in AIC. Recall that a smaller AIC indicates a better model fit balanced with model parsimony.

```
#backward elimination based on AIC
m2 = step(m1)

## Start:  AIC=8219.82
## povty ~ ag + manu + retail + foreign + feemp + hsch + black + hisp
##
##          Df Sum of Sq   RSS    AIC
## <none>                 44402 8219.8
## - retail  1        38 44440 8220.5
## - manu    1       127 44529 8226.6
## - hisp    1       831 45232 8274.7
## - foreign 1       944 45346 8282.4
## - ag      1       975 45376 8284.5
## - hsch    1      2358 46759 8376.6
## - black   1      3208 47610 8432.0
## - feemp   1     32236 76638 9893.4
```

When the explanatory variable *retail* is dropped, the AIC value increases from 8,219.8 to 8,220.5. This indicates that the model without *retail* is not as good a model as the full model with all the explanatory variables *m1*. This holds for all the other explanatory variables as well, and thus none of the explanatory variables are dropped from the full model based on AIC. The final model *m2* is the same as the full model *m1*.

Alternatively, we could use the R function *step()* to perform a backward elimination based on Schwartz's Bayesian information criterion (BIC) by setting the penalty coefficient to the log of the sample size ($k = \log(n)$) and save the result to an *lm* object *m3*. Like AIC, a smaller BIC indicates a good model fit balanced with model parsimony. We thus start with the full model *m1*, which has all the socioeconomic explanatory variables, and we drop the explanatory variable that results in the largest decrease in BIC iteratively until there is no further decrease in BIC:

```
#backward elimination based on BIC
n = nrow(povdf) #n is the sample size
m3 = step(m1, k=log(n))

## Start:  AIC=8274.08
## povty ~ ag + manu + retail + foreign + feemp + hsch + black + hisp
##
##          Df Sum of Sq   RSS    AIC
## - retail  1        38 44440 8268.7
## <none>                 44402 8274.1
## - manu    1       127 44529 8274.8
## - hisp    1       831 45232 8322.9
## - foreign 1       944 45346 8330.7
## - ag      1       975 45376 8332.7
## - hsch    1      2358 46759 8424.9
## - black   1      3208 47610 8480.2
## - feemp   1     32236 76638 9941.7
##
## Step:  AIC=8268.69
## povty ~ ag + manu + foreign + feemp + hsch + black + hisp
##
```

```
##              Df Sum of Sq   RSS    AIC
## - manu        1       102 44542 8267.7
## <none>                    44440 8268.7
## - hisp        1       845 45285 8318.5
## - foreign     1       933 45373 8324.5
## - ag          1      1576 46016 8367.7
## - hsch        1      2404 46844 8422.4
## - black       1      3332 47772 8482.6
## - feemp       1     32207 76647 9934.0
## 
## Step:  AIC=8267.73
## povty ~ ag + foreign + feemp + hsch + black + hisp
## 
##              Df Sum of Sq   RSS    AIC
## <none>                    44542 8267.7
## - hisp        1       893 45436 8320.7
## - foreign     1       987 45529 8327.0
## - ag          1      2211 46754 8408.4
## - black       1      3233 47775 8474.8
## - hsch        1      3572 48115 8496.5
## - feemp       1     32912 77454 9958.2
```

There are three steps in this model selection by BIC. In the first step, the *retail* explanatory variable is dropped from the reference model with all the explanatory variables because the BIC value of 8,268.7 without *retail* is smaller than the BIC value of 8,274.1 for the reference model with *retail*, whereas dropping any of the other explanatory variables would result in a BIC value larger than 8,274.1 for the reference model. In the second step, the reference model without *retail* has a BIC value of 8,268.7, and the *manu* explanatory variable is dropped because the BIC value of 8,267.7 without *manu* is smaller than the BIC value of 8,268.7 for the reference model with *manu*, whereas dropping any of the other explanatory variables would result in a BIC value larger than 8,268.7 for the reference model. In the third and last step, the reference model without *retail* and *manu* has a BIC value of 8,267.7. Because leaving out any of the remaining explanatory variables would result in an increase in the BIC value, the model selection is finished. The final best model is *m3* without *retail* and *manu*, with the following summary of the model fit:

summary(m3)

```
## 
## Call:
## lm(formula = povty ~ ag + foreign + feemp + hsch + black + hisp, 
##     data = povdf)
## 
## Residuals:
##      Min       1Q   Median       3Q      Max 
## -13.1475  -2.2578  -0.3776   1.6626  29.3469 
## 
## Coefficients:
##              Estimate Std. Error t value Pr(>|t|)
## (Intercept) 45.911167   0.858997  53.447  < 2e-16 ***
## ag           0.125505   0.010178  12.331  < 2e-16 ***
```

```
## foreign      -0.174881    0.021227   -8.239 2.55e-16 ***
## feemp        -0.528419    0.011108  -47.573  < 2e-16 ***
## hsch         -0.206914    0.013202  -15.673  < 2e-16 ***
## black         0.079324    0.005320   14.910  < 2e-16 ***
## hisp          0.063941    0.008159    7.837 6.31e-15 ***
## ---
## Signif. codes:  0 '***' 0.001 '**' 0.01 '*' 0.05 '.' 0.1 ' ' 1
##
## Residual standard error: 3.813 on 3063 degrees of freedom
## Multiple R-squared:  0.5847, Adjusted R-squared:  0.5839
## F-statistic: 718.8 on 6 and 3063 DF,  p-value: < 2.2e-16
```

This standard linear regression summary for *m3* provides estimates for the regression coefficients that are similar to those of *m1*. For example, in *m3*, the estimated regression coefficient for *feemp* is −0.528 with standard error 0.011108, compared with an estimate of −0.526 with standard error 0.011166 in *m1*. There is a very slight decrease of the multiple and the adjusted *R*-squared values, but the amount of variation in the response variable explained by this final best model remains about 58 percent. We proceed with this set of six explanatory variables (*ag, foreign, feemp, hsch, black,* and *hisp*) in the remainder of this chapter.

8.1.2.3 Model Diagnostics

Now that we have fitted standard linear regression models and selected a final model *m3*, we perform model diagnostics for the purpose of evaluating the model assumptions. There are four model assumptions to evaluate: linearity, independence, equal variance, and normality. For linearity and equal variance, it is common to use the plot of residuals versus fitted responses. This is the first option in the R function *plot()* applied to *m3*. For normality, it is common to use the normal quantile-quantile (Q-Q) plot of the standardized residuals (Figure 8.2b on the next page), which is the second option in the R function *plot()* applied to *m3*:

After fitting standard linear regression models and selecting a final model, model diagnostics should be performed to evaluate the model assumptions of linearity, independence, equal variance, and normality.

```
par(mfrow=c(1,2))
plot(m3, which=c(1,2), cex=0.1)
```

The normal Q-Q plot (Figure 8.2a) shows a departure from the straight line at the upper end, indicating right skewness in the residuals (i.e., more large positive residuals than a normal distribution would typically have). The right skewness is also reflected in the plot of the residuals versus the fitted responses (Figure 8.2b), while the remaining residuals appear to be scattered fairly randomly.

When model diagnostics like those above indicate possible departure from the standard linear regression assumptions, remedial measures are not always needed due to the robustness of the regression. When remedial measures are needed, a commonly used approach is transformation of the response variable and/or the explanatory variables. For illustration, we take a natural log transformation of the response variable and fit a linear regression model. Then we perform model diagnostics as before by a residual versus fitted response plot and a normal Q-Q plot (Figure 8.3):

```
m3.log = lm(log(povty) ~ ag + foreign + feemp + hsch + black + hisp,
data=povdf)
par (mfrow=c(1,2))
plot(m3.log, which=c(1,2), cex=0.1)
```

The normal Q-Q plot (Figure 8.3a) shows less departure from the straight line at the upper end but more departure at the lower end, indicating a possible overcorrection of the right skewness in the untransformed data. In the plot of the residuals versus the fitted responses (Figure 8.3b), several large negative residuals are marked and there is some indication of smaller variance for larger fitted values (i.e., unequal

Although remedial measures are not always needed when model diagnostics indicate a departure from standard linear regression assumptions, when such measures are necessary, a common measure is transformation of the response and/or explanatory variables.

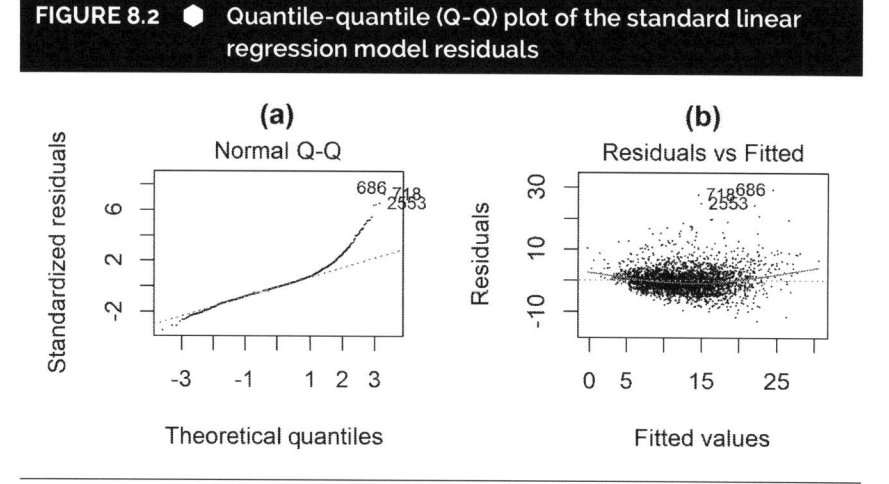

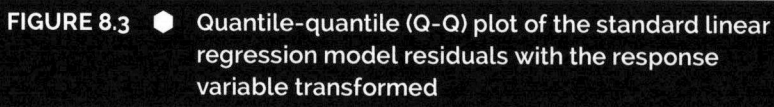

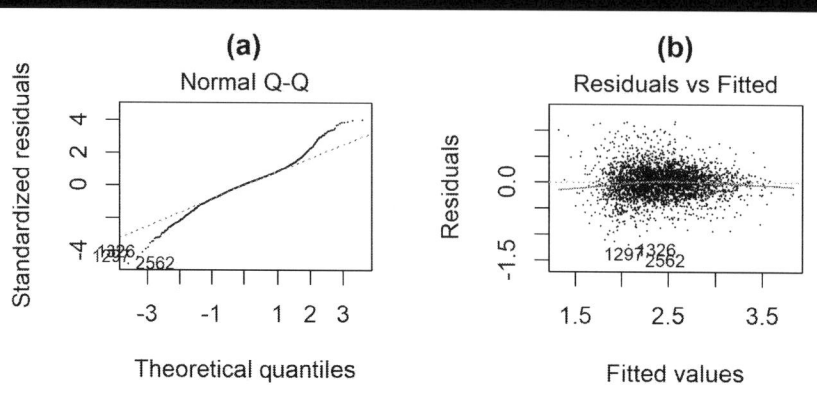

FIGURE 8.2 ● **Quantile-quantile (Q-Q) plot of the standard linear regression model residuals**

FIGURE 8.3 ● **Quantile-quantile (Q-Q) plot of the standard linear regression model residuals with the response variable transformed**

variance). This example demonstrates some of the challenges in model selection and model diagnostics. Taking a remedial measure to correct the departure from one assumption could lead to the departure from another assumption. For the remainder of this chapter, we model the original poverty rate without any transformation.

Thus far, we have evaluated the assumptions of linearity, equal variance, and normality. The independence assumption, however, is not an option in the R function *plot()*; we evaluate the independence assumption in Section 8.1.5.1.

> There are challenges in model selection and model diagnostics, such as that taking a remedial measure to correct a departure from one assumption may lead to a departure from another assumption.

8.1.3 Neighborhood Structure and Spatial Weight Matrix

In Sections 8.1.1 and 8.1.2, we perform exploratory data analysis and standard linear regression analysis of the poverty rate data without considering spatial information in the data. In this section, we create a neighborhood structure and a spatial weight matrix in preparation for spatial analysis. In the following two sections, we perform exploratory spatial data analysis (Section 8.1.4) and carry out spatial linear regression analysis (Section 8.1.5).

Recall that the data frame *povdf* comprises the response variable and the explanatory variables as well as the FIP that identifies the counties in the forty-eight states of the contiguous United States.

```
head(povdf)
```

```
##    FIPS_N    ag black feemp foreign hisp  hsch manu povty retail
## 1  56001  3.13  1.11 62.74    3.80 7.49 21.90 4.15 23.64   9.94
## 2  56015 12.03  0.20 52.08    1.89 8.83 33.43 4.42 13.23  10.94
## 3  56045  5.70  0.12 50.06    0.77 2.06 40.21 7.10  7.89  10.19
## 4  56017  8.03  0.35 59.48    1.31 2.38 36.13 3.13 10.77   6.63
## 5  56039  2.87  0.15 71.88    5.88 6.49 18.91 1.97  5.88  10.95
## 6  56003 10.79  0.11 48.56    2.21 6.17 34.13 5.77 12.11  10.83
```

We now create neighbors and their corresponding spatial weights. First, we import the OpenGIS reference (OGR) data source that contains the .shp, .cpg, .dbf, .prj, .sbn, and .shx files using the R function *readOGR()* from the *rgdal* package (Bivand, Keitt, Rowlingson, & Pebesma, 2018). The resulting pov_shape is a shape object.

```
#read in shapefile
pov_shape = readOGR(dsn=".",layer="pov_shp")
```

```
## OGR data source with driver: ESRI Shapefile
## Source: "C:\...", layer: "pov_shp"
## with 3104 features
## It has 21 fields
```

Because two states, Alaska and Hawaii, are not in the contiguous United States, we identify them by the R function *which()* and delete them from the shape object *pov_shape:*

```
idx = which(!is.na(match(as.numeric(as.character(pov_shape@data$GEOID10)),
      povdf$FIPS_n, nomatch = NULL)))
pov_shapesub = pov_shape[idx,]
```

Since we have created a subset, we set the names of the rows in *pov_shapesub* to be the same as those in *povdf*. This ensures that the names of the neighbors we create next are the same as the names of the observations in *povdf*.

```
row.names(pov_shapesub) = row.names(povdf)
```

With the shape object *pov_shapesub* created and row names set to be the same as in *povdf*, we next convert the polygons in *pov_shapesub* to a neighborhood structure by the R function *poly2nb():*

```
pov_nb = poly2nb(pov_shapesub, row.names = pov_shapesub$FIPS_N) #this
may     take a few minutes
```

The output *pov_nb* is a neighborhood object that explicitly lists who are neighbors with whom and, in our case, which county is a neighbor with which county. We then create spatial weights by the R function *nb2listw()* using the default option of row standardization (*style="W"*) and binary weights (*style="B"*):

```
#W - default row-standardized weights
listw_povW = nb2listw(pov_nb, style="W", zero.policy = TRUE)
#B - binary weights
listw_povB = nb2listw(pov_nb, style="B", zero.policy = TRUE)
```

We specify *zero.policy=TRUE* above because some counties do not have any neighbors, such as Nantucket County in Massachusetts, and the neighborhood object *pov_nb* has entries that are null. The zero policy allows spatial weights to be created for counties with one or more neighbors.

The output *listw_povB* is a spatial weight object, which can be visualized by a map as shown in Figure 8.4. The centroids of all pairs of neighboring counties are connected by lines. The map can be thought of as a network or a graph such that the county centroids are the vertexes and the connecting lines between neighboring counties are the edges.

```
coords = coordinates(pov_shapesub)
plot(listw_povB, coords, col="blue", cex=0.1)
```

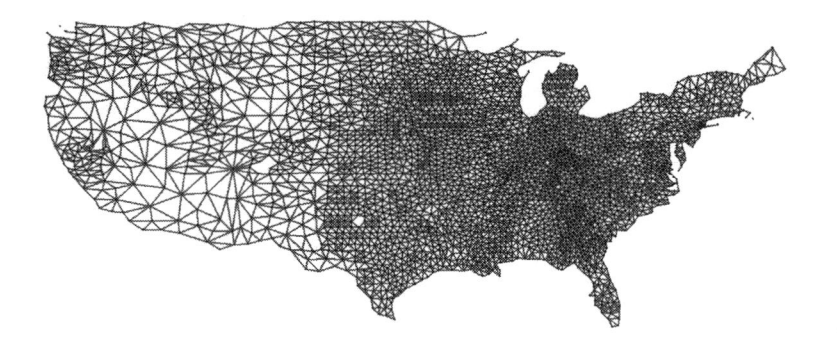

FIGURE 8.4 ● **Neighborhood structure for the counties in the contiguous United States**

8.1.4 Exploratory Spatial Data Analysis

We performed exploratory data analysis by summary statistics and graphical methods in Section 8.1.2. However, standard exploratory data analysis does not take into account the spatial nature of the data. In this section, we consider exploratory spatial data analysis by summary statistics and graphical methods that use the spatial information in the data. A natural graphical method to use for exploratory spatial data analysis is a heatmap, where the levels of a variable are color coded on a map. We can draw the heatmap of the poverty rates as well as heatmaps of the socioeconomic explanatory variables over the 3,070 counties in the contiguous United States.

> A heatmap, which is a natural graphical method used for exploratory spatial data analysis, color codes the levels of a variable on a map.

We use the R function *spplot()* from the *sp* package (Pebesma et al., 2018) to plot the response variable by specifying the *SpatialPolygonsDataFrame* (*pov_shapesub*), the variable to plot (*povty*), and the gray scale from lighter to darker gray for smaller to larger values of the poverty rate (*col.regions=gray.colors(99, start=1, end=0)*):

```
spplot(pov_shapesub, "povty", main="(a)",
    col.regions=gray.colors(99, start=1, end=0), colorkey=TRUE))
```

For illustration purposes, we also use the R function *spplot()* to plot one of the explanatory variables, female employment rate *feemp*:

```
spplot(pov_shapesub, "feemp", main="(b)",
    col.regions=gray.colors(99, start=1,end=0), colorkey=TRUE))
```

The spatial pattern of *povty* (Figure 8.5a) indicates relatively low poverty rates in the northern and western states, whereas the poverty rates are relatively high in the southeastern states. The spatial pattern of *feemp* (Figure 8.5b) indicates relatively high female employment rates in eastern states. The relationship between the poverty and female employment rates shown in Figure 8.5 is not as obvious as in Figure 8.1.

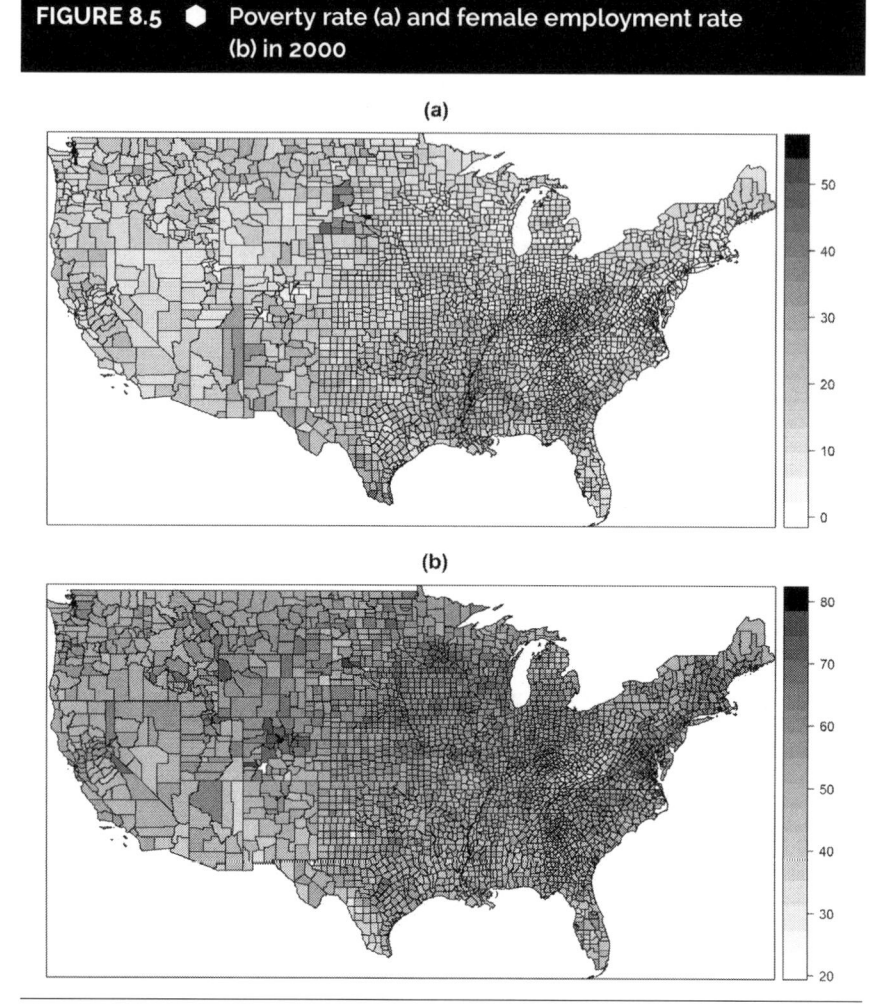

198 Spatial Regression Models for the Social Sciences

FIGURE 8.5 ● Poverty rate (a) and female employment rate (b) in 2000

(a)

(b)

Data source: The U.S. Census Bureau's Decennial Census in 2000.

8.1.4.1 Moran's *I* and Geary's *c*

For exploratory spatial data analysis, summary statistics such as Moran's *I* and Geary's *c* can be used to quantify spatial dependence.

With the neighborhoods created in Section 8.1.3, we use the R function *moran.test()* to estimate Moran's *I* statistic and perform a Moran's *I* test for the null hypothesis that there is no spatial dependence versus a two-sided alternative hypothesis that there is spatial dependence:

```
#Moran's I test based on randomization
moran.test(povdf$povty, listw_povB, zero.policy = TRUE,
alternative = "two.sided")

##
##   Moran I test under randomisation
##
```

```
## data:  povdf$povty
## weights: listw_povB   n reduced by no-neighbour observations
##
## Moran I statistic standard deviate = 53.934, p-value < 2.2e-16
## alternative hypothesis: two.sided
## sample estimates:
## Moran I statistic        Expectation           Variance
##      0.5668859074       -0.0003260515        0.0001106021
```

Based on the output above, the Moran's *I* statistic is 0.5669, indicating a positive spatial dependence among neighboring counties. If there is no spatial dependence, then the expected value and the variance of Moran's *I* statistic are −0.000326 and 0.0001106, respectively. This results in a standard deviate of 53.934 with a *p*-value less than 2.2E−16 (i.e., 2.2×10^{-16}), which is virtually zero. There is very strong evidence for spatial dependence in the poverty rates across counties in the contiguous United States.

Moran's *I* test by *moran.test()* is based on a normal approximation, and the variance estimation is based on randomization. Alternatively, a Monte Carlo test can be performed by the R function *moran.mc()*, where we prespecify the number of Monte Carlo simulations (here, *nsim=999*) and compare Moran's *I* statistic of 0.5669 against the null distribution of Moran's *I* statistic under the assumption of no spatial dependence. We set the randomization seed to 1 so that when the code is rerun we would get the same test result:

```
#Moran's I test based on Monte Carlo
set.seed(1)
moran.mc(povdf$povty, listw_povB, zero.policy = TRUE, nsim=999)

##
##   Monte-Carlo simulation of Moran I
##
## data:  povdf$povty
## weights: listw_povB
## number of simulations + 1: 1000
##
## statistic = 0.56689, observed rank = 1000, p-value = 0.001
## alternative hypothesis: greater
```

This Monte Carlo test shows that the rank of the observed Moran's *I* test statistic of 0.5669 is larger than any of the test statistics from the *nsim=999* simulations and thus has the highest rank. The *p*-value is 1 out of 1,000, which is .001 for a null hypothesis that there is no spatial dependence versus a one-sided alternative that there is positive spatial dependence. That is, there is very strong evidence for positive spatial dependence in the poverty rates among counties. For a two-sided alternative that there is spatial dependence (positive or negative), we double .001 and obtain a *p*-value of .002. There is still very strong evidence for spatial dependence in the poverty rates among counties.

Besides Moran's I, we may use the R function *geary.test()* to estimate the Geary's c statistic and perform a Geary's c test for the null hypothesis that there is no spatial dependence versus a two-sided alternative hypothesis that there is spatial dependence:

```
geary.test(povdf$povty, listw_povB, zero.policy=TRUE,
alternative = "two.sided")

##
##  Geary C test under randomisation
##
## data:  povdf$povty
## weights: listw_povB
##
## Geary C statistic standard deviate = 40.858, p-value < 2.2e-16
## alternative hypothesis: two.sided
## sample estimates:
## Geary C statistic       Expectation          Variance
##      0.4286729712      1.0000000000      0.0001955308
```

Based on this output, Geary's c statistic is 0.4287, indicating a positive spatial dependence among neighboring counties. If there were no spatial dependence, the expected value and the variance of the Geary's c statistic would be 1 and 0.0001955, respectively. This results in a standard deviate of 40.858 with a p-value also virtually zero. There is again very strong evidence for spatial dependence in the poverty rates across counties.

Geary's c test by *geary.test()* is based on a normal approximation, and the variance estimation is based on randomization. Alternatively, a Monte Carlo test can be performed by the R function *geary.mc()*, where we prespecify the number of Monte Carlo simulations (by *nsim=999*) and compare Geary's c statistic of 0.4287 against its null distribution under the assumption of no spatial dependence:

```
set.seed(1)
geary.mc(povdf$povty, listw_povB, zero.policy = TRUE, nsim=999)

##
##  Monte-Carlo simulation of Geary C
##
## data:  povdf$povty
## weights: listw_povB
## number of simulations + 1: 1000
##
## statistic = 0.42867, observed rank = 1, p-value = 0.001
## alternative hypothesis: greater
```

This Monte Carlo test shows that the rank of the observed Geary's c test statistic of 0.4287 is larger than any of the test statistics from the *nsim=999* simulations and thus ranks the highest. The p-value is thus .002 (.001) for a two-sided (one-sided) alternative, and there is very strong evidence for spatial dependence (positive spatial dependence) in the poverty rates across counties.

8.1.4.2 Local Moran's *I*

To apply local Moran's *I* to the data, we use the R function *localmoran()*. The output is extensive, so here we apply the R function *head()* to take a look at the first six counties as an example. We also use the R function *round()* to round the output values to two digits after the decimal point:

```
head(round(localmoran(povdf$povty, listw_povB, zero.policy = TRUE),2))
```

```
##            Ii E.Ii Var.Ii  Z.Ii Pr(z > 0)
## 56001  -4.95    0   5.98 -2.03      0.98
## 56015  -0.14    0   5.98 -0.06      0.52
## 56045   2.61    0   6.97  0.99      0.16
## 56017  -0.04    0   2.99 -0.02      0.51
## 56039   2.09    0   7.97  0.74      0.23
## 56003  -0.05    0   5.98 -0.02      0.51
```

For example, for the county identified as 56001 in the output above (Albany County, Wyoming), the local Moran's *I* (*Ii*) is −4.95, with a virtually zero expectation (*E.Ii*) and a variance of 5.98 (*Var.Ii*). Thus, the standard deviate (*Z.Ii*) is −2.03 and the *p*-value $(1 - \Pr[z > 0])$ is $1 - .98 = .02$ for a one-sided alternative (the *p*-value is .04 for a two-sided alternative). There is moderate evidence of local spatial dependence for this county.

8.1.5 Spatial Linear Regression

8.1.5.1 Diagnostics for Spatial Dependence

In Section 8.1.2, we fitted and selected standard linear regression models to quantify the relationship between poverty rates and the socioeconomic variables. We also carried out model diagnostics using residuals plots to evaluate the model assumptions of linearity, equal variance, and normality (but not yet independence). We are now ready to evaluate the independence assumption.

Here we use row-standardized spatial weights and recall the spatial weights object *listw_povW*. We apply the R function *lm.morantest()* to the residuals of the fitted standard linear regression models and the null hypothesis is that there is no spatial dependence in the residuals.

```
lm.morantest(m3, listw_povW, zero.policy = TRUE, alternative = "two.sided")
```

```
##
##  Global Moran I for regression residuals
##
```

```
## data:
## model: lm(formula = povty ~ ag + foreign + feemp + hsch + black +
## hisp, data = povdf)
## weights: listw_povW
##
## Moran I statistic standard deviate = 25.375, p-value < 2.2e-16
## alternative hypothesis: two.sided
## sample estimates:
## Observed Moran I       Expectation              Variance
##     0.2701415249      -0.0015999042         0.0001146869
```

Based on the output above, Moran's *I* statistic is 0.2701, indicating a positive spatial dependence among neighboring counties. The standard deviate is 25.375 with a *p*-value less than 2.2E–16, which is virtually zero. There is very strong evidence for spatial dependence among the residuals of the standard linear regression model fit. This calls for more complex spatial linear regression analysis.

The next subsection presents spatial lag models and spatial error models including the simultaneous autoregressive (SAR) and conditional autoregressive (CAR) models.

8.1.5.2 Spatial Lag Models

We consider fitting a spatial lag model to the poverty rates data. The R function *LagsarLm()* is applied to the data frame *povdf* and the output is *m3_Lag*. We then apply the R function *summary()* to *m3_Lag* and obtain the results of the spatial lag model fit:

```
m3_lag = lagsarlm(povty ~ ag + foreign + feemp + hsch + black + hisp,
         data=povdf, listw = listw_povW,type="lag",zero.policy=TRUE)
summary(m3_lag, correlation=FALSE)

##
## Call:lagsarlm(formula = povty ~ ag + foreign + feemp + hsch + black +
##     hisp, data = povdf, listw = listw_povW, type = "lag",
##         zero.policy = TRUE)
##
## Residuals:
##      Min       1Q    Median       3Q       Max
## -14.3063  -2.0402   -0.3439   1.4135   31.9339
##
## Type: lag
## Regions with no neighbours included:
##  53055 25019
## Coefficients: (asymptotic standard errors)
##              Estimate Std. Error   z value  Pr(>|z|)
## (Intercept) 31.1324918  1.0845037   28.7067 < 2.2e-16
## ag           0.0963350  0.0094213   10.2252 < 2.2e-16
## foreign     -0.0732789  0.0198759   -3.6868 0.0002271
## feemp       -0.3773675  0.0126215  -29.8988 < 2.2e-16
## hsch        -0.1423252  0.0127948  -11.1237 < 2.2e-16
## black        0.0597204  0.0051484   11.5999 < 2.2e-16
## hisp         0.0313621  0.0077033    4.0712 4.676e-05
##
```

```
## Rho: 0.38852, LR test value: 411.34, p-value: < 2.22e-16
## Asymptotic standard error: 0.018898
##     z-value: 20.559, p-value: < 2.22e-16
## Wald statistic: 422.66, p-value: < 2.22e-16
##
## Log likelihood: -8256.232 for lag model
## ML residual variance (sigma squared): 12.324, (sigma: 3.5106)
## Number of observations: 3070
## Number of parameters estimated: 9
## AIC: 16530, (AIC for lm: 16940)
## LM test for residual autocorrelation
## test value: 46.474, p-value: 9.2848e-12
```

There are five parts to this spatial linear regression output. The initial function call is in the first part. The second part reports the summary statistics of residuals (minimum, first quartile, median, third quartile, and maximum). Here the residual is defined as the difference between an observed response and its fitted value by the spatial linear regression. The third part reports, for each explanatory variable, a fitted regression coefficient (under *Estimate*), its standard errors (under *Std. Error*), the ratio of the two values as a Z-test statistic (under *z value*), and a *p*-value for testing whether the true regression coefficient is zero or not (under *Pr(>|z|)*). For example, the estimated regression coefficient for *feemp* is −0.377 with standard error 0.01262. The Z-test statistic is −29.8988 and the *p*-value is less than 2.2E−16. This tells us that a 1 percent increase in the female employment rate is associated with a 0.377 percent decrease in the poverty rate when all other explanatory variables are held constant. Relative to the standard error of about 1.262 percent, the Z-statistic of −29.898 is very large and the *p*-value is extremely small. There is very strong evidence that the true regression coefficient for female employment rate is not zero.

The fourth part of the output provides the estimate of the spatial correlation coefficient *rho*, which is 0.389. Two hypothesis tests—a likelihood ratio (LR) test and a Wald test—are applied for testing whether the true spatial correlation coefficient *rho* is zero or not. The LR test statistic is 411.34 with a *p*-value of less than 2.2E−16. The Wald test is presented as a Z-test with a z-value of 20.559 and a *p*-value of less than 2.2E−16. Equivalently, the Wald test statistic is 422.66, which is the square of the z-value, and the *p*-value of less than 2.2E−16 is the same as the Z-test. Both the LR test and the Wald test indicate there is very strong evidence that the spatial correlation coefficient *rho* is not zero.

The fifth and last part of the output provides several useful statistics and tests. The log-likelihood value for the fitted spatial lag model is −8,256.232 and the AIC value is 16,530, which is smaller than the AIC value of 16,940 for the standard linear regression model. The maximum likelihood estimate of the error variance *sigma squared* is 12.324, with the error standard deviate *sigma* estimated to be its square root, 3.5106. Finally, the Lagrange multiplier (LM) test for the spatial dependence in the error term has a test value of 46.474 and a small *p*-value, indicating that there is additional spatial dependence unaccounted for by the spatial lag model.

In addition, we may extract the estimated regression coefficients and the corresponding 95 percent confidence intervals by applying the R functions *coef()* and *confint()* to the *m3* object. Using the R function *cbind()*, we combine these results into a table of three columns, one for the estimated regression coefficients and the other two for the lower and upper limits of the 95 percent confidence intervals:

```
cbind(coefest = coef(m3_lag), confint(m3_lag))
```

```
##                   coefest         2.5 %        97.5 %
## rho            0.38852210    0.35148224    0.42556196
## (Intercept)   31.13249177   29.00690361   33.25807994
## ag             0.09633503    0.07786958    0.11480048
## foreign       -0.07327886   -0.11223483   -0.03432288
## feemp         -0.37736753   -0.40210523   -0.35262983
## hsch          -0.14232516   -0.16740243   -0.11724789
## black          0.05972044    0.04962982    0.06981107
## hisp           0.03136205    0.01626383    0.04646028
```

For example, the estimated regression coefficient for *feemp* is -0.377 with a 95 percent confidence interval of $[-0.402, -0.353]$. That is, there is a 95 percent confidence of between a 0.353 percent and 0.402 percent decrease in the poverty rate associated with a 1 percent increase in the female employment rate when all other explanatory variables are held constant. Compared with the results under *m1*, the estimated regression coefficient for *feemp* is still negative but with a smaller magnitude, and the confidence interval is slightly wider in the spatial lag model *m3_Lag* after accounting for spatial dependence.

We have already tested for spatial dependence in the error term and learned that there is strong evidence for spatial dependence. In addition, we may plot the residuals against the fitted responses (Figure 8.6) as follows:

```
plot(m3_lag$fitted.values, m3_lag$residuals, xlab="Fitted values",
ylab="Residuals", main="Residuals vs Fitted", cex=0.1)
abline(h=0, lty=2)
```

In Figure 8.6, we see that the residuals are distributed fairly randomly around the zero horizontal line and that the variation tends to be higher for larger fitted values. This suggests no obvious departure from the linearity assumption, but there is indication of unequal variances among the errors.

FIGURE 8.6 ● Residuals versus fitted values of the spatial lag model

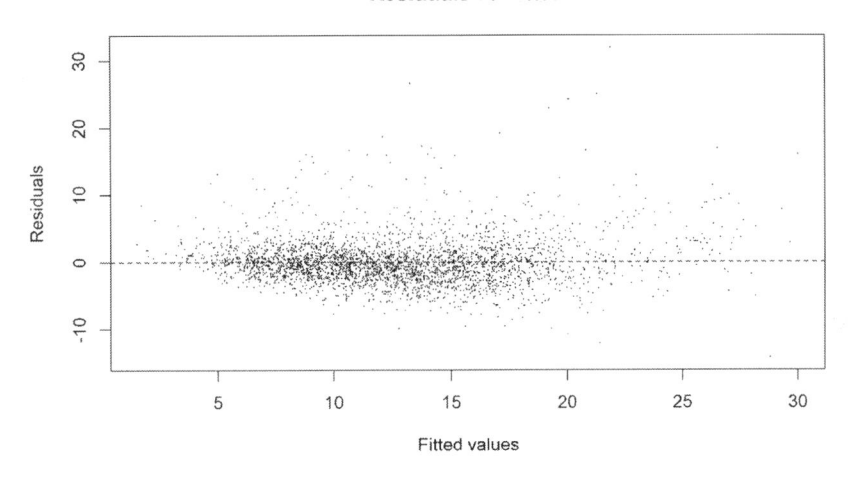

Residuals vs Fitted

We apply the Breusch-Pagan (BP) test for the null hypothesis that the error variance is constant versus the alternative that the error variance is not constant by the R function *bptest.sarlm()*:

```
bptest.sarlm(m3_lag)

##
##   studentized Breusch-Pagan test
##
## data:
## BP = 218.15, df = 6, p-value < 2.2e-16
```

The observed BP test statistic is 218.15 and the *p*-value is extremely small. There is very strong evidence for unequal variance in the error term of the spatial lag model.

8.1.5.3 Spatial Error Models

As an alternative to the spatial lag model, we consider fitting a spatial error model to the poverty rates data. The R function *errorsarlm()* is applied to the data frame *povdf* and the output is *m3_err*. We then apply the R function *summary()* to the *m3_err* object and obtain the results of the spatial error model fit:

```
m3_err = errorsarlm(povty ~ ag + foreign + feemp + hsch + black + hisp,
         data=povdf, listw = listw_povW, zero.policy = TRUE)
summary(m3_err)

##
## Call:errorsarlm(formula = povty ~ ag + foreign + feemp + hsch + black +
##     hisp, data = povdf, listw = listw_povW, zero.policy = TRUE)
```

```
## 
## Residuals:
##       Min        1Q    Median        3Q       Max
## -14.63734  -1.86232  -0.36507   1.41036  29.97123
## 
## Type: error
## Regions with no neighbours included:
##  53055 25019
## Coefficients: (asymptotic standard errors)
##               Estimate Std. Error  z value  Pr(>|z|)
## (Intercept) 41.4409292  1.0717400  38.6670  < 2.2e-16
## ag           0.0765506  0.0126109   6.0702  1.278e-09
## foreign     -0.0671560  0.0271326  -2.4751    0.01332
## feemp       -0.4410192  0.0143178 -30.8021  < 2.2e-16
## hsch        -0.2283387  0.0148294 -15.3977  < 2.2e-16
## black        0.1267843  0.0076816  16.5049  < 2.2e-16
## hisp         0.0893849  0.0123932   7.2124  5.496e-13
## 
## Lambda: 0.6181, LR test value: 597.7, p-value: < 2.22e-16
## Asymptotic standard error: 0.019018
##     z-value: 32.501, p-value: < 2.22e-16
## Wald statistic: 1056.3, p-value: < 2.22e-16
## 
## Log likelihood: -8163.055 for error model
## ML residual variance (sigma squared): 10.989, (sigma: 3.3149)
## Number of observations: 3070
## Number of parameters estimated: 9
## AIC: 16344, (AIC for lm: 16940)
```

There are five parts to this spatial linear regression output. The initial function call is in the first part. The second part reports the summary statistics of residuals (minimum, first quartile, median, third quartile, and maximum). The third part reports, for each explanatory variable, a fitted regression coefficient (under *Estimate*), its standard errors (under *Std. Error*), the ratio of the two values as a Z-test statistic (under *z value*), and a *p*-value for testing whether the true regression coefficient is zero or not (under *Pr(>|z|)*). For example, the estimated regression coefficient for *feemp* is −0.441 with standard error 0.0143178. The Z-test statistic is −30.8021 and the *p*-value is less than 2.2E−16. This tells us that a 1 percent increase in the female employment rate is associated with a 0.441 percent decrease in the poverty rate when all other explanatory variables are held constant. Relative to the standard error of about 1.431 percent, the Z-statistic of −30.8021 is very large and the *p*-value is extremely small. There is very strong evidence that the true regression coefficient for female employment rate is not zero.

The fourth part of the output provides the estimate of the spatial correlation coefficient *Lambda*, which is 0.618. The LR test value is 597.7 with a *p*-value of virtually zero. The Wald test has a *p*-value that is also virtually zero. Both the LR test and the Wald test indicate there is very strong evidence that the spatial correlation coefficient *Lambda* is not zero.

The fifth and last part of the output provides several useful statistics and tests. The log-likelihood value for the fitted spatial lag model is −8,163.055 and the AIC value is 16,344, which is smaller than the AIC value of 16,940 for the standard linear regression model and the AIC value of 16,530 for the spatial lag model. The maximum likelihood estimate of the error variance *sigma squared* is 10.989, with the error standard deviation *sigma* estimated to be its square root, 3.3149.

Unlike the spatial lag model fit, there is no test for spatial dependence in the residuals. Thus, we apply the R function *moran.mc()* to test for spatial dependence in the residuals of the spatial error model:

```
moran.mc(residuals(m3_err), listw_povW, zero.policy=TRUE, nsim=999)
```

```
## 
##  Monte-Carlo simulation of Moran I
## 
## data:  residuals(m3_err)
## weights: listw_povW  
## number of simulations + 1: 1000
## 
## statistic = -0.041249, observed rank = 1, p-value = 0.999
## alternative hypothesis: greater
```

The observed Moran's I test statistic is −0.041249 with an observed rank of 1. Thus, the p-value is $(1 - .999) \times 2$, which is .002. There is still evidence of additional spatial dependence unaccounted for by the spatial error model.

8.1.5.4 Spatial SAR Models

An alternative to *lagsarlm()* is the R function *spautolm()* applied to the data frame *povty*; the output is *m3_sar*. We apply the R function *summary()* to *m3_sar* and obtain the results of the spatial linear regression that assumes a simultaneous autoregressive (SAR) model for the error term:

```
m3_sar = spautolm(povty ~ ag + foreign + feemp + hsch + black + hisp,
data=povdf, listw = listw_povW, zero.policy = TRUE, family="SAR")
summary (m3_sar)
```

```
## 
## Call: spautolm(formula = povty ~ ag + foreign + feemp + hsch + black + 
##     hisp, data = povdf, listw = listw_povW, family = "SAR", 
zero.policy = TRUE)
## 
## Residuals:
##       Min        1Q    Median        3Q       Max
## -14.63734  -1.86232  -0.36507   1.41036  29.97123
## 
## Regions with no neighbours included:
##  53055 25019
## 
```

```
## Coefficients:
##                Estimate Std. Error   z value  Pr(>|z|)
## (Intercept) 41.4409318  1.0717399   38.6670 < 2.2e-16
## ag           0.0765507  0.0126109    6.0702 1.278e-09
## foreign     -0.0671561  0.0271325   -2.4751   0.01332
## feemp       -0.4410193  0.0143178  -30.8021 < 2.2e-16
## hsch        -0.2283387  0.0148294  -15.3977 < 2.2e-16
## black        0.1267842  0.0076816   16.5049 < 2.2e-16
## hisp         0.0893849  0.0123932    7.2124 5.496e-13
##
## Lambda: 0.6181 LR test value: 597.7 p-value: < 2.22e-16
## Numerical Hessian standard error of lambda: 0.02026
##
## Log likelihood: -8163.055
## ML residual variance (sigma squared): 10.989, (sigma: 3.3149)
## Number of observations: 3070
## Number of parameters estimated: 9
## AIC: 16344
```

The output of *m3_sar* is essentially the same as the output of *m3_err*, which is not surprising because the same model is fitted. An advantage of *spautolm()* over *lag-sarlm()* is that *spautolm()* can be used to fit not only a SAR model but also a CAR model—this point is illustrated in Section 8.1.5.5.

8.1.5.5 Spatial CAR Models

In the R function *spautolm()*, we may specify a conditional autoregressive (CAR) model for the error term as follows:

```
m3_car = spautolm(povty ~ ag + foreign + feemp + hsch + black + hisp,
data=povdf, listw = listw_povW, zero.policy = TRUE, family="CAR")
summary (m3_car)

##
## Call: spautolm(formula = povty ~ ag + foreign + feemp + hsch + black +
##     hisp, data = povdf, listw = listw_povW, family = "CAR",
zero.policy = TRUE)
##
## Residuals:
##        Min         1Q     Median         3Q        Max
## -15.18926   -1.86108   -0.28199    1.42546   29.18209
##
## Regions with no neighbours included:
##  53055 25019
##
## Coefficients:
##                Estimate Std. Error   z value  Pr(>|z|)
## (Intercept) 38.8094082  1.1511956   33.7123 < 2.2e-16
## ag           0.0491986  0.0132661    3.7086 0.0002084
## foreign     -0.1045783  0.0290240   -3.6032 0.0003144
## feemp       -0.4027615  0.0149485  -26.9433 < 2.2e-16
## hsch        -0.2400807  0.0153632  -15.6270 < 2.2e-16
## black        0.1620906  0.0085421   18.9754 < 2.2e-16
## hisp         0.1253422  0.0145408    8.6200 < 2.2e-16
##
## Lambda: 0.97084 LR test value: 714.5 p-value: < 2.22e-16
## Numerical Hessian standard error of lambda: 0.016324
##
```

```
## Log likelihood: -8104.653
## ML residual variance (sigma squared): 9.8405, (sigma: 3.137)
## Number of observations: 3070
## Number of parameters estimated: 9
## AIC: 16227
```

Similar to the spatial SAR model fit, the percentages of agricultural workers, Blacks, and Hispanics are positively associated with poverty rates, whereas the percentages of foreign-born residents, female employment, and high school graduates are negatively associated with poverty rates. For example, the estimated regression coefficient for *feemp* is −0.403 with standard error 0.0149485. The Z-test statistic is −26.9433 and the *p*-value is less than 2.2E−16. This tells us that a 1 percent increase in the female employment rate is associated with a 0.403 percent decrease in the poverty rate when all other explanatory variables are held constant. Relative to the standard error of about 1.495 percent, the absolute value of the Z-statistic −26.9433 is very large and the *p*-value is extremely small. There is very strong evidence that the true regression coefficient for female employment rate is not zero.

The output also provides the estimate of the spatial correlation coefficient *Lambda*, which is 0.971. The LR test value is 714.5 with a *p*-value of virtually zero. There is very strong evidence that the spatial correlation coefficient *Lambda* is not zero.

The log-likelihood value for the fitted spatial CAR model is −8,104.653 and the AIC value is 16,227, which is smaller than the AIC values of 16,940, 16,530, and 16,344 for the standard linear regression, the spatial lag model, and the spatial SAR model, respectively. The maximum likelihood estimate of the error variance *sigma squared* is 9.8405, with the error standard deviation *sigma* estimated to be its square root, 3.137.

We apply the R function *moran.mc()* to test for spatial dependence in the residuals of the spatial CAR model:

```
moran.mc(resid(m3_car), listw_povW, zero.policy = TRUE, nsim=999)

##
##  Monte-Carlo simulation of Moran I
##
## data:  resid(m3_car)
## weights: listw_povW
## number of simulations + 1: 1000
##
## statistic = -0.20858, observed rank = 1, p-value = 0.999
## alternative hypothesis: greater
```

The observed Moran's *I* test statistic is −0.20858 with an observed rank of 1. Thus, the *p*-value is .001 × 2, which is .002. There is strong evidence of additional spatial dependence unaccounted for by the spatial CAR model. Even though the spatial

CAR model has a smaller AIC value than the spatial SAR model, their AIC values are similar. The two models' regression coefficients and their standard errors are also similar, leading to similar interpretations of the relationships between poverty and its explanatory variables. There is evidence of spatial dependence in the error term of both the spatial SAR and CAR models.

8.2 GENERAL PROCEDURE FOR SPATIAL SOCIAL DATA ANALYSIS

By now we have covered the methods related to spatial regression, including exploratory spatial data analysis, spatial regression models dealing with spatial dependence, spatial regression models dealing with spatial heterogeneity, spatial regression models dealing with both spatial dependence and spatial heterogeneity, and some advanced spatial regression models. With these many options to choose from for spatial regression but there being potential issues associated with each method, which approach is to be used?

Current literature addresses at least two approaches to choosing the more appropriate model:

- One is a theory-based approach, which suggests that the selection of a spatial regression model should be based on substantive grounds (Doreian, 1980).
- The other is a data-driven approach, which follows statistical procedures in selecting the better model based on data.

> Between theory-based and data-driven approaches, the latter is often preferred because typically the data, not the theoretical concerns, motivate spatial data analysis.

While both approaches are used in spatial regression, the data-driven method is frequently preferred because often it is the data rather than formal theoretical concerns that motivate spatial data analysis (Anselin, 2002, 2003).

Building on the methods covered in this book, we propose a general modeling procedure for studying social science phenomena with the spatial dimension in mind. The procedure not only deals with spatial dependence and spatial heterogeneity but also addresses other common issues associated with regression models. It consists of four aspects:

- data dimensions reduction,
- appropriate spatial weight matrix selection,

- spatial regression modeling with spatial dependence and spatial heterogeneity, and

- multitemporal comparison of variable presence and coefficient influence.

The following subsections address each of these four aspects. It should be noted that this general modeling procedure is just one possible procedure of many, although the four aspects of this procedure are likely familiar to social scientists and the combination of these familiar aspects allows a systematic examination of the response variable. As the last section, this section also serves as a summary of the spatial regression models and methods covered in this book.

8.2.1 Reducing Data Dimensions

Very often a social science phenomenon of interest (the response variable) is associated with a number of factors (explanatory variables), which can be found out by a thorough literature review. While it is important to consider as many of these explanatory variables as possible in data analysis and modeling, using numerous explanatory variables makes "big picture" interpretation of the response variable difficult. It also raises the multicollinearity that affects the interpretability and stability of regression modeling and others. However, there are approaches to dealing with multicollinearity. The three addressed in this book are factor analysis, using theory-based variables, and automated variable selection.

The issue of multicollinearity can be dealt with by factor analysis, using theory-based variables, or by automated variable selection.

Many studies have used factor analysis to examine the relationships among multiple explanatory variables (e.g., Marcouiller et al., 2004). Factor analysis takes a large number of variables and ends up with a smaller subset of latent factors. While researchers can use factor analysis to discover underlying patterns and understand interrelations among a set of variables, the factor analysis method can also be used for reducing data dimensions of conceptually related variables.

When the choice is made to use individual variables, two approaches can be used. The traditional approach is to use theory-based variables only. This approach has the advantage of allowing theories within disciplines to be used to support arguments and data analysis. However, considering this approach from an interdisciplinary perspective, it is argued that this theory-based approach will likely exclude other disciplines' theories that might be relevant because this approach is usually done within a single discipline. The other approach is to use automated variable selection methods such as backward elimination, forward selection,

Using only theory-based variables to reduce data dimensions allows the use of theories within disciplines to support arguments and data analysis.

and stepwise regression (Agresti & Finlay, 2009). This approach, which can be characterized as "data mining," has the strength of considering all the potential variables and selecting a subset of variables based on data in a statistically principled way. Nevertheless, this approach may end up eliminating substantive variables that are conceptually or theoretically sound in explaining the response variable—especially subtle associations overwhelmed by the associations of stronger variables in regression-based approaches.

There is a trade-off between developing models using a comprehensive set of variables pared down to a relevant subset using statistical methodology versus a more parsimoniously specified set of variables derived from purely theoretical grounds (Chi & Marcouiller, 2011). Although these approaches are the two most often used to address reducing the data dimensions of numerous variables, alternative theories may lead to alternatively specified models. Such models reflect an important point that theories behind any phenomenon of interest vary—or at least that the associations that are the most relevant at a given point in time and space vary—and that no single, generalizable construct exists. We recommend, from an interdisciplinary perspective, that researchers start with a comprehensive set of variables and then compare theory-based and data-driven approaches to discover if the theory-based approaches are ignoring any relevant variables.

8.2.2 Selecting an Appropriate Spatial Weight Matrix

Once data dimensions have been reduced, the retained explanatory variables are used to fit a standard linear regression model. In these models, it is assumed that errors are distributed both independently and identically. Yet this assumption may not be reasonable if the data exhibit either spatial dependence or spatial heterogeneity. Accounting for spatial dependence in a spatial regression model and diagnosing spatial dependence in the model's residuals require us to create a neighborhood structure for each areal unit of analysis (census tract, county, etc.) by specifying for each areal unit its neighboring areal units on a lattice (Anselin, 1988b). It is common practice to designate a spatial weight matrix corresponding to the neighborhood structure such that the resulting variance-covariance matrix can be expressed as a function of a small number of estimable parameters relative to the sample size (Anselin, 2002).

Analysis of areal data requires a spatial weight matrix, but there is little theory available to guide neighborhood structure selection.

Although areal data analysis requires a spatial weight matrix, little theory exists to guide the selection of a neighborhood structure in practice. Frequently, researchers define a spatial weight matrix exogenously and then compare several spatial weight matrices before selecting the most appropriate one (Anselin, 2002). As addressed in previous chapters, there are several data-driven approaches for selecting spatial weight matrices. One approach, which is used for the data examples in this book, is based on the strength and statistical significance of spatial dependence (Chi & Zhu, 2008). In this approach, the most appropriate spatial weight matrix is the one that achieves the highest coefficient of spatial dependence in combination with a high level of statistical significance. By and large, however, how to properly or even optimally specify the spatial weight matrix remains an open research question. For social scientists, the familiar spatial weight matrices are the rook's case and queen's case contiguity weight matrices with order 1 or higher, the k-nearest neighbor weight matrices, and the general distance weight matrices and inverse-distance weight matrices with power 1 or higher (Chi & Zhu, 2008). More complex spatial weight matrices, such as economic distance, can be created based on theories and assumptions (Case et al., 1993). Refer to Chapter 2 for more detailed discussion of the spatial weight matrices.

If theories or relevant studies in a field of research suggest or recommend a specific spatial weight matrix, researchers can of course use the said matrix. However, in instances where there is no theoretical guidance or prior research, we suggest readers use a data-driven approach.

8.2.3 Spatial Regression Modeling With Spatial Dependence and Spatial Heterogeneity

Moran's I statistic for regression residuals can be used to diagnose spatial dependence in model errors. If spatial dependence is detected, the LM test and the robust LM test (Anselin, 1988a) can be used to determine the appropriate spatial regression model for further examining the associations of various factors with the response variable. Frequently used spatial regression models include the spatial lag model and the spatial error model. Estimation of spatial lag and spatial error dependence simultaneously is best achieved through a spatial autoregressive moving average (SARMA) model (Anselin & Bera, 1998). In practice, we could use a spatial error model with spatially lagged responses to simultaneously estimate spatial lag and error dependence.

Spatial heterogeneity could refer to the fact that individual variables or the regression coefficients between a response variable and explanatory variables vary systematically across space (Dutilleul, 2011; LeSage, 1999). Frequently, it is found that the associations of the response variable with the numerous explanatory variables vary

Three approaches to dealing with spatial heterogeneity are aspatial methods, geographically weighted regression models, and spatial regime models.

across the studied area. There are several approaches to deal with spatial heterogeneity; three are discussed in Chapter 5:

- The first approach, widely used by sociologists, is to use *aspatial methods,* such as using dummy variables indicating the category of regions, combining dummy variables with explanatory variables, partitioning the study area into several regions that exhibit different spatial patterns, and then separately fitting standard linear regression for each region (Baller & Richardson, 2002). The disadvantage of this approach is that it makes it difficult to practically control spatial dependence when any of the partitioned regions are not contiguous or when they change over time.

- The second approach is using the *geographically weighted regression (GWR) method* (Fotheringham, Charlton, & Brunsdon, 1998), which enables modeling of the spatially varying coefficients. However, GWR does not consider the spatial lag and error dependence in the spatial econometric context; this makes it difficult to consider the spatial lag and error dependence simultaneously.

- The third approach is to apply a *spatial regime model* to estimate coefficients separately for each regime (Anselin, 1990; Patton & McErlean, 2003). With this approach, the spatial Chow test can be used to diagnose each variable's coefficient stability as well as the overall structural stability.

The ideal situation would be to have a model specification of spatial heterogeneity that considers the spatial lag dependence and the spatial error dependence simultaneously. However, to the best knowledge of the authors, no such ideal model specification exists within the currently available statistical software packages. That said, in practice, spatial regimes can be contained within a spatial error model with spatially lagged responses (Chi, 2010a). Such models estimate the coefficients and the spatial lag effects separately for each regime and estimate a spatial error effect for the overall model.

Selection of a spatial regression model should be based on the study's research questions as well as data availability.

Each of these methods of dealing with spatial heterogeneity has strengths and limitations. Selecting a spatial regression model should be based on the research questions and the availability of the data. We recommend the spatial regime approach to understand the phenomenon of interest comprehensively—it considers spatial lag dependence, spatial error dependence, and spatial heterogeneity simultaneously, whereas the other two approaches cannot.

In practice, standard linear regression and spatial regression models could be evaluated based on AIC or BIC for evaluating the model fitting balanced with model parsimony

(Kuha, 2005). An alternative approach to comparing a standard linear regression model and a spatial regression model is to use the likelihood ratio test (LRT) and get a *p*-value, if the spatial regression model can be reduced to a standard linear regression model. The statistical significance can indicate whether one model is better fitted to data than another model is. Refer to Chapters 3 to 5 for more details on model evaluations.

8.2.4 Multitemporal Comparison of Variable Presence and Coefficient Influence

Numerous explanatory variables can be associated with the response variable, and the importance of each explanatory variable may vary over time. Thus, researchers could also consider the temporal variation of the explanatory variables in relation to the response variable. One way to do this is to fit the same set of regression models for different time periods. The estimated coefficients of the regression models can be compared to evaluate the extent of temporal instability. The significance of coefficient drift in different time periods among the regression specifications can be determined by using the Chow test. Furthermore, spatial panel data analysis methods (see Chapter 7) can be used to model spatial and temporal dependence simultaneously.

Study Questions

1. How does the R environment work differently from the statistical software packages that you typically use, such as Stata and SPSS?
2. What packages of R were used in the poverty data example?
3. What is the general procedure of spatial data analysis presented in this chapter?
4. What are the advantages and disadvantages of the theory-based and data-driven approaches for selecting spatial regression models?
5. What methods are appropriate for reducing data dimensions? What are their advantages and disadvantages?
6. What guidelines could be used to select appropriate spatial weight matrices?
7. What methods or approaches could be used to simultaneously model spatial lag and spatial error dependence and spatial heterogeneity?
8. What methods or approaches could be used to incorporate temporal variation into spatial regression modeling?
9. Is a data-driven approach or a theory-driven approach more appropriate in guiding your research?
10. Can you develop a general procedure of spatial data analysis to guide your own research?
11. By following the practical procedure of spatial data analysis that you will develop, how might the results help you make a (spatial) theoretical contribution to your area of research?

APPENDIX A

Spatial Data Sources

Spatial regression analysis is applied to spatial data. An important question is, where do the data come from? We could create our own spatial data by using spatial data collection and analysis tools, which are covered in many geographic analysis books (e.g., Burrough & McDonnell, 1998; Fischer & Nijkamp, 1993; Fotheringham & Rogerson, 1994; Longley, Goodchild, Maguire, & Rhind, 2001; Maguire, Goodchild, & Rhind, 1991; O'Sullivan & Unwin, 2003) and thus are not addressed in this book.

There are also many websites from which we can download spatial data. Depending on the objective of a study and the data quality, we can either use the data directly or integrate the data into a cleaned data set for analysis. Such options are also covered in many geographic analysis books. In this appendix, we provide some spatial data sources that the reader can start with. This list is far from comprehensive by any means and is in the context of the United States only; other sources of data can be obtained from published research in your field.

The data sources listed here fall into one of two types. One is traditional websites where we could navigate through the website to find the data theme(s) we need and download their shapefile, the most often used spatial data type for spatial data analysis in GeoDa, R, and other software packages. The other is interactive web GIS, an online mapping tool by which we can view, visualize, edit, and/or download the data (Fu & Sun, 2011). Web GIS does not require the user to have geographic analysis knowledge and has been gaining popularity due to its user-friendly nature and the easy dissemination of data from the server to end-users.

TRADITIONAL WEBSITES

Federal Geographic Data Committee (FGDC)
http://www.fgdc.gov/

The FGDC oversees geospatial decisions and initiatives across federal government agencies in collaboration with federal, state, tribal, and local governments; communities; constituents; and professional bodies to provide the foundation of standards, data catalogs, and other services related to geospatial data. Through the FGDC's online portal (https://www.GeoPlatform.gov), users can access their geographic data, maps, and online services for free.

U.S. Government's Open Data
https://www.data.gov/

The U.S. General Services Administration manages and hosts this website of open data, collecting government data in machine-readable formats. Some data sets are downloadable, while others are linked to websites or apps that help users access or use them. In addition, researchers can upload their data to this website for others to use.

Census Bureau
https://www.census.gov

The Census Bureau serves as the nation's leading provider of quality data about its people and economy. The Census Bureau is responsible for the U.S. decennial census, American Community Survey, demographic surveys, economics surveys, and sponsored surveys for other government agencies. The boundary files of administrative areas and census areas can be downloaded from https://www.census.gov/geo/maps-data/data/tiger-cart-boundary.html. These boundary files are available in shapefiles.

Social Explorer
http://www.socialexplorer.com/pub/home/home.aspx

Social Explorer collects and harmonizes social data from many sources. It covers a wide range of social topics and presents the data professionally. Users can also create dynamic maps and customizable reports. Social Explorer is used widely among social scientists because it is one of the most comprehensive data sources and presents the data in a user-friendly manner.

Integrated Public Use Microdata Series (IPUMS)
https://www.ipums.org/

IPUMS integrates census and survey data from around the world. It creates and harmonizes the world's largest accessible census and survey microdata and the most comprehensive area-level census data. It is popular among social scientists. Both Social Explorer and IPUMS host a vast amount of social data, but the former appears to be more user-friendly while the latter has more comprehensive data.

INTERACTIVE WEB GIS

Census Data Mapper

http://datamapper.geo.census.gov/map.html

The Census Data Mapper allows users to customize maps (using census data) through six easy steps. It is straightforward to create custom color maps based on a myriad of themes (e.g., age/sex, population/race, family/housing); data tables (e.g., gender and age); colors; and classification systems.

Census Interactive Population Map

http://www.census.gov/2010census/popmap/

The Interactive Population Map provides population, ethnicity, race, age, and household data for specific locations in map form for all fifty U.S. states, the District of Columbia, and Puerto Rico. The site also allows users to compare data on locations from census tract to national levels.

Census Flows Mapper

http://flowsmapper.geo.census.gov/map.html

This tool is a web mapping application that provides users with a simple tool to view, save, and print county-to-county migration flow maps of the United States. The data come from the American Community Surveys. (Note: This site requires Adobe Flash Player.)

Census Metro/Micro Thematic Map Viewer

http://www.census.gov/population/metro/data/thematic_maps.html

This web mapping application uses 2010 Census tract–level data in both metropolitan and micropolitan areas in the United States, District of Columbia, and Puerto Rico. After the parameters are created, the user can zoom in to obtain specific information on city statistics compared with national statistics.

Census OnTheMap for Emergency Management

http://onthemap.ces.census.gov

If users want to know the demographics of areas hit or affected by disasters, this is the site to visit. Users can analyze data at aggregated geographic levels, including state, county, city, ZIP code, census tract, census block, school district, and so on. This mapping tool also has graphic functionality that allows for polygons, simple radii, donut radii, and plumes for a single or layered data set.

Net Migration Patterns for U.S. Counties
http://netmigration.wisc.edu

This mapping tool allows users to make maps and charts of migration patterns across the United States. Net migration estimates can be selected based on age, race, and sex for all decades from 1950 to 2010. Data sets from this site can also be downloaded for other uses. This site is available in part by a joint effort among the University of Wisconsin–Madison, Michigan Technological University, and the University of New Hampshire.

Atlas of Rural and Small-Town America
http://www.ers.usda.gov/data-products/atlas-of-rural-and-small-town-america/go-to-the-atlas.aspx

The U.S. Department of Agriculture (USDA) provides statistical information in four broad categories: people, jobs, agriculture, and county classifications. The atlas allows users to view over sixty socioeconomic indicators at the county level, zoom in and out from the county to regional levels, print maps, download spreadsheets, and perform multiple other functions. The site also has USDA data files on topics such as GMOs, agricultural productivity, and research funding.

County Health Rankings & Roadmaps
http://www.countyhealthrankings.org

This site allows users to find out how healthy a county is and the factors that drive health care outcomes. Users can view one county or compare counties from across the United States. Some of the topics included are length of life, quality of life, health behaviors, socioeconomic factors, and the physical environment. Data sets include information from 2008 to 2014 and are downloadable.

Land Developability
http://www.landdevelopability.org

This site aggregates the layers of land use and development for political or geographic areas. The index represents the proportion of lands available for future development or conversion. The data elements include surface water, wetlands, federal and state lands, Indian reservations, built-up lands, and steep slopes. This site is an ongoing project conducted at The Pennsylvania State University.

Appendix B: Results Using Forty Spatial Weight Matrices is available on the website at: **study.sagepub.com/researchmethods/quantitative-statistical-research/chi**

GLOSSARY

Areal data are spatial data observed or aggregated over regular cells or irregular areal regions.

Areal data analysis is the focus of this book because it is the spatial approach currently most used in the social sciences.

Autocorrelation is the correlation of a variable with itself at different time points or spatial locations.

Conditional autoregressive (CAR) models are spatial models in which the distribution of a response variable (or regression error) at one location is specified by conditioning on the values of its neighbors, and the neighbors' spatial effect is considered to be exogenous.

Diff-criterion statistic is based on a set of model-fitting measures, including AIC_c, AIC, BIC, and CV.

Exploratory spatial data analysis (ESDA) displays and summarizes data spatially, helping researchers choose potential models and statistical methods.

G statistic is a measure of the concentration (or lack of concentration) of the sum of the study area's attributes.

Geary's c is a measure of dissimilarity between neighboring areal units, or spatial autocorrelation.

Geographic analysis extracts or creates new information from spatial data and examines spatial data locations, attributes, and feature relations.

Geographically weighted regression (GWR) is capable of estimating one set of coefficients for each areal unit under suitable conditions.

Geostatistical data are spatial data from point locations continuous in space.

LM test/robust LM test can help indicate the appropriateness of a spatial regression model with respect to spatial lag dependence and spatial error dependence.

Local Indicator of Spatial Association (LISA) can be used to evaluate the local variation in spatial patterns (or, spatial heterogeneity).

MLE method chooses the set of parameter estimates that has resulted in the maximum likelihood of the observed data.

Moran's I is a measure of similarity between neighboring areal units, or spatial autocorrelation.

Multilevel linear regression (MLR) models address the limitation of not being able to interpret results at both levels by incorporating both individual-level and aggregated-level associations.

Ordinary least squares (OLS) estimation chooses the model fitting that has resulted in the least squares of errors.

Simultaneous autoregressive (SAR) models are spatial models in which the relations among the response variables at all locations are explained simultaneously and the spatial effects are considered to be endogenous.

Spatial autocorrelation refers to the correlation of the same attribute between two locations.

Spatial autoregressive moving average (SARMA) model simultaneously models spatial lag and spatial error dependence.

Spatial Chow test can be used to test the structural stability of each variable as well as the overall structural stability.

Spatial cross-regressive model assumes a linear relation between the response variable and the explanatory variables and their associated spatially lagged explanatory variables.

Spatial data refer to data that are referenced geographically and represent phenomena located in space.

Spatial data analysis describes, models, and explains spatial data and enables us to make inferences and predictions.

Spatial error models account for spatial dependence by an error term and an associated spatially lagged error term.

Spatial error model with spatially lagged responses (SEMSLR) is a spatial error model that includes spatially lagged response variables.

Spatial heterogeneity refers to differences across space in the mean, variance, or spatial correlation structures.

Spatial moving average (SMA) models are spatial models in which the error process is modeled by a linear combination of white noises at neighboring locations, akin to the moving average models in time series.

Spatial interaction data are the "flows" between origins and destinations.

Spatial lag models relate explanatory variables and a response variable as in a standard linear regression model, except the response variable is auto-regressed on spatially lagged response variables.

Spatial panel data are geographically referenced and have observations at each areal unit over multiple time points.

Spatial point patterns consist of event locations in a spatial domain of interest.

Spatial regime error model (SREM) is a model that combines the spatial regime model and the spatial error model.

Spatial regime error and lag model (SRELM) is a relatively more flexible model that deals with spatial dependence and spatial heterogeneity simultaneously by considering spatial lag dependence, spatial error dependence, and spatial heterogeneity.

Spatial regime lag model (SRLM) is a model that combines the spatial regime model and the spatial lag model.

Spatial regime standard linear regression (SRSLR) model considers a separate set of coefficients for each areal type, or regime.

Spatial weight is used in a spatial weight matrix to relate a variable at one areal unit to that same variable at a neighboring unit per a specified neighborhood structure. Conducting exploratory spatial data analysis and fitting spatial regression models often involve a spatial weight matrix.

Spatial regression forecasting models can be estimated by adding the spatially lagged terms to a standard regression forecasting model.

Spatio-temporal regression models refer to regression models that consider both spatial and temporal dependence exhibited in the data.

REFERENCES

Agresti, A., & Finlay, B. (2009). *Statistical methods for the social sciences* (4th ed.). Upper Saddle River, NJ: Pearson and Prentice Hall.

Akaike, H. (1973). *Information theory and an extension of the maximum likelihood principle.* Paper presented at Proceedings of the 2nd International Symposium on Information Theory, Akademiai Kaido, Budapest, Hungary.

Alba, R. D., & Logan, J. R. (1993). Minority proximity to whites in suburbs: An individual-level analysis of segregation. *American Journal of Sociology, 98*, 1388–1427.

Aldstadt, J., & Getis, A. (2006). Using AMOEBA to create a spatial weights matrix and identify spatial clusters. *Geographical Analysis, 38*, 327–343.

Alfes, K., Shantz, A. D., & Ritz, A. (2018). A multilevel examination of the relationship between role overload and employee subjective health: The buffering effect of support climates. *Human Resource Management, 57*, 659–673.

Alho, J. M., & Spencer, B. D. (2005). *Statistical demography and forecasting.* New York, NY: Springer.

Ali, K., Partridge, M. D., & Olfert, M. R. (2007). Can geographically weighted regressions improve regional analysis and policy making? *International Regional Science Review, 30*, 300–329.

Allison, P. D. (1999). *Multiple regression.* Thousand Oaks, CA: Pine Forge Press.

Amara, M., & Jemmali, H. (2018). Household and contextual indicators of poverty in Tunisia: A multilevel analysis. *Social Indicators Research, 137*, 113–138.

Anselin, L. (1988a). Lagrange multiplier test diagnostics for spatial dependence and spatial heterogeneity. *Geographical Analysis, 20*, 1–17.

Anselin, L. (1988b). *Spatial econometrics: Methods and models.* Dordrecht, the Netherlands: Kluwer Academic.

Anselin, L. (1990). Spatial dependence and spatial structural instability in applied regression analysis. *Journal of Regional Science, 30*, 185–207.

Anselin, L. (1992). *SpaceStat tutorial: A workbook for using SpaceStat in the analysis of spatial data.* Santa Barbara: National Center for Geographic Information and Analysis, University of California.

Anselin, L. (1995). Local indicators of spatial association—LISA. *Geographical Analysis, 27*, 93–115.

Anselin, L. (1996). The Moran scatterplot as an ESDA tool to assess local instability in spatial association. In M. Fischer, H. J. Scholten, & D. Unwin (Eds.), *Spatial analytical perspectives on GIS: GISDATA 4* (pp. 111–125). London, UK: Taylor & Francis.

Anselin, L. (2002). Under the hood: Issues in the specification and interpretation of spatial regression models. *Agricultural Economics, 27*, 247–267.

Anselin, L. (2003). Spatial externalities, spatial multipliers, and spatial econometrics. *International Regional Science Review, 26*, 153–166.

Anselin, L. (2005). *Exploring spatial data with GeoDa™: A workbook.* Urbana: Spatial Analysis Laboratory, University of Illinois at Urbana-Champaign.

Anselin, L., & Bera, A. (1998). Spatial dependence in linear regression models with an introduction to spatial econometrics. In A. Ullah & D. Giles (Eds.), *Handbook of applied economic statistics* (pp. 237–289). New York, NY: Marcel Dekker.

Anselin, L., Bera, A. K., Florax, R. J. G. M., & Yoon, M. J. (1996). Simple diagnostic tests for spatial dependence. *Regional Science and Urban Economics, 26*, 77–104.

Ansong, D., Ansong, E. K., Ampomah, A. O., & Adjabeng, B. K. (2015). Factors contributing to spatial inequality in academic achievement in Ghana: Analysis of district-level factors using geographically weighted regression. *Applied Geography, 62*, 136–146.

Armstrong, J. S. (2001). Introduction. In J. S. Armstrong (Ed.), *Principles of forecasting: A handbook for researchers and practitioners* (pp. 1–12). Boston, MA: Kluwer Academic.

Assunção, R. M., Schmertmann, C. P., Potter, J. E., & Cavenaghi, S. M. (2005). Empirical Bayes estimation of demographic schedules for small areas. *Demography*, *42*, 537–558.

Baddeley, A., Rubak, E., & Turner, R. (2015). *Spatial point patterns: Methodology and applications with R*. Boca Raton, FL: CRC Press.

Bailey, A. (2005). *Making population geography*. London, UK: Hodder.

Bailey, T. C., & Gatrell, A. C. (1995). *Interactive spatial data analysis*. Harlow, UK: Longman Scientific & Technical.

Ballas, D., Clarke, G. P., & Wiemers, E. (2005). Building a dynamic spatial microsimulation model for Ireland. *Population, Space and Place*, *11*, 157–172.

Baller, R. D., Anselin, L., Messner, S. F., Deane, G., & Hawkins, D. F. (2001). Structural covariates of U.S. county homicide rates: Incorporating spatial effects. *Criminology*, *39*, 561–590.

Baller, R. D., & Richardson, K. K. (2002). Social integration, imitation, and the geographic patterning of suicide. *American Sociological Review*, *67*, 873–888.

Baltagi, B., & Li, D. (2004). Prediction in the panel data model with spatial autocorrelation. In L. Anselin, R. J. G. M. Florax, & S. Rey (Eds.), *Advances in spatial econometrics: Methodology, tools, and applications* (pp. 283–295). New York, NY: Springer.

Baltagi, B. H., & Yang, Z. L. (2013). Standardized LM tests for spatial error dependence in linear or panel regressions. *Econometrics Journal*, *16*, 103–134.

Bardenheier, B. H., Shefer, A., Barker, L., Winston, C. A., & Sionean, C. K. (2005). Public health application comparing multilevel analysis with logistic regression: Immunization coverage among long-term care facility residents. *Annals of Epidemiology*, *15*, 749–755.

Bellani, D., Esping-Andersen, G., & Nedoluzhko, L. (2017). Never partnered: A multilevel analysis of lifelong singlehood. *Demographic Research*, *37*, 53–100.

Bennett, K. J., Probst, J. C., & Pumkam, C. (2011). Obesity among working age adults: The role of county-level persistent poverty in rural disparities. *Health and Place*, *17*, 1174–1181.

Bera, A. K., & Jarque, C. M. (1980). Efficient tests for normality, homoscedasticity and serial independence of regression residuals. *Economics Letters*, *6*, 255–259.

Bera, A. K., & Yoon, M. J. (1993). Specification testing with locally misspecified alternatives. *Econometric Theory*, *9*(4), 649–658.

Berry, B. J. L., & Kasarda, J. D. (1977). *Contemporary urban ecology*. New York, NY: Macmillan.

Bilecen, B., & Cardona, A. (2018). Do transnational brokers always win? A multilevel analysis of social support. *Social Networks*, *53*, 90–100.

Bille, A. G., Salvioni, C., & Benedetti, R. (2018). Modelling spatial regimes in farms technologies. *Journal of Productivity Analysis*, *49*, 173–185.

Bivand, R., Keitt, T., Rowlingson, B., & Pebesma, E. (2018). Package 'rgdal'. R package version 1.3-4. Retrieved from ftp://mozilla.c3sl.ufpr.br/CRAN/web/packages/rgdal/rgdal.pdf

Blanchard, T. C. (2007). Conservative Protestant congregations and racial residential segregation: Evaluating the closed community thesis in metropolitan and nonmetropolitan counties. *American Sociological Review*, *72*, 416–433.

Boarnet, M. G. (1994a). An empirical model of intra-metropolitan population and employment growth. *Papers in Regional Science*, *73*, 135–152.

Boarnet, M. G. (1994b). The monocentric model and employment location. *Journal of Urban Economics*, *36*, 79–97.

Boarnet, M. G. (1997). Highways and economic productivity. Interpreting recent evidence. *Journal of Planning Literature*, *11*, 476–486.

Boarnet, M. G. (1998). Spillovers and the locational effects of public infrastructure. *Journal of Regional Science*, *38*, 381–400.

Boarnet, M. G., Chalermpong, S., & Geho, E. (2005). Specification issues in models of population and employment growth. *Papers in Regional Science*, *84*, 21–46.

Breusch, T. S., & Pagan, A. R. (1979). A simple test for heteroscedasticity and random coefficient variation. *Econometrica*, *47*, 1287–1294.

Brown, D. L., Fuguitt, G. V., Heaton, T. B., & Waseem, S. (1997). Continuities in size of place preferences in the United States, 1972–1992. *Rural Sociology*, *62*, 408–428.

Brueckner, J. K. (2003). Airline traffic and urban economic development. *Urban Studies*, *40*, 1455–1469.

Burrough, P. A., & McDonnell, R. A. (1998). *Principles of geographical information systems*. New York, NY: Oxford University Press.

Cardille, J. A., Ventura, S. J., & Turner, M. G. (2001). Environmental and social factors influencing wildfires in the upper Midwest, USA. *Ecological Applications, 11*, 111–127.

Carlino, G. A., & Mills, E. S. (1987). The determinants of county growth. *Journal of Regional Science, 27*, 39–54.

Case, A. C., Rosen, H. S., & Hines, J. R., Jr. (1993). Budget spillovers and fiscal policy interdependence: Evidence from the states. *Journal of Public Economics, 52*, 285–307.

Cervero, R. (2003). Road expansion, urban growth, and induced travel: A path analysis. *Journal of the American Planning Association, 69*, 145–163.

Charles, C. Z. (2003). The dynamics of racial residential segregation. *Annual Review of Sociology, 29*, 167–207.

Chen, D. R., & Truong, K. (2012). Using multilevel modeling and geographically weighted regression to identify spatial variations in the relationship between place-level disadvantages and obesity in Taiwan. *Applied Geography, 32*, 737–745.

Chi, G. (2009). Can knowledge improve population forecasts at subcounty levels? *Demography, 46*, 405–427.

Chi, G. (2010a). The impacts of highway expansion on population change: An integrated spatial approach. *Rural Sociology, 75*, 58–89.

Chi, G. (2010b). Land developability: Developing an index of land use and development for population research. *Journal of Maps, 2010*, 609–617.

Chi, G. (2012). The impacts of transport accessibility on population change across rural, suburban and urban areas: A case study of Wisconsin at subcounty levels. *Urban Studies, 49*, 2711–2731.

Chi, G., & Marcouiller, D. W. (2011). Isolating the effect of natural amenities on population change at the local level. *Regional Studies, 45*, 491–505.

Chi, G., & Marcouiller, D. W. (2013). Natural amenities and their effects on migration along the urban-rural continuum. *The Annals of Regional Science, 50*(3), 861–883.

Chi, G., & Parisi, D. (2011). Highway expansion effects on urban racial redistribution in the post-civil-rights period. *Public Works Management and Policy, 16*, 40–58.

Chi, G., & Voss, P. R. (2005). Migration decision-making: A hierarchical regression approach. *Journal of Regional Analysis and Policy, 35*, 11–22.

Chi, G., & Voss, P. R. (2011). Small-area population forecasting: Borrowing strength across space and time. *Population, Space and Place, 17*, 505–520.

Chi, G., & Wang, D. (2017). Small-area population forecasting: A geographically weighted regression approach. In D. Swanson (Ed.), *The frontiers of applied demography* (pp. 449–471). Cham, Switzerland: Springer.

Chi, G., & Wang, D. (2018). Population projection accuracy: The impacts of sociodemographics, accessibility, land use, and neighbour characteristics. *Population, Space and Place, 24*(5), e2129.

Chi, G., & Zhu, J. (2008). Spatial regression models for demographic analysis. *Population Research and Policy Review, 27*, 17–42.

Cho, S. H., Lambert, D. M., & Chen, Z. (2010). Geographically weighted regression bandwidth selection and spatial autocorrelation: An empirical example using Chinese agriculture data. *Applied Economics Letters, 17*, 767–772.

Chow, G. C. (1960). Tests of equality between sets of coefficients in two linear regressions. *Econometrica, 28*, 591–605.

Christaller, W. (1966). *Central places in southern Germany* (C. W. Baskin, Trans.). Englewood Cliffs, NJ: Prentice Hall.

Clark, D., & Hunter, W. (1992). The impact of economic opportunity, amenities and fiscal factors on age-specific migration rates. *Journal of Regional Science, 32*, 349–365.

Cliff, A., & Ord, K. (1972). Testing for spatial autocorrelation among regression residuals. *Geographical Analysis, 4*, 267–284.

Cliff, A. D., & Ord, K. J. (1973). *Spatial autocorrelation*. London, UK: Pion Limited.

Cliff, A. D., & Ord, K. J. (1981). *Spatial processes: Models and applications*. London, UK: Pion Limited.

Clogg, C., Petkova, E., & Haritou, A. (1995). Statistical methods for comparing regression coefficients between models. *American Journal of Sociology, 100*, 1261–1293.

Cowen, D. J., & Jensen, J. R. (1998). Extraction and modeling of urban attributes using remote sensing technology. In D. Liverman, E. F. Moran, R. R. Rindfuss, & P. C. Stern (Eds.), *People and pixels: Linking remote* sensing and social science (pp. 164–188). Washington, DC: National Academies Press.

Cressie, N. (1993). *Statistics for spatial data*. New York, NY: John Wiley.

DaVanzo, J. (1981). Microeconomic approaches to studying migration decisions. In G. F. DeJong & R. W. Gardner (Eds.), *Migration decision making: Multidisciplinary approaches to microlevel studies in developed and developing countries* (pp. 90–129). New York, NY: Pergamon.

Diez-Roux, A. V., Nieto, F. J., Muntaner, C., Tyroler, H. A., Comstock, G. W., Shahar, E., . . . Szklo, M. (2017). Neighborhood environments and coronary heart disease: A multilevel analysis. *American Journal of Epidemiology*, *185*, 1187–1202.

Doreian, P. (1980). Linear models with spatially distributed data: Spatial disturbances or spatial effects? *Sociological Methods and Research*, *9*, 29–60.

Draper, N. R., & Smith, H. (1998). *Applied regression analysis*. New York, NY: John Wiley.

Dutilleul, P. R. L. (2011). *Spatio-temporal heterogeneity: Concepts and analyses*. New York, NY: Cambridge University Press.

Ekbrand, H., & Hallerod, B. (2018). The more gender equity, the less child poverty? A multilevel analysis of malnutrition and health deprivation in 49 low- and middle-income countries. *World Development*, *108*, 221–230.

Elhorst, J. P. (2001). Dynamic models in space and time. *Geographical Analysis*, *33*, 119–140.

Elhorst, J. P. (2003). Specification and estimation of spatial panel data models. *International Regional Science Review*, *26*, 244–268.

Elhorst, J. P. (2010a). Spatial panel data models. In M. M. Fischer & A. Getis (Eds.), *Handbook of applied spatial analysis* (pp. 377–407). Berlin, Germany: Springer.

Elhorst, J. P. (2010b). Applied spatial econometrics: Raising the bar. *Spatial Economic Analysis*, *5*(1), 9–28.

Elhorst, J. P., & Freret, S. (2009). Evidence of political yardstick competition in France using a two-regime spatial Durbin model with fixed effects. *Journal of Regional Science*, *49*, 931–951.

Elliott, P., & Wartenberg, D. (2004). Spatial epidemiology: Current approaches and future challenges. *Environmental Health Perspectives*, *112*, 998–1006.

Entwisle, B. (2007). Putting people into place. *Demography*, *44*, 687–703.

Ertur, C., Le Gallo, J., & Baumont, C. (2006). The European regional convergence process, 1980–1995: Do spatial regimes and spatial dependence matter? *International Regional Science Review*, *29*, 3–34.

Evans, C. R., Williams, D. R., Onnela, J. P., & Subramanian, S. V. (2018). A multilevel approach to modeling health inequalities at the intersection of multiple social identities. *Social Science & Medicine*, *203*, 64–73.

Fingleton, B., & Lopez-Bazo, E. (2006). Empirical growth models with spatial effects. *Papers in Regional Science*, *85*, 177–198.

Fischer, M. M., & Nijkamp, P. (1993). *Geographic information systems, spatial modelling and policy evaluation*. Berlin, Germany: Springer.

Florax, R. J. G. M., & Folmer, H. (1992). Specification and estimation of spatial linear regression models. *Regional Science and Urban Economics*, *22*, 405–432.

Florax, R. J. G. M., & Van der Vlist, A. J. (2003). Spatial econometric data analysis: Moving beyond traditional models. *International Regional Science Review*, *26*, 223–243.

Fossett, M. (2005). Urban and spatial demography. In D. L. Poston & M. Micklin (Eds.), *Handbook of population* (pp. 479–524). New York, NY: Springer.

Fotheringham, A. S., Brunsdon, C., & Charlton, M. (2002). *Geographically weighted regression: The analysis of spatially varying relationships*. West Sussex, UK: John Wiley.

Fotheringham, A. S., Charlton, M., & Brunsdon, C. (1998). Geographically weighted regression: A natural evolution of the expansion method for spatial data analysis. *Environment and Planning A: Economy and Space*, *30*, 1905–1927.

Fotheringham, A. S., & Rogerson, P. (1994). *Spatial analysis and GIS*. London, UK: Taylor & Francis.

Fotheringham, A. S., & Wong, D. W. S. (1991). The modifiable areal unit problem in multivariate statistical analysis. *Environment and Planning A: Economy and Space*, *23*, 1025–1034.

Fox, J. (1997). *Applied regression analysis, linear models, and related methods*. Thousand Oaks, CA: Sage.

Fox, J. (2008). *Applied regression analysis and generalized linear models*. Thousand Oaks, CA: Sage.

Fraser, L. K., Clarke, G. P., Cade, J. E., & Edwards, K. L. (2012). Fast food and obesity. *American Journal of Preventive Medicine, 42*, e77–e85.

Freret, S., & Maguain, D. (2017). The effects of agglomeration on tax competition: Evidence from a two-regime spatial panel model on French data. *International Tax and Public Finance, 24*, 1100–1140.

Freudenburg, W. R. (1992). Addictive economies: Extractive industries and vulnerable localities in a changing world economy. *Rural Sociology, 57*, 305–332.

Frisbie, W. P., & Kasarda, J. D. (1988). Spatial processes. In N. J. Smelser (Ed.), *Handbook of sociology* (pp. 629–666). Newbury Park, CA: Sage.

Frisbie, W. P., & Poston, D. L. (1975). Components of sustenance organization and nonmetropolitan population change: A human ecological investigation. *American Sociological Review, 40*, 773–784.

Fu, P., & Sun, J. (2011). *Web GIS: Principles and applications*. Redlands, CA: ESRI Press.

Fuguitt, G. V., & Beale, C. L. (1996). Recent trends in nonmetropolitan migration: Toward a new turnaround? *Growth and Change, 27*, 156–174.

Fuguitt, G. V., & Brown, D. L. (1990). Residential preferences and population redistribution. *Demography, 27*, 589–600.

Fuguitt, G. V., Brown, D. L., & Beale, C. L. (1989). *Rural and small town America*. New York, NY: Russell Sage Foundation.

Fuguitt, G. V., & Zuiches, J. J. (1975). Residential preferences and population distribution. *Demography, 12*, 491–504.

Galster, G. C. (1988). Residential segregation in American cities: A contrary review. *Population Research and Policy Review, 7*, 93–112.

Galston, W. A., & Baehler, K. J. (1995). *Rural development in the United States: Connecting theory, practice, and possibilities*. Washington, DC: Island Press.

Geary, R. C. (1954). The contiguity ratio and statistical mapping. *The Incorporated Statistician, 5*, 115–145.

Getis, A. (1984). Interaction modeling using second-order analysis. *Environment and Planning A: Economy and Space, 16*, 173–183.

Getis, A. (1995). Spatial filtering in a regression framework: Examples using data on urban crime, regional inequality, government expenditures. In L. Anselin & R. J. G. M. Florax (Eds.), *New directions in spatial econometrics* (pp. 172–185). Berlin, Germany: Springer Verlag.

Getis, A. (2008). A history of the concept of spatial autocorrelation: A geographer's perspective. *Geographical Analysis, 40*(3), 297–309.

Getis, A., & Aldstadt, J. (2004). Constructing the spatial weights matrix using a local statistic. *Geographical Analysis, 36*, 90–104.

Getis, A., & Ord, J. K. (1996). Local spatial statistics: An overview. In P. A. Longley & M. Batty (Eds.), *Spatial analysis: Modelling in a GIS environment* (pp. 261–277). New York, NY: John Wiley.

Goetz, A. R. (1992). Air passenger transportation and growth in the U.S. urban system, 1950–1987. *Growth and Change, 23*(2), 217–238.

Goetz, A. R., & Sutton, C. J. (1997). The geography of deregulation in the U.S. airline industry. *Annals of the Association of American Geographers, 87*, 238–263.

Goetz, S. J., & Swaminathan, H. (2006). Wal-Mart and county-wide poverty. *Social Science Quarterly, 87*, 211–226.

Goodchild, M. F. (1992). Geographical data modeling. *Computers & Geosciences, 18*, 401–408.

Goodchild, M. F., & Janelle, D. G. (2004). *Spatially integrated social science*. Oxford, UK: Oxford University Press.

Gordon, D. (1978). Capitalist development and the history of American cities. In W. Tabb & L. Sawers (Eds.), *Marxism and the metropolis* (pp. 25–63). New York, NY: Oxford University Press.

Graaff, T. D., Florax, R. J. G. M., Nijkamp, P., & Reggiani, A. (2001). A general misspecification test for spatial regression models: Dependence, heterogeneity, and nonlinearity. *Journal of Regional Science, 41*, 255–276.

Graif, C., & Sampson, R. J. (2009). Spatial heterogeneity in the effects of immigration and diversity on neighborhood homicide rates. *Homicide Studies, 13*(3), 242–260.

Graves, P. (1983). Migration with a composite amenity. *Journal of Regional Science, 23*, 541–546.

Graves, P. E. (1979). A life-cycle empirical analysis of migration and climate by race. *Journal of Urban Economics, 6*, 135–147.

Graves, P. E. (1980). Migration and climate. *Journal of Regional Science, 20,* 227–237.

Graves, P. E., & Linneman, P. D. (1979). Household migration: Theoretical and empirical results. *Journal of Urban Economics, 6,* 383–404.

Green, M., & Flowerdew, R. (1996). New evidence on the modifiable areal unit problem. In P. Longley & M. Batty (Eds.), *Spatial analysis: Modelling in a GIS environment* (pp. 41–54). Cambridge, UK: GeoInformation International.

Green, R. K. (2007). Airports and economic development. *Real Estate Economics, 35,* 91–112.

Greene, W. H. (2000). *Econometric analysis.* Upper Saddle River, NJ: Prentice-Hall.

Greenlee, R. T., & Howe, H. L. (2009). County-level poverty and distant stage cancer in the United States. *Cancer Causes and Control, 20,* 989–1000.

Griffith, D. A. (1987). *Spatial autocorrelation: A primer.* Washington, DC: Association of American Geographers.

Griffith, D. A. (2008). Spatial-filtering-based contributions to a critique of geographically weighted regression (GWR). *Environment and Planning A: Economy and Space, 40,* 2751–2769.

Hall, P. (1988). The city of theory. In R. LeGates & F. Stout (Eds.), *The city reader* (pp. 391–393). New York, NY: Routledge.

Harris, P., Fotheringham, A. S., & Juggins, S. (2010). Robust geographically weighted regression: A technique for quantifying spatial relationships between freshwater acidification critical loads and catchment attributes. *Annals of the Association of American Geographers, 100,* 286–306.

Haug, S. (2008). Migration networks and migration decision-making. *Journal of Ethnic and Migration Studies, 34,* 585–605.

Hawley, A. H. (1950). *Human ecology: A theory of community structure.* New York, NY: Ronald Press.

Heisig, J. P., Schaeffer, M., & Giesecke, J. (2017). The costs of simplicity: Why multilevel models may benefit from accounting for cross-cluster differences in the effects of controls. *American Sociological Review, 82,* 796–827.

Henry, M. S., Barkley, D. L., & Bao, S. (1997). The hinterland's stake in metropolitan growth: Evidence from selected southern regions. *Journal of Regional Science, 37,* 479–501.

Hepple, L. W. (1998). Exact testing for spatial autocorrelation among regression residuals. *Environment and Planning A, 30,* 85–107.

Hill, R. C. (1977). Capital accumulation and urbanization in the United States. *Comparative Urban Research, 4,* 39–60.

Hsu, C. Y., Chang, S. S., & Yip, P. (2017). Individual-, household- and neighbourhood-level characteristics associated with life satisfaction: A multilevel analysis of a population-based sample from Hong Kong. *Urban Studies, 54,* 3700–3717.

Huang, B., Wu, B., & Barry, M. (2010). Geographically and temporally weighted regression for modeling spatio-temporal variation in house prices. *International Journal of Geographical Information Science, 24*(3), 383–401.

Hudson, J. C. (1972). *Geographical diffusion theory.* Evanston, IL: Department of Geography, Northwestern University.

Hugo, G., Champion, A., & Lattes, A. (2003). Toward a new conceptualization of settlements for demography. *Population and Development Review, 29,* 277–297.

Humphrey, C. R. (1980). The promotion of growth in small urban places and its impact on population change. *Social Science Quarterly, 61,* 581–594.

Humphrey, C. R., & Sell, R. R. (1975). The impact of controlled access highways on population growth in Pennsylvania nonmetropolitan communities, 1940–1970. *Rural Sociology, 40,* 332–343.

Iceland, J., & Nelson, K. A. (2008). Hispanic segregation in metropolitan America: Exploring the multiple forms of spatial assimilation. *American Sociological Review, 73,* 741–765.

Irwin, M. D., & Kasarda, J. D. (1991). Air passenger linkages and employment growth in U.S. metropolitan areas. *American Sociological Review, 56,* 524–537.

Isaaks, E., & Srivastava, R. (1989). *An introduction to applied geostatistics.* New York, NY: Oxford University Press.

Isserman, A. M., Feser, E., & Warren, D. E. (2009). Why some rural places prosper and others do not. *International Regional Science Review, 32,* 300–342.

Jaret, C. (1983). Recent neo-Marxist urban analysis. *Annual Review of Sociology, 9*, 499–525.

Jensen, J. R., Cowen, D. J., Halls, J., Narumalani, S., Schmidt, N. J., Davis, B. A., & Burgess, B. (1994). Improved urban infrastructure mapping and forecasting for BellSouth using remote sensing and GIS technology. *Photogrammetric Engineering and Remote Sensing, 60*, 339–346.

Johnson, K. M. (1999). The rural rebound. *PRB Reports on America, 1*, 1–21.

Johnson, K. M. (2001, August). *More coffins than cradles: The continuing high incidence of natural decrease in American counties.* Paper presented at the annual meeting of the Rural Sociological Society, Albuquerque, NM.

Johnson, K. M., & Beale, C. L. (1994). The recent revival of widespread population growth in nonmetropolitan areas of the United States. *Rural Sociology, 59*, 655–667.

Kasarda, J. D., & Lindsay, G. (2011). *Aerotropolis: The way we'll live next.* New York, NY: Farrar, Straus and Giroux.

Kennan, J., & Walker, J. R. (2003, April). *The effect of expected income on individual migration decisions.* Paper presented at the annual meeting of Population Association of America, Boston, MA.

Kim, K.-K., Marcouiller, D. W., & Deller, S. C. (2005). Natural amenities and rural development: Understanding spatial and distributional attributes. *Growth and Change, 36*, 275–298.

Kim, T. K., Solomon, P., & Zurlo, K. A. (2009). Applying hierarchical linear modeling (HLM) to social work administration research. *Administration in Social Work, 33*, 262–277.

Koenker, R. W., & Bassett, G. W. (1982). Robust tests for heteroscedasticity based on regression quantiles. *Econometrica, 50*, 43–61.

Krugman, P. (1991). *Geography and trade.* Cambridge, MA: MIT Press.

Krygier, J., & Wood, D. (2005). *Making maps: A visual guide to map design for GIS.* New York, NY: Guilford.

Kuha, J. (2005). AIC and BIC: Comparisons of assumptions and performance. *Sociological Methods and Research, 33*, 188–229.

Land Information and Computer Graphics Facility. (2000). *Mapping growth management factors: A practical guide for land use planning.* Madison: University of Wisconsin–Madison.

Land Information and Computer Graphics Facility. (2002). *Population and land allocation: Evolution of geospatial tools helps citizens engage in land-planning process.* Madison: University of Wisconsin–Madison.

Langford, M., Maguire, D. J., & Unwin, D. J. (1991). The areal interpolation problem: Estimating population using remote sensing in a GIS framework. In I. Masser & M. Blakemore (Eds.), *Handling geographical information: Methodology and potential applications* (pp. 55–77). London, UK: Longman Scientific & Technical.

Langford, M., & Unwin, D. J. (1994). Generating and mapping population density surfaces within a geographical information system. *The Cartographic Journal, 31*, 21–26.

Law, M., & Collins, A. (2015). *Getting to know ArcGIS desktop.* Redlands, CA: ESRI Press.

Lee, L., & Yu, J. (2010). Some recent developments in spatial panel data models. *Regional Science and Urban Economics, 40*(5), 255–271.

LeSage, J. P. (1999). A spatial econometric examination of China's economic growth. *Geographic Information Sciences, 5*, 143–153.

LeSage, J. P., & Pace, R. K. (2009). *Introduction to spatial econometrics.* Boca Raton, FL: CRC Press.

Levernier, W., Partridge, M. D., & Rickman, D. S. (2000). The causes of regional variations in U.S. poverty: A cross-country analysis. *Journal of Regional Science, 40*, 473–497.

Lewis, P. H. (1996). *Tomorrow by design: A regional design process for sustainability.* New York, NY: John Wiley.

Li, S.-M., & Wu, F. (2004). Contextualizing residential mobility and housing choice: Evidence from urban China. *Environment and Planning A: Economy and Space, 36*, 1–6.

Lichter, D. T., & Johnson, K. M. (2007). The changing spatial concentration of America's rural poor population. *Rural Sociology, 72*, 331–358.

Lim, U. (2016). Regional income club convergence in US BEA economic areas: A spatial switching regression approach. *Annals of Regional Science, 56*, 273–294.

Liu, J., Dietz, T., Carpenter, S. R., Alberti, M., Folke, C., Moran, E., . . . Taylor, W. W. (2007). Complexity of coupled human and natural systems. *Science, 317*, 1513–1516.

Liu, J., Khattak, A. J., & Wali, B. (2017). Do safety performance functions used for predicting crash frequency vary across space? Applying geographically weighted regressions to account for spatial heterogeneity. *Accident Analysis and Prevention, 109*, 132–142.

Lobao, L. M., Hooks, G., & Tickamyer, A. R. (2008). Poverty and inequality across space: Sociological reflections on the missing-middle subnational scale. *Cambridge Journal of Regions, Economy and Society, 1*, 89–113.

Loftin, C., & Ward, S. K. (1983). A spatial autocorrelation model of the effects of population density on fertility. *American Sociological Review, 48*, 121–128.

Logan, J., Oakley, D., & Stowell, J. (2008). School segregation in metropolitan regions, 1970–2000: The impacts of policy choices on public education. *American Journal of Sociology, 113*, 1611–1644.

Logan, J. R. (2012). Making a place for space: Spatial thinking in social science. *Annual Review of Sociology, 38*(1), 507–524.

Logan, J. R., & Molotch, H. L. (1987). *Urban fortunes: The political economy of place*. Berkeley: University of California Press.

Longley, P. A., Goodchild, M. F., Maguire, D. J., & Rhind, D. W. (2001). *Geographical information systems and science*. New York, NY: John Wiley.

Longley, P. A., & Tobón, C. (2004). Spatial dependence and heterogeneity in patterns of hardship: An intra-urban analysis. *Annals of the Association of American Geographers, 94*, 503–519.

Lundgren, L., & Rankin, B. (1998). What matters more: The job training program or the background of the participant? An HLM analysis of the influence of program and client characteristics on the wages of inner-city youth who have completed JTPA job training. *Evaluation and Program Planning, 21*, 111–120.

Lutz, W. (1994). *Population-development-environment: Understanding their interactions in Mauritius*. New York, NY: Springer-Verlag.

Maguire, D. J., Goodchild, M. F., & Rhind, D. W. (1991). *Geographical information systems: Principles and applications*. New York, NY: Longman Scientific & Technical.

Marcouiller, D. W. (1998). Environmental resources as latent primary factors of production in tourism: The case of forest-based commercial recreation. *Tourism Economics, 4*, 131–145.

Marcouiller, D. W., Clendenning, J. G., & Kedzior, R. (2002). Natural amenity-led development and rural planning. *Journal of Planning Literature, 16*, 515–542.

Marcouiller, D. W., Kim, K.-K., & Deller, S. C. (2004). Natural amenities, tourism and income distribution. *Annals of Tourism Research, 31*, 1031–1050.

Massey, D. S., & Denton, N. A. (1993). *American apartheid: Segregation and the making of the underclass*. Cambridge, MA: Harvard University Press.

Matthews, S., & Parker, D. M. (2013). Progress in spatial demography. *Demographic Research, S13*, 271–312.

McGranahan, D. A. (2008). Landscape influence on recent rural migration in the U.S. *Landscape and Urban Planning, 85*, 228–240.

McKenzie, R. D. (1924). The ecological approach to the study of the human community. *American Journal of Sociology, 30*, 287–301.

Mennis, J. (2003). Generating surface models of population using dasymetric mapping. *The Professional Geographer, 55*, 31–42.

Mennis, J. L., & Jordan, L. (2005). The distribution of environmental equity: Exploring spatial nonstationarity in multivariate models of air toxic releases. *Annals of the Association of American Geographers, 95*, 249–268.

Meuer, J., & Rupietta, C. (2017). Integrating QCA and HLM for multilevel research on organizational configurations. *Organizational Research Methods, 20*, 324–342.

Millar, R. B. (2011). *Maximum likelihood estimation and inference*. Chichester, UK: John Wiley.

Mollenkopf, J. (1975). The postwar politics of urban development. In W. Tabb & L. Sawers (Eds.), *Marxism and the metropolis* (pp. 117–152). New York, NY: Oxford University Press.

Mollenkopf, J. (1981). Neighborhood political development and the politics of urban growth: Boston and San Francisco 1958–78. *International Journal of Urban and Regional Research, 5*, 15–39.

Møller, J., & Waagepetersen, R. P. (2003). *Statistical inference and simulation for spatial point processes*. Boca Raton, FL: Chapman & Hall/CRC.

Moore, D. S. (2010). *The basic practice of statistics*. New York, NY: Freeman.

Moran, P. (1948). The interpolation of statistical maps. *Journal of the Royal Statistical Society B, 10*, 243–251.

Moran, P. A. P. (1950). Notes on continuous stochastic phenomena. *Biometrika, 37*, 17–23.

Mur, J., & Lauridsen, J. (2007). Outliers and spatial dependence in cross-sectional regressions. *Environment and Planning A, 39*, 1752–1769.

Myers, C. A., Slack, T., Martin, C. K., Broyles, S. T., & Heymsfield, S. B. (2015). Regional disparities in obesity prevalence in the United States: A spatial regime analysis. *Obesity, 23*, 481–487.

Myers, R. J., & Jayne, T. S. (2012). Multiple-regime spatial price transmission with an application to maize markets in Southern Africa. *American Journal of Agricultural Economics, 94*, 174–188.

Nord, M., Luloff, A. E., & Jensen, L. (1995). Migration and the spatial concentration of poverty. *Rural Sociology, 60*, 399–415.

Oliveira, S., Pereira, J. M. C., San-Miguel-Ayanz, J., & Lourenço, L. (2014). Exploring the spatial patterns of fire density in southern Europe using geographically weighted regression. *Applied Geography, 51*, 143–157.

Ord, J. K., & Getis, A. (1995). Local spatial autocorrelation statistics: Distributional issues and an application. *Geographical Analysis, 27*, 286–306.

O'Sullivan, D., & Unwin, D. (2003). *Geographic information analysis*. Hoboken, NJ: John Wiley.

O'Sullivan, D., & Unwin, D. (2010). *Geographic information analysis* (2nd ed.). Hoboken, NJ: John Wiley.

Pacheco, A. I., & Tyrrell, T. J. (2002). Testing spatial patterns and growth spillover effects in clusters of cities. *Journal of Geographical Systems, 4*, 275–285.

Páez, A., Uchida, T., & Miyamoto, K. (2002). A general framework for estimation and inference of geographically weighted regression models: 2. Spatial association and model specification tests. *Environment and Planning A: Economy and Space, 34*, 883–904.

Partridge, M. D., Rickman, D. S., Ali, K., & Olfert, M. R. (2008a). The geographic diversity of U.S. nonmetropolitan growth dynamics: A geographically weighted regression approach. *Land Economics, 84*, 241–266.

Partridge, M. D., Rickman, D. S., Ali, K., & Olfert, M. R. (2008b). Lost in space: Population growth in the American hinterlands and small cities. *Journal of Economic Geography, 8*, 727–757.

Patton, M., & McErlean, S. (2003). Spatial effects within the agricultural land market in Northern Ireland. *Journal of Agricultural Economics, 54*, 35–54.

Pebesma, E., Bivand, R., Rowlingson, B., Gomez-Rubio, V., Hijmans, R., Sumner, M., . . . O'Rourke, J. (2018). Package 'sp'. R package version 1.3-1. Retrieved from https://cran.r-project.org/web/packages/sp/sp.pdf

Perroux, F. (1955). Note sur la Notion de pole de croissance [Note on the concept of growth pole]. *Economie Appliquee, 8*, 307–320.

Pittenger, D. B. (1976). *Projecting state and local populations*. Cambridge, MA: Ballinger.

R Development Core Team. (2008). *R: A language and environment for statistical computing*. Vienna, Austria: R Foundation for Statistical Computing.

Rasker, R., Gude, P. H., Gude, J. A., & Noort, J. (2009). The economic importance of air travel in high-amenity rural areas. *Journal of Rural Studies, 25*, 343–353.

Raudenbush, S. W., & Bryk, A. S. (2002). *Hierarchical linear models: Applications and data analysis methods*. Thousand Oaks, CA: Sage.

Reibel, M. (2007). Geographic information systems and spatial data processing in demography: A review. *Population Research and Policy Review, 26*, 601–618.

Riahi, K., & Nakicenovic, N. (2007). Special issue: Greenhouse gases—integrated assessment. *Technological Forecasting and Social Change, 74*(7), 873–1108.

Robinson, W. S. (1950). Ecological correlations and the behavior of individuals. *American Sociological Review, 15*, 351–357.

Rocconi, L. M. (2013). Analyzing multilevel data: Comparing findings from hierarchical linear modeling and ordinary least squares regression. *Higher Education, 66*, 439–461.

Rotarou, E. S. (2018). Does municipal socioeconomic development affect public perceptions of crime?

A multilevel logistic regression analysis. *Social Indicators Research*, *138*, 705–724.

Rugh, J. S., & Massey, D. S. (2010). Racial segregation and the American foreclosure crisis. *American Sociological Review*, *75*, 629–651.

Sampson, R. J., Morenoff, J. D., & Earls, F. (1999). Beyond social capital: Spatial dynamics of collective efficacy for children. *American Sociological Review*, *64*, 633–660.

Schabenberger, O., & Gotway, C. A. (2005). *Statistical methods for spatial data analysis*. Boca Raton, FL: Chapman & Hall/CRC Press.

Schwartz, G. (1978). Estimating the dimension of a model. *Annals of Statistics*, *6*, 461–464.

Shaw, R. P. (1975). *Migration theory and fact: A review and bibliography of current literature*. Philadelphia, PA: Regional Science Research Institute.

Shoff, C., Chen, V. Y.-J., & Yang, T.-C. (2014). When homogeneity meets heterogeneity: The geographically weighted regression with spatial lag approach to prenatal care utilisation. *Geospatial Health*, *8*(2), 557–568.

Shryock, H. S. (1964). *Population mobility within the United States* (Vol. 2). Chicago, IL: Community and Family Study Center, University of Chicago.

Smith, S. K., Tayman, J., & Swanson, D. A. (2013). *A practitioner's guide to state and local projections*. Dordrecht, the Netherlands: Springer.

Stedman, R. C., & Hammer, R. B. (2006). Environmental perception in a rapidly growing amenity-rich region: The effects of lakeshore development on perceived water quality in Vilas County, Wisconsin. *Society & Natural Resources*, *19*, 137–151.

Stein, M. L. (1999). *Interpolation of spatial data: Some theory for Kriging*. New York, NY: Springer.

Suvak, M. K., Walling, S. M., Iverson, K. M., Taft, C. T., & Resick, P. A. (2009). Multilevel regression analyses to investigate the relationship between two variables over time: Examining the longitudinal association between intrusion and avoidance. *Journal of Traumatic Stress*, *22*, 622–631.

Tayman, J. (1996). The accuracy of small-area population forecasts based on a spatial interaction land-use modeling system. *Journal of the American Planning Association*, *62*, 85–98.

Thiede, B., Kim, H., & Valasik, M. (2018). The spatial concentration of America's rural poor population: A postrecession update. *Rural Sociology*, *83*, 109–144.

Tickamyer, A. R., & Duncan, C. M. (1990). Poverty and opportunity. *Annual Review of Sociology*, *16*, 67–86.

Timmins, T. L., Hunter, A. J. S., Cattet, M. R. L., & Stenhouse, G. B. (2013). Developing spatial weight matrices for incorporation into multiple linear regression models: An example using grizzly bear body size and environmental predictor variables. *Geographical Analysis*, *45*, 359–379.

Tobler, W. (1970). A computer movie simulating urban growth in the Detroit region. *Economic Geography*, *46*, 234–240.

Trewartha, G. (1953). A case for population geography. *Annals of the Association of American Geographers*, *43*, 71–97.

Treyz, G. I., Rickman, D. S., Hunt, G. L., & Greenwood, M. J. (1993). The dynamics of U.S. internal migration. *Review of Economics and Statistics*, *75*, 209–214.

Tso, G. K. F., & Guan, J. J. (2014). A multilevel regression approach to understand effects of environment indicators and household features on residential energy consumption. *Energy*, *66*, 722–731.

Upton, G. J. G., & Fingleton, B. (1985). *Spatial data analysis by example*. Chichester, UK: John Wiley.

Vaughan, A. S., Rosenberg, E., Shouse, R. L., & Sullivan, P. S. (2014). Connecting race and place: A county-level analysis of White, Black, and Hispanic HIV prevalence, poverty, and level of urbanization. *American Journal of Public Health*, *104*, 77–84.

Voss, P. R. (2007). Demography as a spatial social science. *Population Research and Policy Review*, *26*, 457–476.

Voss, P. R., & Chi, G. (2006). Highways and population change. *Rural Sociology*, *71*, 33–58.

Voss, P. R., Long, D. D., Hammer, R. B., & Friedman, S. (2006). County child poverty rates in the US: A spatial regression approach. *Population Research and Policy Review*, *25*, 369–391.

Waller, L. A., & Gotway, C. A. (2004). *Applied spatial statistics for public health data*. New York, NY: John Wiley.

Weber, B., Jensen, L., Miller, K., Mosley, J., & Fisher, M. (2005). A critical review of rural poverty literature:

Is there truly a rural effect? *International Regional Science Review, 28*, 381–414.

Weinmayr, G., Dreyhaupt, J., Jaensch, A., Forastiere, F., & Strachan, D. P. (2017). Multilevel regression modelling to investigate variation in disease prevalence across locations. *International Journal of Epidemiology, 46*, 336–347.

Wheeler, D., & Tiefelsdorf, M. (2005). Multicollinearity and correlation among local regression coefficients in geographically weighted regression. *Journal of Geographical Systems, 7*, 161–187.

Wilson, T., & Rees, P. (2005). Recent developments in population projection methodology: A review. *Population, Space and Place, 11*, 337–360.

Wimberley, R. C., & Morris, L. (2002). The regionalization of poverty: Assistance for the Black Belt South? *Southern Rural Sociology, 18*, 294–306.

Wisconsin Legislative Reference Bureau. (2005). *State of Wisconsin blue book 2005–2006.* Madison: Wisconsin Department of Administration.

Wu, J., & Gopinath, M. (2008). What causes spatial variations in economic development in the United States? *American Journal of Agricultural Economics, 90*, 392–408.

Xu, H. W. (2014). Comparing spatial and multilevel regression models for binary outcomes in neighborhood studies. *Sociological Methodology, 44*, 229–272.

Yamagata, Y., Murakami, D., Yoshida, T., Seya, H., & Kuroda, S. (2016). Value of urban views in a bay city: Hedonic analysis with the spatial multilevel additive regression (SMAR) model. *Landscape and Urban Planning, 151*, 89–102.

Yang, T. C., & Matthews, S. A. (2012). Understanding the non-stationary associations between distrust of the health care system, health conditions, and self-rated health in the elderly: A geographically weighted regression approach. *Health Place, 18*, 576–585.

Yu, D. (2006). Spatially varying development mechanisms in the greater Beijing area: A geographically weighted regression investigation. *Annals of Regional Science, 40*(1), 173–190.

Yu, D., Peterson, N. A., & Reid, R. J. (2009). Exploring the impact of non-normality on spatial non-stationarity in geographically weighted regression analyses: Tobacco outlet density in New Jersey. *GIScience & Remote Sensing, 46*(3), 329–346.

Yu, D., Wei, Y. D., & Wu, C. (2007). Modeling spatial dimensions of housing prices in Milwaukee, WI. *Environment and Planning B: Planning and Design, 34*, 1085–1102.

Zeng, Z., & Xie, Y. (2004). Asian Americans' earnings disadvantage reexamined: The role of place of education. *American Journal of Sociology, 109*, 1075–1108.

Zhu, J., Huang, H.-C., & Reyes, P. E. (2010). On selection of spatial linear models for lattice data. *Journal of the Royal Statistical Society: Series B, 72*, 389–402.

Zipf, G. K. (1946). The P1 P2/D hypothesis: On the intercity movement of persons. *American Sociological Review, 11*, 677–686.

INDEX

Adaptive bandwidth, 131
Adjusted R^2, 59
Age
   mobility and, 26
   population change affected by, 26–29, 62
Aggregated quantitative data, 1
AIC. *See* Akaike's information criterion
Airport, 30–31, 62–63
Akaike's information criterion, 59, 66–68, 88–89, 117, 144, 161, 190, 214
AIC_c, 131
AMOEBA method, 39–40, 88
Applied demography, 10
Areal data, 6–7, 35, 79, 183
Areal data analysis
   definition of, 3, 6
   geostatistics versus, 7
   models for, 79
   neighborhood structure for, 34
   spatial weight matrix for, 40, 212
Areal unit, 140
Aspatial data analysis, 5
Aspatial regression methods
   data, 115–116
   data example, 116–122
   data partitioning, 116
   dummy variables, 115–116
   overview of, 115–116
   spatial regime models versus, 124–125
Autocorrelation
   definition of, 42
   spatial. *See* Spatial autocorrelation

Backwash effect, 68
Bayesian information criterion (BIC), 59, 67–68, 88–89, 117, 131, 161, 191–192, 214
Bayesian methods, 168
Breusch-Pagan test, 58, 67, 205

Capital, 11
Capitalism, 10–11
CAR. *See* Conditional autoregressive model
Census Bureau, 218
Census Data Mapper, 219
Census Flows Mapper, 219
Census Interactive Population Map, 219
Census Metro/Micro Thematic Map Viewer, 219
Census OnTheMap for Emergency Management, 219
Census summary files, 2
Census tracts, 14
Census Urban Areas, 14
Center for Spatially Integrated Social Science Classics, 3
Central place theory, 9
Coefficient drift, 215
Conditional autoregressive model, 79, 202, 208–210
Contiguity-based neighborhood structure, 34
Correlation, 22, 24–25, 42–43, 45, 187–188, 203, 206, 209
County, 10, 13–14, 16, 18, 23, 33, 63, 115, 124, 184–187, 196, 201, 212, 219–220
Country health rankings & roadmaps, 220

Data
   areal, 6
   geostatistical, 7
   regional, 6
   spatial. *See* Spatial data
   spatial interaction, 7
Data dimensions reduction, in spatial social data analysis, 211–212
Data examples
   exploratory spatial data analysis, 49–53
   introduction to, 7–18
   spatial dependence, 60–65
Data-driven approach, to spatial social data analysis, 210, 213
Data-mining, 212
Data partition, 43, 122–126
Demographic characteristics, population growth affected by, 23
Demographic data, 23
Demographic survey databases, 2
Demography, population change as spatial process in, 9
Diagnostics
   for geographically weighted regression, 131–132
   for multilevel regression models, 103–104

235

for spatial cross-regressive models, 93–94
for spatial dependence, 58–59, 201–202
for spatial error model, 77
for spatial lag models, 67
for standard linear regression models, 57–58, 63–65, 69, 77, 193–195
Diff-criterion, 131–132, 134, 178
Disease mapping, 6
Distance-based neighborhood structure, 34–35
Distance-based spatial weight matrix, 41
Dummy variables, in aspatial regression methods, 115–116

Economic geography model, 9
EDA. *See* Exploratory data analysis
Edge effect, 123
Elhorst's spatio-temporal linear regression model, 157, 160–161
Employment growth, infrastructure investment and, 60
Environmental planning, 9
Equilibrium theory, 32
Explanatory variables
  description of, 1, 22
  dummy variables and, 122
  in geographically weighted regression, 131
  interaction variables and, 122
  for multilevel regression models, 100–102
  population change affected by, 23–33, 60–63
  response variables and, 114, 215
  in spatial lag models, 65
  in spatial regime models, 122, 124
  spatially lagged, 94, 161
  temporal variation of, 215
  temporally lagged, 161
Exploratory data analysis
  applications of, 22–23
  exploratory spatial data analysis versus, 43
  graphs used for, 187–188
  methods of, 22–23
  for poverty, 185–188, 195
  practices in, 22
Exploratory spatial data analysis
  data example of, 49–53
  exploratory data analysis versus, 43
  Geary's c in, 46, 198–201
  graphical methods, 197
  graphics in, 44
  heatmap for, 197
  mapping variables or residuals in, 44
  Moran's I statistic, 40, 42, 44–46, 198–201
  neighborhood structure for. *See* Neighborhood structure
  for poverty, 197–201
  spatial data in, 43–44
  for variable of interest, 114

Factor analysis, 22, 211
Federal Geographic Data Committee (FGDC), 217–218
First-order serial and spatial autoregressive distributed lag model, 160, 162, 170
Fixed spatial weight matrix, 38
Fixed-effects spatial error model, 161
Fixed-effects spatial lag model, 161
Forecasting. *See also* Spatial regression forecasting models
  applications of, 167–168
  geographically weighted regression for, 176–181
  practical considerations in, 171
Forest, 23, 25, 31–32, 52–53, 63, 72, 80–81, 92, 95–96, 133–134, 171, 178
F-test, 190
Future Directions in Spatial Demography, 10

G statistic, 48–49
Geary's c statistic
  description of, 46
  for exploratory spatial data analysis, 198–201
  local, 48
General distance weight matrix, 38, 72, 74, 90, 149, 171, 213,
General first-order serial and spatial autoregressive distributed lag model, 170
GeoDa, 2, 44
Geographic analysis
  definition of, 5
  examples of, 5–6
Geographic information systems, 2, 6, 9, 40, 219–220
Geographically weighted regression
  adaptive bi-square kernel function, 131
  data example for, 133–138
  description of, 127, 129, 139
  diagnostics for, 131–132
  explanatory variables in, 131
  for exploratory analysis, 132
  fitting of, 131
  for forecasting, 176–181
  limitation of, 132–133
  local coefficients of, 133–134
  local R^2 for, 181
  local weight matrix in, 130–131

regression coefficients of, 129
spatial error models versus, 131
for spatial heterogeneity, 214
spatial lag models versus, 131
spatial regime models versus, 138
spatial weight matrices for, 130–131
specifications of, 129–130
strength of, 132–133
t-values, 138
Geostatistical data, 7
Geostatistics, 3, 6–7
GIS. *See* Geographic information systems
Growth pole theory, 9, 68
GWR models. *See* Geographically weighted regression

Heatmap, 197
Heteroscedasticity, 58, 67
Hierarchical linear model, 107
Histogram, 187–188
Homoscedasticity, 58, 63, 193, 195, 201
Human capital model, 26–27
Human ecology, sociological, 10
Human geography
  description of, 3
  population change in, 9
Humanities, 4

In-migration rate, 26
Integrated Public Use Microdata Series (IPUMS), 218
Interaction term, 22
Inverse-distance weight matrix, 213

Jarque-Bera test, 58

K statistics, 47
Kelejian-Robinson test, 96
Koenker-Bassett test, 58
K-nearest neighbor weight matrix, 38, 41, 48, 49, 213

Lagrange multiplier test, 24, 59, 64, 69, 77, 87, 204, 213
Land developability, 32–33, 63, 74, 92, 97, 118, 120–121, 134, 178, 220
Land developability index, 9, 25, 33
Land use and development
  population growth affected by, 23, 32–33, 63
  spatial lag models and, 74–75
  urban status and, 119
Land use patterns, 9
Large-scale global trend. *See* Spatial heterogeneity

Lattice data, 6
Lattice data analysis, 3, 6
Life-cycle literature, 32
Likelihood ratio test, 59, 67, 161, 203, 215
Linear regression models, standard, 56–59
Linearity, 58, 63, 193, 195, 201, 204
LISA. *See* Local indicator of spatial association
LM. *See* Lagrange multiplier
Local indicator of spatial association (LISA)
  definition of, 47
  G statistic, 48–49
  Geary's c statistic, 48
  Moran's I statistic, 47–48
Local interaction. *See* Spatial autocorrelation
Local Moran's I, 47–48, 201
Location, 5–7, 10, 30, 42–43, 79, 123, 131
Location theory, 73
Log-likelihood value, 203, 207
LRT. *See* Likelihood ratio test

MATLAB, 161
MAUP. *See* Modifiable areal unit problem
Maximum likelihood, model fitting via
  spatial error models, 76
  spatial lag models, 66–67
  spatial regime models, 125
Maximum log-likelihood, 66
Measurement error, 43
Metropolitan and Micropolitan Statistical Areas, 14
Migration, 7, 9, 10, 16–28, 26–27, 30, 31–32, 62, 86, 104, 105, 107, 110, 125
Minor civil divisions (MCDs)
  definition of, 8, 13
  neighborhood structure and, 35
  population change at, 14–18
  in Wisconsin, 13–18, 26, 28–30, 49–52, 95, 116–118, 133–134, 173
Maximum Likelihood Estimate (MLE) method, 66
Modifiable areal unit problem (MAUP), 68
Monte Carlo simulations, 199
Moran scatterplot, 50–51
Moran's I plot of errors, 58
Moran's I statistic
  calculation of, 63, 78
  description of, 40, 42, 44–46, 209
  for exploratory spatial data analysis, 198–201
  local, 47–48, 201
  for spatial auto-regressive models, 164
  for spatial cross-regressive models, 97, 99
  for spatial regime lag models, 150
  of spatial regime model residuals, 128
  for spatial regression forecasting models, 172

Multicollinearity, 22, 24, 58, 211
Multidirectional optimal ecotope-based algorithm, 88
Multilevel regression models
 advantages of, 110
 data example for, 104–110
 diagnostics for, 103–104
 explanatory variables for, 100–102
 formula for, 100
 limitations of, 104
 purpose of, 100
 reliability estimates of level 1 coefficients in, 109
 results of, 108

Natural amenities, population growth affected by, 23, 31–32, 63
Negative spatial autocorrelation, 42
Negative spatial lag effect, 68
Neighborhood structure
 for areal data analysis, 34
 construction of, 35
 contiguity-based, 34
 definition of, 34
 description of, 33–34
 distance-based, 34–35
 minor civil divisions and, 35
 for poverty, 195–197
 selection of, 212
 spatial weight matrix conversion of, 35–39
Neo-Marxists, 10
Net Migration Patterns for U.S. Counties, 220
Normal distribution, 22, 56–58, 93, 101, 106, 124, 130, 158, 177, 193
Normality, 58, 63, 132, 193, 195, 201

Observation, 4–5, 39, 48, 56, 58, 60, 67, 86, 93, 100, 104–105, 115–116, 124, 130–132, 140–143, 156–157, 176, 178, 187, 196
Old age, population change and, 27–29, 62
OLS estimation. *See* Ordinary least squares estimation
OLS residuals, 67
OpenGIS reference, 195
Ordinary least squares estimation, 25, 57, 125
 in spatial error models, 76
 in spatial lag models, 66
 residuals, 67

Pearson's correlation analysis, 24–25
Place poverty, 184
Place stratification, 10

Population change
 age effects on, 26–29, 62
 airport proximity effects on, 30–31, 62–63
 in demography, 9, 11
 description of, 8
 explanatory variables that affect, 23–33, 60–63
 factors that affect, 23–33
 in human geography, 9
 land use and development effects on, 23, 32–33, 63
 land use patterns and, 9
 at minor civil division level, 8, 14–18
 Moran's I statistic of, 50
 multilevel regression model application, 104–110
 natural amenities effect on, 23, 31–32, 63
 old age and, 27–29, 62
 previous change effects on, 26, 62
 in sociology, 9, 11
 spatial dependence, 60–65
 spatial error model with spatially lagged responses applied to, 89–92
 spatial lag effects in, 69–74
 spatial lag models, 80–82
 as spatial process, 8–11
 standard linear regression models, 60–65
 unemployment effects on, 30, 62
 in Wisconsin, 16–18
 Wisconsin as study example of, 11–13
Population forecasting, 26
Population geography, 9
Population growth
 airport proximity effects on, 30–31, 62–63
 aspatial regression methods, 116–122
 employment opportunities and, 30
 explanatory variables associated with, 23–33
 geographically weighted regression with application to, 133–137
 land use and development effects on, 23, 32–33
 natural amenities effect on, 23, 31–32, 63
 socioeconomic conditions and, 23
 spatial regime models, 126
 spatial regression forecasting models, 171, 173–176
 spatio-temporal regression models, 167
Population redistribution, 10, 30
Positive spatial autocorrelation, 42
Positive spatial lag effect, 68, 72
Poverty
 county-level, 184–186
 exploratory data analysis for, 185–188, 195
 exploratory spatial data analysis for, 197–201
 histogram of, 187–188

neighborhood structure for, 195–197
place, 184
social problems associated with, 184
socioeconomic variables and, 185, 201
spatial distribution of, 184
spatial error models for, 205–207
spatial lag models for, 202–205
spatial linear regression for, 197–201
standard linear regression for, 188–195
in United States, 184–210
Previous change, in population change, 26, 62
Principal component analysis (PCA), 22
Principal factor analysis (PFA), 24
Proximity, 11, 23, 25, 30–31, 62, 72, 80, 97, 120, 133, 178
Python, 2

Quantile-quantile (Q-Q) plot, 193–194
Queen's contiguity weight matrix, 34, 213

R
  description of, 183–184
  statistical exploratory data analysis, 185–188
  U.S. poverty data example, 184–210
R function, 185–188, 196, 199–200, 205
R^2, 59
Random-effects spatial error model, 161
Random-effects spatial lag model, 161
Regional data, 6
Regional economics, 9
Regional science, 3
Regression coefficients
  spatial heterogeneity of. See Spatial heterogeneity
  in standard linear regression models, 114
Regression models. See also Linear regression models; Spatial regression models
  at aggregated levels, 98
  coefficients of, 215
  at individual levels, 98
  multilevel. See Multilevel regression models
  spatio-temporal. See Spatio-temporal regression models
  two-level, 101
Remote sensing, 2–3, 6, 24
Residuals
  spatial error models, 82
  spatial lag models, 205
  spatial regime error and lag model, 152
  spatial regime error models, 149
  spatial regime lag models, 147
  spatial regime standard linear regression model, 125–126
  spatial regression forecasting models, 175
  spatio-temporal regression models, 166
  standard linear regression models, 57–58, 63–65, 69, 77
Response variables
  explanatory variables associated with, 215
  temporally lagged, 161–163
rgdal, 195
Robust Lagrange multiplier test, 59, 69, 77
Rook's contiguity weight matrix, 34, 213
Rural demography, 10
Rural sociology, 9

SAR. See Simultaneous autoregressive model
SARMA model. See Spatial autoregressive moving average model
Scale effect, 15
Scatterplot, 187–188
Schwartz's criterion (SC). See Bayesian information criterion (BIC)
Segregation studies, 10
SEMSLR. See Spatial error model with spatially lagged responses
Simultaneous autoregressive (SAR) model, 79, 202, 207–208
SMA. See Spatial moving average model
Small-scale spatial variation. See spatial autocorrelation
Social Explorer, 218
Social sciences, spatial thinking in, 3–4
Socioeconomic conditions
  data sources, 23
  population growth affected by, 23
  poverty and, 185, 201
Sociological databases, 2
Sociological human ecology, 10
Sociology, population change as spatial process in, 9, 11
Software packages, 2, 44
SpaceStat, 2
Spatial analysis. See also Geographic analysis; Spatial data analysis
  definition of, 5
  techniques of, 3
Spatial assimilation, 10
Spatial association, 47. See also Local indicator of spatial association (LISA)
Spatial autocorrelation
  definition of, 42
  Geary's c in, 46

of infrastructure investment, 60
measurement of, 44
Moran's *I*, 42, 45–52, 58, 63, 70, 78, 80, 89, 95, 97, 162, 164, 171, 198–202, 207, 209
negative, 42
positive, 42
in simultaneous autoregressive models, 79
spatial dependence versus, 41, 58
spatial weight matrix and, 40
Spatial autoregressive moving average (SARMA) model, 87, 213
Spatial Breusch-Pagan (BP) test, 67, 205
Spatial Chow test, 123, 144
Spatial covariance, 42–43
Spatial cross-regressive models
data example, 95–98
definition of, 93
diagnostics for, 93–94
explanatory variables, 95
fitting of, 93–94
formula for, 93
indications for, 94
Moran's *I* statistic for, 97, 99
need for, 94
results of, 96–97
spatial weight matrices for, 95
Spatial data
definition of, 5
in exploratory spatial data analysis, 43–44
sources of, 217–220
visualizing of, 43–44
Spatial data analysis. *See also* Exploratory spatial data analysis
areal data, 6
definition of, 5
geostatistical data, 7
spatial point patterns, 6
types of, 6–7
Spatial demographic analysis
description of, 11
resources for, 2
Spatial demography, 9–11
Spatial dependence
accounting for, 59–60
data example for, 60–65
description of, 42
diagnostics for, 58–59, 201–202
G statistic for measurement of, 48–49
population change and, 60–65
for poverty, 204
spatial autocorrelation versus, 41
spatial error model and, 77

spatial error model with spatially lagged responses for. *See* Spatial error model with spatially lagged responses
spatial regression modeling with, 212–215
Spatial diffusion effects, 69
Spatial diffusion theory, of population geography, 9
Spatial econometrics, 6, 79
Spatial effects
introduction to, 4–7
large-scale, 43
microscale, 43
small-scale, 43
in social sciences, 3
Spatial error dependence
description of, 59
spatial error model with spatially lagged response, 92
spatial lag dependence and, 87
spatial regime model and, 125
spatial regression models, 156
Spatial error model(s)
components of, 159
definition of, 74, 76
description of, 40, 85
diagnostics for, 77
enriched, 162
equation for, 169
fitting of, 76, 161
fixed-effects, 161
formula for, 76
geographically weighted regression versus, 131
need for, 77–78
for poverty, 205–207
random-effects, 161
residuals for, 82
response variable for, 159
spatial dependence and, 77
spatial lag models and, 78–79, 87
spatial weight matrix for, 78
Spatial error model with spatially lagged responses
data example for, 89–92
definition of, 86
description of, 143
fitting of, 87–88
formula for, 86–87
indications for, 87
need for, 87
results of, 91
spatial weight matrices for, 88–90
Spatial heterogeneity
approaches for, 214
aspatial methods for, 214

aspatial regression methods. *See* Aspatial regression methods
  definition of, 113, 213
  description of, 42–43
  geographically weighted regression for, 214
  in individual variables, 114
  in relations between explanatory variables and response variables, 114
  spatial dependence and, 139–140
  spatial regime model for, 214
  spatial regression modeling with, 213–215
  types of, 113–114
Spatial heteroscedasticity, 88, 125, 144
Spatial homogeneity, 43
Spatial information analysis, 5. *See also* Geographic analysis
Spatial interaction. *See* Spatial autocorrelation
Spatial interactive data, 7
Spatial interactive data analysis, 3, 6
Spatial lag coefficient, 68
Spatial lag dependence
  description of, 59
  spatial error dependence and, 87
  spatial error model with spatially lagged response, 92
  spatial regression models and, 156
Spatial lag effects
  negative, 68
  population change as data example of, 69–74
  positive, 68, 72
Spatial lag models
  cautions about, 68–69
  components of, 158
  definition of, 65
  description of, 85
  diagnostics for, 67
  explanatory variables in, 65
  fixed-effects, 161
  formula for, 65, 158
  geographically weighted regression versus, 131
  need for, 67
  population change as data example, 80–82
  for poverty rates, 202–205
  random-effects, 161
  residuals of, 205
  spatial error models and, 78–79, 87
  spatial weight matrix for, 68, 73–74
Spatial linear regression model
  fitting of, 66–67
  output from, 203, 206–207
  for poverty, 201–210
Spatial moving average (SMA) model, 79

Spatial panel data
  analysis of, 161, 215
  definition of, 156
  models of, 161
Spatial point data, 7
Spatial point data analysis, 3, 6
Spatial point patterns, 6
Spatial process effects, 8–11, 104, 168
Spatial regime, 47, 140, 214
Spatial regime error and lag model
  coefficients of, 152
  formula for, 142
  residuals of, 152
  results of, 147
Spatial regime error models
  coefficients of, 148
  description of, 141–142
  residuals of, 149
  results of, 147–148
  for spatial heterogeneity, 214
Spatial regime error standard linear regression, 144
Spatial regime lag models
  coefficients of, 146
  data example for, 144–152
  description of, 140–141
  Moran's *I* statistics for, 150
  residuals of, 147
  results of, 145
Spatial regime models
  advantages of, 124–125
  aspatial models versus, 124–125
  data example for, 126
  data partition method, 122–123
  explanatory variables in, 122, 124
  fitting of, 125
  geographically weighted regression versus, 137
  limitations of, 127–129
  methods of, 122–125
  Moran's *I* statistic of, 128
  social science applications of, 125
  spatial error dependence and, 125
Spatial regime standard linear regression model
  description of, 123
  formula for, 123–124
  residuals, 125–126
Spatial regression forecasting models
  applications of, 167–168
  building of, 169
  definition of, 168–170
  explanatory variables in, 169, 174
  fitting of, 173, 175
  population growth in, 171, 173–176

residuals of, 175
spatial weight matrices for, 171
steps involved in, 168–169
Spatial regression models
  accessibility to, 2
  fitting of, 157
  methodological perspective of, 1
  neighborhood structure for, 34–35
  practical perspective of, 1
  rapid increase in, 1–2
  reasons for studying, 1
  spatial dependence for, 212–215
  spatial error dependence, 156
  spatial heterogeneity for, 213–215
  spatial lag dependence, 156
  spatial weight matrix in, 35
  theoretical perspective of, 1
Spatial social data analysis
  data dimensions reduction, 211–212
  data-driven approach, 210
  factor analysis, 211
  general procedure for, 210–215
  spatial weight matrix for, 212–213
  theory-based approach, 210
  theory-based variables for data dimension reduction, 211
Spatial spillover effects, 69
Spatial statistical software packages, 2
Spatial statistics, 5
Spatial structure. *See* Spatial heterogeneity
Spatial thinking
  application areas for, 4
  perspectives on, 3–4
  rapid increase in, 4
  in social sciences, 3–4
Spatial variation, 113–114. *See also* Spatial heterogeneity
Spatial weight matrix (matrices)
  for areal data analysis, 40, 212
  data example for, 171–176
  data-driven approach to, 213
  definition of, 35
  distance-based, 41
  economic distance, 213
  fixed, 38
  for geographically weighted regression, 130–131
  issues associated with, 40–41
  neighborhood structure conversion to, 35–39
  reasons for using, 39
  selection of, 39–40, 70, 213
  spatial autocorrelation and, 40
  for spatial cross-regressive models, 95
  for spatial error model, 78
  for spatial error model with spatially lagged responses, 88–90
  for spatial lag models, 68, 73–74
  for spatial regime lag models, 141
  for spatial regression forecasting models, 171
  for spatial social data analysis, 212–213
  for spatio-temporal regression model, 162
  thresholds for, 48
  variable, 38
Spatially lagged explanatory variables, 161
Spatio-temporal regression models
  approaches for, 157
  data example for, 163–167
  definition of, 156
  effects in, 163
  Elhorst's, 157, 160–161
  fitting of, 161–162
  population growth in, 164, 167
  reasons for using, 156
  residuals of, 166
  spatial dimension of, 156
  spatial panel data analyzed using, 156
  spatial weight matrices for, 162
  temporal dimension of, 156–157
Spread effect, 68
SPSS, 66
Squared inverse distance function, 38
SRELM. *See* Spatial regime error and lag model
SREM. *See* Spatial regime error models
SRLM. *See* Spatial regime lag models
SRSLR model. *See* Spatial regime standard linear regression model
Standard linear regression models
  assumptions of, 63, 193
  components of, 157–158
  description of, 56–58
  diagnostics for, 57–58, 63–65, 69, 77, 193–195
  evaluation of, 59
  fitting of, 188–190
  formula for, 157–158
  linearity of, 193
  measures of fit of, 59
  Moran's *I* statistics in, 165
  population change as data example for, 60–65
  for poverty, 188–195
  Q-Q plot, 193–194
  regression coefficients in, 114
  remedial measures for, 193–194
  residuals for, 57–58, 63–65, 69, 77
  selection of, 190–193
  spatial cross-regressive model in form of, 93
  urban-rural classifications, 119–121

Stata, 66
Stationarity. *See* Spatial homogeneity
Statistical inference, 1, 22, 57, 156
Statistical instability, 47, 126, 146, 215
Statistical software packages, 2
Suburbanization, 10

Temporally lagged explanatory variables, 161, 163
Temporally lagged response variables, 161–162
Theory-based approach, to spatial social data analysis, 210
TIGER system. *See* Topologically integrated geographic encoding and reference system
Tobler's first law of geography, 9, 73
Topologically integrated geographic encoding and reference system, 2
Transportation accessibility
   population growth affected by, 23, 30–31, 62–63, 73
T-test statistic, 189
Turnaround migration, 16, 31

Unemployment, population change affected by, 30, 62
Urban-rural continuum, 17, 26, 30–33, 117, 118–122, 144, 146, 151
U.S. Census Bureau, 16
U.S. Department of Agriculture, 220
U.S. Government's Open Data, 218

Variable spatial weight matrix, 38

Wald test, 203
Websites, for spatial data, 217–218
Wisconsin
   history of, 11–13
   land developability in, 33
   minor civil divisions in, 13–18, 26–30, 49–52, 95, 116–118, 133–134, 173
   natural amenities in, 32
   population change in, 16–18
   Public Use Microdata Areas (PUMA), 104–106

Z-test statistic, 203, 209

Printed in Poland
by Amazon Fulfillment
Poland Sp. z o.o., Wrocław
23 December 2020

c6bf5752-8529-43f7-9886-dcb1b21d355aR01